Situating Josephus' *Life* within Ancient Autobiography

Education, Literary Culture, and Religious Practice in the Ancient World

Series Editors: Sean A. Adams (University of Glasgow, UK) and Catherine Hezser (SOAS, University of London, UK)

Editorial Board: Jim Aitken (University of Cambridge, UK), Jeanne-Nicole Saint-Laurent (Marquette University, USA), David Carr (Union Theological Seminary, New York, USA), Raffaella Cribiore (NYU, USA), Matthew Goff (Florida State University, USA), Marc Hirshman (Hebrew University of Jerusalem, Israel), Sylvie Honigman (Tel Aviv University, Israel), Jan Stenger (Julius Maximilian University of Würzburg, Germany).

This interdisciplinary series provides a space for the exploration and advancement of the study of education and literary culture in antiquity and its intersection(s) with religious practice. Specifically, it covers the geography of the Mediterranean basin from the beginning of literary culture until late antiquity. Books in the series are at the cutting edge of research, challenging traditional scholarly boundaries by engaging with the lived elements of literary culture, religion, and education.

By advancing theoretical and methodological approaches from inter/transdisciplinary perspectives, books in this series make important contributions to discussions of textuality, history, material culture, and cultural studies. Interactions with material and literary culture are core elements to this series and scholars will wrestle with how practices change over time and locality. Attention to interreligious and intercultural interaction will deepen our understanding of religious experiences, communities, institutions, and individuals in antiquity.

Lived Wisdom in Jewish Antiquity, Elisa Uusimäki

Reading, Writing and Bookish Circles in the Ancient Mediterranean, Edited by Jonathan D.H. Norton, Garrick V. Allen, and Lindsey A. Askin

Situating Josephus' *Life* within Ancient Autobiography

Genre in Context

Davina Grojnowski

BLOOMSBURY ACADEMIC
LONDON • NEW YORK • OXFORD • NEW DELHI • SYDNEY

BLOOMSBURY ACADEMIC
Bloomsbury Publishing Plc
50 Bedford Square, London, WC1B 3DP, UK
1385 Broadway, New York, NY 10018, USA
29 Earlsfort Terrace, Dublin 2, Ireland

BLOOMSBURY, BLOOMSBURY ACADEMIC and the Diana logo are trademarks of
Bloomsbury Publishing Plc

First published in Great Britain 2023
This paperback edition published 2025

Copyright © Davina Grojnowski, 2023

Davina Grojnowski has asserted her right under the Copyright, Designs and
Patents Act, 1988, to be identified as Author of this work.

For legal purposes the Acknowledgements on p. vii constitute an extension of
this copyright page.

Series design: Charlotte James
Cover image © Vladimir Zapletin/iStock

All rights reserved. No part of this publication may be reproduced or transmitted
in any form or by any means, electronic or mechanical, including photocopying,
recording, or any information storage or retrieval system, without prior
permission in writing from the publishers.

Bloomsbury Publishing Plc does not have any control over, or responsibility for, any
third-party websites referred to or in this book. All internet addresses given in this
book were correct at the time of going to press. The author and publisher regret any
inconvenience caused if addresses have changed or sites have ceased to exist,
but can accept no responsibility for any such changes.

A catalogue record for this book is available from the British Library.

Library of Congress Control Number: 2023932728.

ISBN: HB: 978-1-3503-2016-1
PB: 978-1-3503-2019-2
ePDF: 978-1-3503-2017-8
eBook: 978-1-3503-2018-5

Series: Education, Literary Culture, and Religious Practice in the Ancient World

Typeset by Deanta Global Publishing Services, Chennai, India

To find out more about our authors and books visit www.bloomsbury.com and
sign up for our newsletters

Contents

List of tables — vi
Acknowledgements — vii

1 State of the question — 1
2 Genre theory — 27
3 Josephus' literary milieu — 57
4 Opening features and subject — 79
5 External features — 95
6 Internal features — 117
7 Conclusions of the analysis — 157
8 A new reading — 169

Bibliography — 185
Index — 201

Tables

1	Josephus	88
2	Xenophon	90
3	Libanius	91

Acknowledgements

This book did not write itself, and many people have contributed to the writing process. Professor Joan Taylor and Professor Richard Burridge have both generously offered their opinions of earlier drafts, and I am grateful for their insightful comments. Similar thanks must be extended to the anonymous peer reviewer; the inconsistencies that an astute reader might find in my arguments remain because I refused to listen to people who perhaps knew better. Special thanks go to Michelle Fletcher and Rosie Andrious, who were always available for advice or champagne. Sean Adams encouraged the original proposal and was also helpful and readily available throughout. It was a delight to work with the editors and their team at Bloomsbury, greatly facilitating the publishing process.

I also thank my family for their continued support, and I thank my husband for his endless patience with my choice of career. I dedicate this book to my children in the hopes that one day, they will understand that not every book needs to include funny pictures.

1

State of the question

In the late first, post-Christian century, one of the most prolific authors of the Flavian era was Flavius Josephus, born Joseph ben Matityahu. Soon after the fall of Jerusalem, Josephus composed his *Judean War* (*War*), a detailed history of events resulting in the destruction of Jerusalem's temple in 70 CE. But Josephus could offer more than contemporary historiography; he subsequently composed his masterful historiographical feat, the twenty-book-long *Judean Antiquities of the Jews* (*Ant.*). He included the history of the Judean people from its biblical beginnings up to the outbreak of revolt. Attached to the *Antiquities,* we can read Josephus' autobiography, *Life,* and a few years later, Josephus wrote *Against Apion,* an apologetic treatise.[1]

This is a standard introduction of Josephus' literary accomplishments, and it is easy to understand. I can offer my readers such a straightforward introduction to Josephus' works because the genre descriptions attributed to the individual ancient texts are contemporary, established terms that are also perfectly acceptable for ancient literature. If it were this simple, of course, then this book, and many others, would not be necessary. Admittedly, our understanding of historiography recognizes features different to ancient expectations, and vice versa, Herodotus would struggle with our understanding of historiography.[2] Nevertheless, the concept of genre helps us organize, categorize and ultimately interpret literature from other eras and cultures, if we understand and respect a range of features and expectations paradigmatic of a given society.

---

1 On the genre of *Against Apion,* see in more detail John M. G. Barclay, *Against Apion: Translation and Commentary* (Leiden: Brill, 2007), xxx–xxxvi, and Steve Mason, '*Contra Apionem* in Social and Literary Context', in *Josephus'* Contra Apionem: *Studies in Its Character and Context,* ed. by L. H. Feldman and J. R. Levison (Leiden: Brill, 1996).
2 Even though Herodotus is colloquially referred to as the 'Father of History', nevertheless his understanding of historiography differed from contemporary interpretations. See Arnaldo Momigliano, *The Classical Foundations of Modern Historiography with a Foreword by Riccardo di Donato* (Berkeley: University of California Press, 1990) and the relevant chapters in *The Cambridge Companion to Herodotus,* ed. by Carolyn Dewald and John Marincola (Cambridge: Cambridge University Press, 2006).

This book focuses on the genre of Josephus' *Life*, a book I have just nonchalantly described as his autobiography. In our current editions, the final book of Josephus' *Antiquities of the Jews* transitions into *Life*, although nowadays it is often published separately.³ Josephus begins the narrative by presenting his Hasmonean and priestly genealogy, his education and early career highlights, including a trip to Neronian Rome to free two imprisoned priests (*Life* 1–16).⁴ Upon his return to Jerusalem, Josephus was sent to Galilee during the early stages of violent uprisings (17–29). Josephus describes the situation in Galilee (30–61) and introduces John of Gischala, his local rival (43–5). The next part of the narrative elaborates on Josephus' and John's quarrels. Roughly the second half of *Life* focuses on a delegation sent from Jerusalem to depose Josephus (190–335). At the pivotal point of the narrative, Josephus announces his plans to return to Jerusalem. He claims emotional despair, accusing unnamed (although John is implied) envious citizens of plotting his downfall. In the same night, however, Josephus experienced a vision encouraging him to remain in Galilee (208–9). Revitalized, Josephus plays cat and mouse with the delegation before finally confronting them. He also sends a counter-delegation to Jerusalem to plead his case (266–70). Two-thirds through the narrative, Josephus prominently and notably digresses from the narrative and verbally attacks his opponent and literary colleague, Justus of Tiberias (336–67). Justus had also written an account of the war against Rome and Josephus accuses him of spreading lies – Josephus sees himself forced to mount a literary self-defence. Not Josephus, as claimed by Justus, but the accuser himself had instigated the revolt of Tiberias against Rome. Josephus holds the city of Tiberias responsible. The digression ends with more accusations against Justus, his sources and his credibility. The final part of *Life*'s active narrative highlights Josephus' successes and victories against his opponents, both individuals (e.g. John of Gischala) or cities (e.g. Tiberias) (368–410). The narrative of Josephus' short career in Galilee ends with the arrival of Vespasian and the Roman army; for more information, Josephus refers his readers to *Jewish War* (411–13). *Life*'s final paragraphs include an account of Josephus' marriages, his relationship with the Flavian imperial family members and his life in Rome after Jerusalem's destruction (414–30).

---

3   For manuscript traditions, see Heinz Schreckenberg, *Die Flavius-Josephus-Tradition in Antike Und Mittelalter* (Leiden: Brill, 1972), 31. See further, Chapter 4, for discussions of using the epilogue of *Antiquities* as a prologue for *Life*. See also further, Chapter 1, for scholars reading *Life* as an 'appendix' or 'addition' to *Antiquities*.
4   As will be discussed in greater detail, especially in Chapters 4 and 7, Josephus proudly and distinctly frames his *Life*-narrative with suggestive and repetitive genre-claiming terminology (e.g. 'my life', 'ancestry', 'events of my life') in order to direct his audience's interpretative process.

The problem in referring to *Life* as an autobiography lies in the fact that even though in our modern society, the existence of, and appreciation for, autobiography as a literary genre is taken for granted, the ancient literary landscape had different expectations – as did some scholars. On the whole, scholars have felt decidedly uncomfortable referring to Josephus' *Life* as an autobiography: Mathias Gelzer does not consider it a 'proper autobiography', William Weber accuses Josephus of 'watering down' the genre, David Barish suggests it is an 'autobiography of sorts', Tessa Rajak prefers 'partial autobiography'.[5] Steve Mason's acceptance of *Life* as an autobiography may have gone far to establish an accepted genre-affiliation for *Life*, but scholars largely omit clarifying whether this amounted to the existence or recognition of a literary genre with boundaries and expectations and how *Life*, and Josephus as its author, compared to any potential genre-expectations.[6] An uneasy restlessness still lingers, exacerbated by the lack of a consensus on the status of autobiography as a genre in antiquity overall; Christopher Pelling's statement doubting the existence of the genre during the early Empire comes to mind.[7]

But is it important? This study rests on the basic tenet that recognizing and knowing a work's genre fundamentally influences our interpretative process. The importance of genre for understanding and interpretation had already been recognized in antiquity. Isocrates (436–338 BCE) introduces his *Antidosis* by pointing out that without understanding or recognizing the genre, the subsequent content and recognition process would strike an audience as strange or odd, obstructing understanding and interpretation (*Antid.* 1). We see an example of such an interpretative misunderstanding in the election of North Korea's Kim Yong-Un as the Sexiest Man Alive 2012 – by the spoof online newspaper *The Onion*.[8] Unaware that the newspaper reports are satire, thus misunderstanding

---

5   Mathias Gelzer, *Kleine Schriften 3 vols.* (Wiesbaden: Franz Steiner Verlag, 1962–4), 300; Wilhelm Weber, *Josephus Und Vespasian: Untersuchungen Zu Dem Jüdischen Krieg Des Flavius Josephus* (Berlin, Stuttgart: Verlag von W. Kohlhammer, 1921), 92n.1; David A. Barish, 'The Autobiography of Josephus and the Hypothesis of a Second Edition of His Antiquities', *Harvard Theological Review* 71 (1978): 61–75 (64); Tessa Rajak, *Josephus – the Historian and His Society* (London: Duckworth, 2002), 6. Rajak qualifies her statement by adding that *Life* was an autobiography, 'not of the interior, modern kind', demonstrating awareness of the uneasiness that rests between modern and ancient expectations.
6   For example, Steve Mason, 'Josephus's *Autobiography* (Life of Josephus)', in *A Companion to Josephus*, ed. by Honora Howell Chapman and Zuleika Rodgers (Chichester: John Wiley & Sons, Ltd., 2016).
7   Christopher B. R. Pelling, 'Was There an Ancient Genre of "Autobiography"? Or, Did Augustus Know What He Was Doing?', in *The Lost Memoirs of Augustus and the Development of Roman Autobiography*, ed. by Christopher Smith and Anton Powell (Swansea: The Classical Press of Wales, 2009), 41. Pelling echoes a similar statement put out by Tim Whitmarsh, *The Second Sophistic* (Oxford: Oxford University Press, 2005).
8   http://www.theonion.com/articles/kim-jongun-named-the-onions-sexiest-man-alive-for,30379/

the generic implications, the *People's Daily* newspaper in China ran the story of the election as a factual report from a Western newspaper. Or to take an example from ancient literature: the genre of the *Scriptores historiae augustae* (*SHA*) has been frequently debated, to derive a better understanding and interpretation of the partially scurrilous contents.[9] Recently, Dennis Pausch has suggested that previous discussions had misunderstood the genre of the *SHA*, reading the text either as historiography or as a collection of imperial biographies; consequently scholars had asked the wrong questions and made misguided judgements of the text and its contents.[10] Previous focal point, so Pausch, had been the issue of reliability, and the many contradictions and fictional elements within the *SHA* had led scholars to conclude that the author (be he historian or biographer) must have been incompetent, unknowledgeable and unskilled. Instead, Pausch suggests that the genre and purpose of the *SHA* may have been misunderstood by a modern audience and that all these fictional elements and contradictions were in fact purposefully included by the author who realized his work more as a historical novel, mixing fact with an entertaining story.[11]

Revised genre assumptions must necessarily take into due consideration the ancient literary and social milieu, not the modern. Presuming to understand a text's genre based on modern assumptions does a disservice to ancient literature (see the qualifiers and hesitations attributed to *Life*'s status as autobiography). Such a warning and admonition, to approach ancient texts respectfully, unhindered by modern assumptions, is not unique to this study and need not be repeated unnecessarily. Still, proper knowledge of the ancient literary landscape and its genre system is an essential prerequisite for the modern scholar's interpretative process, because it prevents judgements such as were levelled against Josephus' *Life*.[12]

However, the ambiguity surrounding the existence of an ancient genre of autobiography is partly to blame for the unclear genre associations. A study

---

9 The *Scriptores historiae augustae* are a collection of ostensible biographies of Roman emperors and heirs, from Hadrian to Numerianus (117–284 CE). Purporting to have been written by six different authors, the collection is now surmised to have had a single author only. The narratives gradually descend into partially scurrilous accounts of the imperial figures, forcing scholars to question the (in)competence of the author and the genre of the texts, which in turn impacts on credibility and historicity. See further Adolf Lippold, *Die Historia Augusta* (Stuttgart: Steiner Verlag, 1998) and John F. Matthews, 'Historia Augusta', in *OCD*[3] with further references.
10 Dennis Pausch, 'Libellus Non Tam Diserte Quam Fideliter Scriptus? Unreliable Narrative in the Historia Augusta', *Ancient Narrative* 8 (2009): 115–35 (116).
11 Ibid., 118–19 cf. 132: 'a literary work with historical context'. See Chapter 2 for a brief discussion of modern genre theory as well as a note on authorial intent and reader-response theories.
12 Cf. Sean Adams, *The Genre of Acts and Collected Biography* (Cambridge: Cambridge University Press, 2013), 3.

informed by genre theory will prove helpful in pulling together disparate discussions and aligning them and will develop a theoretical framework to guide interpretation. How would authors know how to compose their autobiography, and how could their audiences determine genre and interpret these compositions? Did expectations change? How were they transmitted? Were there certain features indicative of the genre, if it even existed? Asking these questions will benefit our interpretive approaches to Josephus and his *Life*. This book reacts to the ambiguity surrounding the genre of autobiography in antiquity. It also reacts to our inherent need to categorize and classify literature to facilitate interpretation and bases its approach firmly on the interpretive aid of genre theory.

The genre of *Life* has been commented on by generations of scholars. For ease of reading and reference, the following survey on the ways colleagues have judged *Life*'s participation in a genre has been separated into smaller units. This structure is of course highly artificial and by no means exhaustive, as every study touches on several different issues. Colleagues commenting directly on the genre of Josephus' *Life* and its value as an autobiography will be discussed first alongside *Life*'s relationship with *Antiquities*. Understanding the relationship between the texts is fundamental to any discussion of *Life*.[13] Was *Life* attached to *Antiquities* as an afterthought, thus composed independently and connected to *Antiquities* for practical reasons, or should we view *Life* as flavoured by the foregoing history and vice versa? For many scholars of previous generations, *Life* was an appendix to *Antiquities*, a reaction to Josephus' compatriot Justus of Tiberias.[14] Subsequent scholars including Shaye Cohen, Rajak or Per Bilde used a different approach, setting *Life* into a wider Greco-Roman context and to varying degrees appreciating its generic status as an autobiography closely related to and informed by the *Antiquities*, culminating in Steve Mason's understanding of *Life* as a study of character.

As if to unbalance these assessments, other arguments suggest a different genre altogether, an encomium for example or a biography, leading us towards a larger question: if there is this much variety in the genre-labelling of a fully extant book, what does that suggest for the genre autobiography in antiquity?

---

13 This study fully accepts a contemporaneous publication date of *Antiquities* 20 and *Life* in 93–4 CE. An overview of scholarship debating the publication date of *Life* would require a chapter in and of itself. Steve Mason, *Life of Josephus; Translation and Commentary* (Leiden, Boston: Brill, 2001), and idem., 'Josephus's *Autobiography*', offer a full review of the discussion. All translations from *Life* are taken from Mason's recent translation and commentary.

14 See Chapter 6 for a discussion of *Life*'s purpose as a response to the allegations raised by Justus of Tiberias in his history of the war.

How is it possible that respected scholars have such widely differing opinions? A review of different approaches to genre and autobiography in antiquity will establish that while we can trace a rise of interest in ancient autobiography and see scholarly attempts at categorization and explanation of previously inexplicable features, others remain unconvinced that autobiography the genre existed to a recognizable degree in ancient literature. A gap remains open between theoretical discussions of genre and a practical analysis of texts in light of their genre-fulfilling features. This study aims to bridge this gap by submitting *Life* and a selection of comparative texts to a detailed literary analysis based firmly on genre theory. It is a foundational tenet of this study that genre remains integral to interpretation and that genres can be recognized by the inclusion or omission of a range of generic features.[15]

The genre of Josephus' *Life*

Any study of ancient autobiography must begin with Misch's seminal collection of first-person narratives.[16] Misch understands autobiography as a platform for the individual author to survey and assess his life – autobiography becomes the product of the author's self-awareness and self-consciousness, exhibiting a deep, inwards-directed process of self-revelation. With such a baseline, Misch does not approve of *Life*. He reads it as a mundane recollection of Josephus' career, whose prologue and epilogue (*Life* 1–29, 414–30) offer only a bare appearance of autobiography. The lack of deeper self-examination is replaced with a (perceived) apologetic tendency, leading Misch to conclude that this shapeless work ('formlos') does not deserve to carry the title βίος.[17] Misch's prescriptive approach to autobiography, searching for the sole defining feature of internal self-examination and self-consciousness, causes him to reject *Life* and the entire discussion is limited to a mere summary of the text.

Subsequent scholarly assessments of *Life* have felt also uneasy with the designation autobiography, preferring to think of *Life* as a secondary appendix to *Antiquities*, an afterthought, an apology, disconnected, written two decades after the publication of *Antiquities*' final book to defend the author – Josephus

---

15 See Chapter 2 for an overview of modern and ancient genre theory.
16 Georg Misch, *Geschichte Der Autobiographie; Das Altertum*, 2nd revised edn (Leipzig, Berlin: B.G. Teubner, 1931).
17 Ibid., 189. Misch classifies Josephus as one of many 'kleine Menschen' who fail to contribute originality, whose literary results are merely 'abgeleitete Formen', ibid., 190. In *Life*, Misch sees merely a collection of a superficial nature and internal inconsistencies,

– against accusations levelled by his compatriot and literary competitor Justus of Tiberias.[18] Their assessments are based largely on their decidedly modern expectations of autobiography as a balanced, self-reflecting, insightful, well-rounded narrative, exhibiting an author's sense of decorum. What many scholars perceived as boastful, unashamed bragging coloured their estimation of Josephus as a person and historian.[19]

Mathias Gelzer claims that *Life* is 'keineswegs eine richtige Selbstbiographie', given its unbalanced structure and the omission of much detail; individual passages, such as *Life* 80–4, bring about Gelzer's disapproval, 'ein Schwall von Selbstruhm' clearly offends him.[20] R. J. H. Shutt echoes his colleague's sentiments, suggesting that *Life* was not as much an autobiography in the ordinary sense (whose sense?) as an account of Josephus' career with a special reference to those aspects of his career that were criticized by Justus of Tiberias.[21] David Barish offers an almost identical assessment of this 'autobiography of sorts'; he judges *Life*'s structural imbalance and focus on Josephus' military career highlights, and suggests it would prove more beneficial to consider *Life* 'both an account of the war and an autobiography'.[22]

Josephus' character has in an inversion of the wider scholarly opinion become the preferred explanation for *Life*'s purpose and its relationship with *Antiquities*.[23] This acceptance comes hand in hand with reading *Life* as an

---

18 The theory had been comprehensively formulated at the beginning of the twentieth century by Richard Laqueur, *Der Jüdische Historiker Flavius Josephus: Ein biographischer Versuch auf neuer quellenkritischer Grundlage* (Giessen: Münchow'sche Verlagsbuchhandlung, 1920). The theory has been taken up and modified by subsequent scholars including Weber, *Josephus und Vespasian*; H. St. John Thackeray, *Josephus: The Man and the Historian. With a Preface by George Foot Moore, The Hilda Stich Strook Lectures (Established 1926) at the Jewish Institute of Religion* (New York: Jewish Institute of Religion Press, 1929), 17–19; G. C. Richards, 'The Composition of Josephus' Antiquities', *The Classical Quarterly* 33 (1939): 36–40; Gelzer, *Kleine Schriften*; Tessa Rajak, 'Josephus and Justus of Tiberias', in *Josephus, Judaism and Christianity*, ed. by Louis Feldman and Gohei Hata (Leiden: Brill, 1987). Cf. also Solomon Zeitlin, 'A Survey of Jewish Historiography: From the Biblical Books to the "Sefer ha-Kabbalah" with Special Emphasis on Josephus (Continued)', *The Jewish Quarterly Review* 60, no. 1 (1969): 37–68.
19 In addition to the scholars discussed in this section, see also Detlef Dormeyer, 'Die Vita des Josephus als Biograpie eines gescheiterten Herrschers', in *Internationales Josephus-Kolloquium 2002*, ed. by Folker Siegert and Jürgen U. Kalms (Münster: LIT Verlag, 2003), 26, in whose opinion Josephus' Selbstgerechtigkeit', which leaves reality far behind ('eine Häufung von realitätsfernen Übertreibungen'), makes him appear rather unsympathetic. Rowland J. H. Shutt, *Studies in Josephus* (London: SPCK, 1961), 126, suggests that Josephus' pride and 'unsatisfactory sides of his character' occasionally impacted on his ability and neutrality as an historian.
20 Gelzer, *Kleine Schriften*, 68.
21 Shutt, *Studies in Josephus*, 6, 14–15.
22 Barish, 'The Autobiography of Josephus', 64.
23 The development of this perspective can be seen in Rajak's work, who in 1983 admits that her previous interpretation of the relationship between Justus and Josephus was no longer tenable. It has by no means, however, been universally accepted in contemporary scholarship. Pere Villalba Varneda, 'The Early Empire', in *Political Autobiographies and Memoirs in Antiquity: A Brill Companion*, ed. by Gabriele Marasco (Leiden, Boston: Brill, 2011), 334 suggests that a response

autobiography, meant to highlight the author's character and deeds. Per Bilde and Shaye Cohen were some of the first scholars to set *Life* in its literary context and its relationship to *Antiquities* (see the following review), and Steve Mason's interpretation of *Life* as a celebration of character fully developed this thought to great critical acclaim.[24]

In his seminal analysis of Josephus' treatment of source material and the relationship between *Life* and *War*, Cohen attempts to place *Life* in the Greco-Roman autobiographical tradition.[25] Despite having previously stated that there was no independent, fixed genre of autobiography, thus implying the lack of guidelines, expectations, or conventions bound up with the notion of a genre, and that autobiography's relationship (if indeed it even existed) with biography was unclear, Cohen looks to what may or may not be considered 'appropriate' to an autobiography, or what was considered 'normal' for autobiographies.[26] Cohen aligns *Life* with other autobiographies ('like most autobiographies' they shared first-person narrative, lack of long speeches, a standardized account of youth).[27] Cohen confidently concludes that *Life* was an autobiography in both form and content.[28] He implicitly acknowledges the existence of at the very least a framework of literary guidelines or expectations recognizable to both author and audience, and perhaps without realizing, places *Life* into a generic context by highlighting its similarities and connections to other texts – we are confronted by the paradox of autobiography not being an 'independent, fixed genre' but nevertheless capable of demonstrating sufficient features 'appropriate' to the concept of autobiography that go beyond the author writing about himself.[29]

---

to Justus of Tiberias as the underlying reason conditions the book's structure and Joseph Geiger recently reiterated the view that *Life* was published in a second edition roughly a decade after *Ant.* 20, motivated by the actions of Justus: 'Jewish Biography', in *Oxford Handbook for Ancient Biography*, ed. by Koen De Temmerman (Oxford: Oxford University Press, 2020), 69–70.

24 'die beste Antwort . . . hat u.E. Steve Mason gegeben': Folker Siegert, Heinz Schreckenberg and Manuel Vogel, *Flavius Josephus, Aus Meinem Leben (Vita). Kritische Ausgabe, Übersetzung und Kommentar von Folker Siegert, Heinz Schreckenberg, Manuel Vogel und dem Josephus Arbeitskreis des Institutum Judaicum Delitzschianum* (Tübingen: Mohr Siebeck, 2001), 3.

25 Shaye Cohen, *Josephus in Galilee and Rome – His Vita and Development as a Historian*, 2nd edn (Boston, Leiden: Brill Academic Publishers, 2002), 101–9. Cohen merges autobiography with biography to create a larger pool of comparative literature for his analysis of *Life's* aims, methods, structure and style. As I will explain in Chapter 2, this study finds it possible to analyse *Life* without extending the pool of comparative literature to biographical works.

26 Ibid., 103–4.

27 Ibid., 105.

28 Ibid., 105–9, esp. 109.

29 Ibid., 101. Cohen also actively connects *Life* to *Antiquities*. This is relevant as at a later stage, we shall be discussing *Life's* connection with *Antiquities*. Cohen notes that in *Life*, Josephus portrays himself as an active follower of the Pharisees and as far more religious than he had portrayed himself in *War's* parallel sections (ibid., 144–51. In *War* 2.568–3.408, Josephus himself becomes an actor in his own historiographical narrative; the passages/time narrated overlaps with the events narrated in *Life*). Cohen argues that this rather devout portrayal of Josephus in *Life* connects to the religious,

Bilde, several years later, also plainly calls *Life* an autobiography. He states the obvious, long periods of Josephus' life are missing in *Life*, clearly because Josephus wanted to include only what was important to him.[30] However, in contrast to earlier scholars such as Gelzer or Shutt, in Bilde's estimation, this imbalance does not disqualify *Life* as an autobiography. The issue does, however, pose an intellectual problem: *Life* claims to cover all of Josephus' life events but does not fulfil that promise.[31] Either *Life* is not a true autobiography, so Bilde, or it is an autobiography of a 'very special nature'.[32] Bilde firmly rejects earlier readings of *Life* written to refute the accusations raised by Justus of Tiberias. Clearly, the events that Josephus does include constituted the highlight of his career, a period during which he played the leading role in the history of his people; despite the evident imbalance which had caused earlier generations of scholars to reject *Life* as an autobiography, Bilde firmly claims that *Life* must be a 'genuine autobiography'. After this successful thought experiment, Bilde moves on to connect *Life* to *Antiquities*. Looking closely at Josephus' own statements, Bilde concludes that *Life* has dual purposes: first, establishing a priestly heritage for the author which allowed him to compose *Antiquities*, and second, establishing his own participation as the author of *War*.[33] *Life* as a genuine autobiography is dependent on the unusual history of its author and his writings – which the autobiography will thusly elucidate and justify.

Mason's approach, lastly, firmly connects *Life* to *Antiquities* and at the same time understands *Life* as an autobiography separate from its mother-work, it

---

pro-Pharisaic nationalistic outlook he had detected in *Antiquities*. He argues that *Life*'s presentation of a pious, educated, Pharisaic, Josephus acts as a continuation of the same emphasis in *Antiquities*. The aim of this slanted emphasis, so Cohen, was directed at Josephus' Pharisaic audience, a rising rabbinical faction located in Yavneh. For example, Josephus presents himself as a precocious youth who was learned in the ancestral laws (*Life* 8) and who had chosen to follow Pharisaic teachings (12). His men keep the Sabbath (159, 161); such pious behaviour is contrasted with that of his opponents, who attempt to kill Josephus in a synagogue (302).

30 Per Bilde, *Flavius Josephus between Jerusalem and Rome: His Life, His Works and Their Importance* (Sheffield: JSOT, 1988), 33.
31 Ibid., 107–10. Compare here James S. McLaren, *Turbulent Times?: Josephus and Scholarship on Judaea in the First Century CE* (Sheffield: Sheffield Academic Press, 1998), 30, who similarly argues that Josephus clearly omitted many more important events from his life. The contents of *Life*, so McLaren, make it difficult to accept that Josephus gave us an account of his whole life despite his promise to offer 'events of my whole life'. McLaren suggests that Josephus' authorial decisions in selecting passages to include or omit reflect a strong 'apologetical element' to defend Josephus' credentials and attack his rival, notably Justus of Tiberias (77). Zeitlin, 'A Survey of Jewish Historiography', suggests that Josephus had no need to repeat certain events, having narrated them previously in *War*.
32 Bilde, *Josephus*, 108.
33 Ibid., 110–13. Rajak, *Josephus*, 146–55, similarly, understands *Life* as Josephus' effort as a survivor of the war to explain to a Judean aristocracy why he had failed as a commander in the war and why he had been rejected by the authorities in Jerusalem.

being fashionable at the time to append an autobiography to a longer work.[34] In his discussion, in the vein of Bilde's earlier deliberations, Mason surmises that his literary accomplishments convinced Josephus to celebrate himself as one of only a handful of men to have mastered his ancestral traditions – *Life* must be read as a celebration of himself as a fitting end to a historiographical masterpiece. As such, Josephus focuses on scoring points with his character, not with historical truths or facts.[35] *Life*, thusly, is unequivocally a part of *Antiquities*. They are connected by the lack of an independent title or individual prologue, convincing Mason to use *Antiquities*' epilogue (*Ant.* 20.262-7) as a surrogate prologue.[36] In Mason's opinion, *Life* survived as an autobiography where others perished only because of its connection to *Antiquities*.[37] In his new translation of *Life* as part of the Brill translation and commentary series, Mason briefly sketches the development of autobiography through from the Hellenistic period but sees the emergence of a 'full-fledged' autobiography only in the Roman period, which due to its highly competitive culture was well suited for the genre. Mason confidently speaks of a 'genre' of autobiography, popular among the Roman aristocracy, and even traces a number of precursors (e.g. inaugural or funerary speeches) but despite his genre terminology, he does not clarify how far he understands this genre as having generated boundaries or generic expectations. Mason's readers do come away with the impression that the Roman aristocracy easily recognized and composed autobiography, and that Josephus' *Life* was written in reaction to this literary trend, that is, in keeping with genre conceptions. Mason highlights some basic parallels to other texts but does not embark on a systematic comparative

---

34 Mason, *Life*, xii, xlii. Mason refers to other authors incorporating autobiographical sections into larger corpuses including Cicero (*Brutus* 88.301-97.333), Sallust (*B Cat.* 3-4), Ovid (*Tristia* 1.10), although these were all decidedly shorter than Josephus' *Life*. However, see further, Chapter 5.

35 Mason, *Life*, xxxviii. Idem., 'An Essay in Character: The Aim and Audience of Josephus' Vita', in *Internationales Josephus-Kolloquium 1997*, ed. by Folker Siegert and Jürgen U. Kalms (Münster: LIT Verlag, 1998). Pnina Stern also suggests that Josephus wished to portray himself as a 'vir bonus' by using his character and education as example: 'Life of Josephus: The Autobiography of Flavius Josephus', *Journal for the Study of Judaism* 41 (2010): 63-93, esp. 72, 77. Some scholars were at times too preoccupied with the question of where Josephus was lying more or less, including Uriel Rappaport, 'Where Was Josephus Lying – in His Life or in the War?' in *Josephus and the History of the Greco-Roman Period: Essays in Memory of Morton Smith*, ed. by Fausto Parente and Joseph Sievers (Leiden, New York: E.J. Brill, 1994) and Rajak, *Josephus*, 4; cf. Zeitlin, 'A Survey of Jewish Historiography'.

36 Mason, *Life*, xiv. Barish, 'The Autobiography of Josephus', 69, had been one of the earliest scholars to argue for the integrity of *Antiquities*' epilogue. Dormeyer, 'Vita', 16n.7 argues that the epilogue should not be used to replace a prologue.

37 Mason, *Life*, xv. Mason sees further evidence that *Life* was composed as part of *Antiquities*, as Josephus mentions his patron Epaphroditus in the prologue of *Antiquities* and the epilogue of *Life*, as well as in a number of shared expressions Josephus uses only in the last books of *Antiquities* and *Life*. Eusebius similarly, quoting a passage from *Life*, refers to Josephus' *Antiquities* (*Hist. Ecc.* 3.10.8-11). Mason insists that the genre 'flourished' among the Roman aristocrats, leading Josephus, who understood himself as part of the aristocracy, to 'embrace' the genre.

approach and we do not learn much about the genre and its features as a whole. Mason's main focus lies instead on the value of rhetoric and comparing themes from *Life* to Plutarch's *Precepts of Statecraft*.

Other genres for *Life*

Most of the scholars noted in the section earlier assume that autobiography was a recognized genre at the time of *Life*'s composition and deliberate in how far *Life* was a 'good' autobiography, imposing an artificial generic hierarchy onto ancient literature. *Life*'s precarious association with autobiography, however, is evidenced by considerations of *Life* participating in other genres. Mireille Hadas-Lebel, for example, despite announcing that *Life* introduces itself as 'une véritable autobiographie' and promises to adhere to the laws of the autobiographical genre, subsequently asks whether *Life* really deserves the genre title.[38] She bases this challenge on the above-mentioned narrative imbalance; Josephus had a lifetime of events from which to narrate and chose to focus only on a brief six-month period with essentially non-relevant events. Hadas-Lebel instead declares that *Life*, given its reaction to and focus on Justus of Tiberias, written in a fit of passion and anger, should instead be considered a polemic history ('œuvre de polémique historique').[39] Rajak similarly struggles with the lack of proportion and connection within the narrative. She suggests that in contrast to *War* and the relevant generic conventions (for historiography), there existed 'little by way of direct precedent'.[40] This side note in Rajak's discussion exemplifies the questions asked in the present study: if indeed there was so little precedent, if autobiography did not really exist at the time of *Life*'s composition, how did Josephus know what and how to write? How would his audience understand him – and would they understand him exactly as he had intended?

Jerome Neyrey suggests yet another genre.[41] Neyrey focuses on Josephus' presentation of his character as an ideal example of the Greco-Roman literary encomium, defined by Neyrey as 'a speech of praise, either of some person

---

38 Mirelle Hadas-Lebel, 'Le récit autobiographique chez Flavius Josèphe', in *L'invention de l'autobiograhphie d'Hésiode á Saint Augustine*, ed. by Marie-François Baslez, Philippe Hoffmann and Laurent Pernot (Paris: Presses de l'École normale supérieure, 1993), 125.
39 Ibid., 130.
40 Rajak, *Josephus*, 155
41 Jerome Neyrey, 'Josephus' *Vita* and the Encomium: A Native Model of Personality', *Journal for the Study of Judaism* 25 (1994): 177-206 (177). He also, reasonably, requests that we understand ancient authors and their literature on their own terms.

or place'. He begins by presenting a detailed list of 'fixed categories', taken from *progymnasmata* and literary critics such as Aristotle (384–322 BCE), Cicero (106–43 BCE), and Quintilian (35–90s CE), of how to characterize a person in a literary context, including origin, birth, deeds of the body and soul.⁴² Subsequently, Neyrey uses the list as a template to analyse Josephus' presentation of himself and others in *Life*. He concludes that *Life* fulfils 'all and only' aforementioned particulars.⁴³ Neyrey's approach is weakened by several factors. He rejects ancient authors' own genre designations; since they describe characters by adhering to the set of conventions as proscribed in various *progymnasmata*, they must be writing encomia, not history. He does not offer any practical examples from other encomia on the basis of which to compare either his list of characterization categories or *Life*. Neyrey also omits to offer any other genre-defining features of the encomium and, as will be shown in due course, a genre cannot be defined by only one work or one feature (method of characterization), but rather requires a variety of recognizable features.⁴⁴

This marginalization of the genre category of autobiography is also found in Detlev Dormeyer's work.⁴⁵ Dormeyer confidently refers to *Life* as the 'erste erhaltene Autobiographie der Antike' and suggests that since Josephus had already offered his audiences a narrative of his involvement in the war in *War* 2.568–3.408, *Life* written in the first-person style must offer his audiences something new.⁴⁶ Dormeyer makes his genre suggestion for *Life* (even though he had already claimed autobiography as a genre-label for *Life*): Josephus had chosen the genre 'ancient biography of a failed ruler', divided into the three traditional sections ancestry/childhood, public appearance, and demise/taking leave of public duties.⁴⁷ Josephus characterizes himself as an ancient ruler, surrounding himself with terms such as στρατηγός, εὐεργέτης, σωτήρ. Dormeyer with some insight demonstrates how Josephus presents himself as an ethical character guided by divine direction and concludes that Josephus used this language to portray himself as a failed ruler, following the concept found in the Hebrew Bible, the humiliation and elevation of a just man as found in the

---

42 Neyrey, 'Josephus' *Vita*', 179–88.
43 Ibid., 205. But see Dormeyer, 'Vita', 17, who argues that *Life*'s opening section, characterised by the use of self-praise straight from the onset, is unusual for a first-century encomium.
44 As an afterthought, Neyrey, 'Josephus' *Vita*', 204, does offer 'purpose' as a second defining feature. However, his suggestion of Josephus' aim of praise and blame is kept so general that it warrants only a few sentences in Neyrey's wider argument.
45 Dormeyer, 'Vita'.
46 Ibid., 15–16.
47 Ibid., 16. *Life* 30–413 forms the constituent part of this genre, evidenced by the change of style from encomium to historiographical *hypomnema* including dramatic events, multiple characters and a main character able to make mistakes and learn.

story of Joseph.⁴⁸ A side comment suggests that Josephus was trying to promote himself as the bearer of Judean cultural memory, in competition to the developing rabbinic movement.⁴⁹ While Dormeyer confidently states that Josephus was the first to use the form of ruler-biography for an autobiography and that *Life* was aiming at something new, he does not offer examples or parallels, or more detailed systematic parameters for this genre, nor does he explain how Josephus was able to adapt these forms and genres in the first place.⁵⁰ Dormeyer relegates a relevant and important observation to his footnotes, suggesting that Augustus' *Res Gestae* represented a Latin pendant to the Greek encomium, noting that it had been *usus* to narrate only successful deeds as opposed to *commentarii* which might include events or actions with moderate success. *Life*, so Dormeyer, is the 'first extant witness for the transferal of the historiographical *commentarii* and *bios*-style into the autobiographical I-style.'⁵¹ Admittedly, it took this author several re-readings to grasp the importance of Dormeyer's rather convoluted structure; he suggests that somehow, Josephus blended different genre-styles into something new. Again, however, more detailed explorations of this important genre-announcement are missing.

Tim Whitmarsh has recently revived the argument of *Life* as an apologia, citing Josephus' own words, 'being a victim of false testimony, I face the necessity of making a defense' (*Life* 338).⁵² Arguing that autobiography did not exist in antiquity, but that authors injected *apologia* with autobiographical narrative, Whitmarsh grants that Josephus' *Life* comes closest to what he would consider an autobiography. However, it remains a fundamentally apologetic work and despite the autobiographical framework, its prime focus is an *apologia* against the accusations raised by Justus of Tiberias (see earlier). While Whitmarsh's larger argument will be discussed later, his evidence against Josephus strikes me as unconvincing. Whitmarsh refers to a passage roughly three quarters into the narrative, disregarding Josephus' suggestive terminology when introducing *Life*.⁵³ Without wishing to anticipate the thrust of this study's arguments, it is pertinent to note that an audience would have already formed their generic interpretative framework by the time the narrative arrived at the passage referred to by Whitmarsh. As already noted by Mason, Josephus consciously creates the

---

48 Ibid., 25–6.
49 Ibid., 27. This theory interestingly stands in contrast to Cohen's assumption that Josephus was trying to promote an image of himself as especially devout in order to ingratiate himself with the Pharisaic movement.
50 Ibid., 16.
51 Ibid., 15n.4.
52 Whitmarsh, *Second Sophistic*, 80.
53 See in more detail, Chapters 4 and 7.

impression of a defence speech in this passage only; the digression against Justus (*Life* 336–76) is clearly demarcated and the defensive tone does not cross into the main narrative.⁵⁴

Two of the most recent contributions to the debate of autobiography, Josephus, and *Life* have appeared in compilations devoted to autobiography in antiquity, and exemplify the disparate range of scholarship possible for *Life* and the genre in general. Martina Hirschberger's chapter discusses Josephus' representation of himself in the *War*.⁵⁵ Her contributions to *Life* as such are brief. The majority of her article analyses how Josephus separates and mixes the different personas that he represents: 'das Erzähler-Ich' and 'das erzählte Er' – the omniscient narrator and actor.

Also moving away from *Life* as autobiography is Pere Villalba Varneda's chapter, in which he presents *Life* as 'the only extant "autobiography" from the first century AD written in the *commentarius* genre, of the Hellenistic *bios* tradition and of the "I-style": *Life* could be the first example of the autobiographical genre'.⁵⁶ However, according to Varneda, Josephus' true autobiography cannot be found in *Life*, because the text does not measure up to his expectations of what an autobiography should do and be, and he claims that '*Life* does not satisfy the perspectives of researchers seeking to go into greater depths about the author's intentions and actions'.⁵⁷ Varneda instead suggests that an evaluation of 'the sum of his unilateral contributions constitute the real "autobiography", which suggests our obligation to finding out how he portrays himself throughout his literary corpus'.⁵⁸ The remainder of the chapter offers his readers a synthesis of *Life* and corresponding passages of the *War*. Based on his approach of combing through the Josephan corpus in order to extract personal information, Varneda here does not use autobiography as a genre category, in fact he suggests that 'even if autobiography *stricto sensu* was not a literary genre in classical antiquity, the *commentarii* and the other writings of a personal nature . . . with the aim of letting the account rest upon a rational and edifying basis, constituted its

---

54 Mason, *Life*, 138n.1384.
55 Martina Hirschberger, 'Historiograph im Zwiespalt - Iosephus' Darstellung Seiner Selbst im Ἰουδαϊκὸς Πόλεμος', in *Antike Autobiographien: Werke-Epochen-Gattungen*, ed. by Michael Reichel (Köln: Böhlau Verlag GmbH & Cie, 2005).
56 Villalba Varneda, 'Early Empire', 327. See Thomas M. Bolin, *Freedom Beyond Forgiveness: The Book of Jonah Re-Examined* (Sheffield: Sheffield Academic Press, 1997), 52, who criticizes such masses of generic associations. This, so Bolin, can lead to 'classifications of such breadth and bulk as to be of little or no use in interpretation'.
57 Villalba Varneda, 'Early Empire', 327. Compare with Misch, *Geschichte*, earlier. We might justifiably ask why Josephus should have been concerned with satisfying scholarly research ambitions.
58 Villalba Varneda, 'Early Empire', 327.

beginnings.'⁵⁹ *Life*, so Varneda, in that sense, confusingly despite not being Josephus' true autobiography, could be the first example of the autobiographical genre. Varneda, however, does not clarify in detail how, when or why *Life*, despite not fully satisfying researchers and being only 'of the moment', nevertheless can constitute the first example of the genre autobiography within a development process.

Finally, Sean Adams attempts to bridge the divide between autobiography and historiography.⁶⁰ Well-versed in the particulars of genre theory, Adams accepts *Life* as an autobiography but simultaneously argues that some genres were more compatible than others and could therefore be joined together. He uses *Life* as well as the (now fragmentary) autobiography of Nicolaus of Damascus (born *c.* 63 BCE) which most scholars assume had also been composed and published together with Nicolaus' larger historiographical *Universal History*.⁶¹ Adams argues briefly that *Life* had been composed with an emphasis on contemporaneous rhetorical themes and motives; in addition to the close relationship to historiography (*Life*'s connection to *Antiquities*), it suggests that we might read *Life* as participating in other genres (rhetoric, historiography) as well as autobiography.⁶²

Excursus

*The terms 'memoir(s)' and 'autobiography' are frequently, and confusingly, used interchangeably. Historically, in the nineteenth century, autobiography inverted the generic status quo and superseded the contemporaneous term 'memoir' as genre name.*⁶³ *The rise in critical scholarship on the genre of autobiography in the 1970s then relegated the memoir to a subgenre of autobiography, effectively ignoring it.*⁶⁴ *Georges Gusdorf, for example, explicitly lists the memoir separately from his canon of autobiography and is highly dismissive of it.*⁶⁵ *For Gusdorf, there is no art or*

---

59 Ibid., 358.
60 Sean A. Adams, *Greek Genres and Jewish Authors: Negotiating Literary Culture in the Greco-Roman Era* (Waco: Baylor University Press, 2020), 249–54.
61 See further, Chapter 3.
62 Adams, *Greek Genres*, 254.
63 'autobiography', first used in 1797: 'Autobiography, N.', in *Oxford English Dictionary* (Oxford University Press).
64 James M. Cox, 'Recovering Literature's Lost Ground through Autobiography', in *Autobiography: Essays Theoretical and Critical*, ed. by James Olney (Princeton: Princeton University Press, 1980), 124–5.
65 Georges Gusdorf, 'Conditions and Limits of Autobiography', in *Autobiography: Essays Theoretical and Critical*, ed. by James Olney (Princeton: Princeton University Press, 1980), 28.

literary ability involved in the memoir; he expects evidence of self-consciousness and the evolution of the author's character, as opposed to the historical narrative of the author provided by a memoir.[66] Subsequently, perceptions of autobiography changed again, from a life account of the author's inner self, and the memoir, a historical account of the author, to autobiography, a historically correct account of the author's life, and the memoir, a partial account which does not demand checked facts.[67] A memoir in contemporary literary theory has become an account of a defined period within the life of the author, as remembered by the author.[68] Henry Louis Gates, Jr., himself author of a memoir, reflects the conceptual shifts by contrasting Gusdorf's perceptions about old men writing their memoirs (plural), with writing a memoir (singular) about a certain time and place in his life because at the age of forty-two, he considered himself too young to write an autobiography of how he became the person that he is.[69]

Scholarship on *Life* qua autobiography has travelled considerably; while earlier generations did not accept *Life* and rejected its status as an autobiography in the modern sense, more recent contributions feel comfortable using autobiography in reference to *Life*. However, the fragility in the relationship between autobiography and *Life* is twofold. First, scholars are of course happy to use the term 'autobiography' for want of a better description of *Life*, which after all is a text by and about the author. However, an aspect missing in their discussions is whether, or how far, these texts form a literary genre in the sense that there existed a set of conventions or guidelines generating expectations and allowing a framework within which to compose and recognize, and consequently interpret, a text. Second, we see an equally confident trend in different generic affiliations for *Life*.

The genre of autobiography in antiquity

One of the key problems in reading Josephus' *Life* as autobiography is the question of whether autobiography existed as a genre. The following overview attempts to

---

66 Ibid., 39–40.
67 Ben Yagoda, *Memoir, a History* (New York: Riverhead Books, 2009), 2.
68 Ibid., 1; William Zinsser, *Inventing the Truth: The Art and Craft of Memoir. Revised and Expanded 2nd Edition* (Boston, New York: Mifflin Company, 1995), 3, 11. Cf. Ronald Mellor, *Roman Historians* (London: Routledge, 1999), 165: memoirs of public figures need not include spiritual development but instead offer the author's inside perspective on political and military affairs.
69 Henry Louis Jr. Gates, 'Lifting the Veil', in *Inventing the Truth: The Art and Craft of Memoir. Revised and Expanded 2nd Edition*, ed. by William Zinsser (Boston, New York: Mifflin Company, 1995), 147.

review a selection of contributions which use, or attempt to use, a genre-based approach, or alternatively those scholars who do not acknowledge the existence of the genre in antiquity, but rather see the texts in question as precursors to the modern genre. The overview does not claim to be a comprehensive review of scholarship pertaining to ancient autobiography but merely wishes to highlight several positions and approaches.

Scholars have approached ancient autobiography from a variety of angles, although the small, largely fragmentary state of evidence adds a level of complexity to all discussions. Its origins are traced back to classical Greece, occasioned by the rise of individuals and their positions of power above the masses. Arnaldo Momigliano points to the 'disturbing presence of individuals' in the fifth and fourth centuries BCE who elicited the interest of their contemporaries.[70] Nevertheless, rather than argue for a streamlined development from classical Greece through to the Roman Empire, which the edited collections imply, Peter Scholz considers that the genre was decidedly more popular in Rome and developed rather independently of possible Greek predecessors due to social and cultural differences.[71] Greek democratic ideology did not afford individuals large portions of power; hence, those few individuals who did hold positions of greater power had to justify their public actions.[72] In contrast, the senatorial Roman society valued family traditions and family achievements and was generally more vocal about the individual's achievements.[73] This striving for

---

70 Arnaldo Momigliano, *The Development of Greek Biography* (Cambridge, MA: Harvard University Press, 1971), 40. See also idem., *Classical Foundations*, 14. See *contra* Joseph Geiger, *Cornelius Nepos and Ancient Political Biography* (Stuttgart: Franz Steiner Verlag Wiesbaden GmbH, 1985), 79, who argues along the same lines as Peter Scholz, 'Autobiographien Hellenistischer Herrscher und Republikanischer Nobiles', in *Die Griechische Biographie in Hellenistischer Zeit*, ed. by Michael Erler and Stefan Schorn (Berlin, New York: Walter de Gruyter, 2007). Geiger asserts that the Greeks did not write autobiography because contemporaneous biography was not interested in the individual but rather in the typical and characteristic within a series. Hence autobiography could not develop. A similar train of thought can be found in Christopher Gill's study of the Greek sense of the individual: Christopher Gill, *Greek Thought* (Oxford: Oxford University Press, 1995).

71 Scholz, 'Autobiographien'. See also Mason, *Life*, xlii; cf. Jürgen Malitz, 'Autobiographien und Biographie römischer Kaiser im ersten Jahrhundert nach Christus', in *Propaganda - Selbstdarstellung - Repräsentation im römischen Kaiserreich des 1. Jhr. n. Chr.*, ed. by Gregor Weber (Stuttgart: Steiner Verlag, 2003), 227, who argues for only few predecessors in Greco-Hellenistic times; instead, autobiography became popular in the late Republic. *Contra* Mellor, *Roman Historians*, 165-6, who argues that there were clear Hellenistic precedents for Roman autobiography, and Gabriele Marasco, 'The Hellenistic Age: Autobiography and Political Struggles', in *Political Autobiographies and Memoirs in Antiquity: A Brill Companion*, ed. by Gabriele Marasco (Leiden, Boston: Brill, 2011), 118, who suggests that autobiography did develop in the early Hellenistic period but was not transmitted, alongside much other contemporaneous literature, because of its short-term, localized importance.

72 Scholz refers to Isocrates or Demetrius of Phaleron (350–280 BCE), who composed an account about his ten years in power over Athens, περὶ τῆς δεκαετίας; Scholz, 'Autobiographien', 386-8, *FGrH* 228.

73 Scholz, 'Autobiographien', 391. Also Mason, *Life*, xli–ii; Mellor, *Roman Historians*, 167.

personal, political and military achievements and reputations allows Scholz to suggest that by the first century BCE, the publication of autobiography in Rome was 'selbstverständlich'.[74] While he notes a higher level of conformity in Greek autobiography, Scholz realizes that 'die römische Autobiographie tritt uns . . . vielgestaltig entgegen.'[75] Here he lists the differences between Quintus Lutatius Catulus' short *De consulatu et de rebus gestis liber,* focusing on his consulate and military campaigns with Marius, and the longer *De vita sua* of Rutilius Rufus, which covers many more aspects of the author's life and deeds in five books. While he does not refer to genre theory on a larger scale, Scholz discusses the literature based on basic genre theory, employing the relevant terminology, looking at the origins and development of the genre out of other genres, and also considers other aspects of genre theory such as cross-generic influences, the audience, or other generic characteristics of both genres, and clearly sees an independent genre of autobiography in classical literature.

Geoffrey Lewis sets out to reconstruct the content of lost imperial autobiographies by examining their literary precedents in Republican Rome; his aim is to demonstrate the survival and simultaneous adaptation of the genre.[76] Lewis emphasizes the generic struggle he faces: he considers the question of fullness and imbalance, that is, how little of a life account can constitute an autobiography.[77] In order to solve his conundrum, Lewis divides his investigation

---

74 Scholz, 'Autobiographien', 393. Cf. also Peter Scholz, 'Sulla's *Commentarii* - eine literarische Rechtfertigung. Zu Wesen und Funktion der autobiographischen Schriften in der späten Römischen Republik', in *Formen Römischer Geschichtsschreibung von den Anfängen bis Livius,* ed. by Ulrich Eigler, et al. (Darmstadt: Wissenschaftliche Buchgesellschaft, 2003). See here also Mellor, *Roman Historians,* 168, for whom it was a 'common' occurrence for Republican Roman figures to write memoirs. Cicero, *Att.* 21.2, demonstrates how many publications he had circulated about his own consulship.
75 Ibid., 392. Cf. Jeffrey Tatum, 'The Late Republic: Autobiographies and Memoirs in the Age of the Civil Wars', in *Political Autobiographies and Memoirs in Antiquity: A Brill Companion,* ed. by Gabriele Marasco (Leiden, Boston: Brill, 2011), 162, who speaks of the many different 'guises' of autobiography. Scholz also continuously, and inconsistently, switches between autobiography and memoir. Cf. also Misch, *Geschichte,* who alternates between 'Autobiographie' and 'Selbstbiographie', or Tatum, 'Late Republic', 163, and Cohen, *Josephus,* 104, who switch from memoir to autobiography and back. Cf. Gerhard Dobesch, 'Nikolaus von Damaskus und die Selbstbiographie des Augustus', *Grazer Beiträge* 7 (1987): 90-174 (93) who uses 'Memoiren' and 'Selbstbiographie' in consecutive sentences.
76 Geoffrey Lewis, 'Imperial Autobiography: Augustus to Hadrian', ANRW II.34, no. 1 (1993): 626-706 (632).
77 Ibid., 630, cf. Momigliano, *Development,* 11: 'autobiographies can never include the whole life from birth to death.' Bilde, *Josephus,* 109-10, displays a similar way of thinking influenced by modern assumptions of autobiography having to span the entire lifetime of the author, by suggesting that *Life* was autobiography only of a 'very special kind' because it concentrated only on the decisive events of Josephus' life. Johannes Engels, 'Die Hypomnemata - Schriften und die Anfänge der politischen Biographie und Autobiographie in der Griechischen Literatur', *Zeitschrift für Papyrologie und Epigraphik* 96 (1993): 19-36 (21), on the other hand offers a more encompassing, less prescriptive definition: 'Die Beschreibung des ganzen Lebens - oder der politisch relevanten Teile davon - einer individuellen Person vorzüglich aus dem Kreis der ἄνδρες πολιτικοὶ καὶ στρατηγοί (der politisch-militärischen Elite), die nicht bloße literarische Fiktion sein darf, durch eine andere Person (oder durch die beschriebene Person selbst als Autobiographie) . . .'

into 'autobiographic writings', that is, *commentarii* and other accounts that convey information about certain aspects of the author's life, such as a limited military period (e.g. Trajan's *Dacica*), and comprehensive (imperial) autobiography (e.g. Augustus' *De vita sua*).[78] Despite struggling with the concept of genre and the formulation of a working definition for himself, Lewis does not discuss genre theory in much detail. This omission is also reflected by his inconsistent use of terminology: the work of Agrippina the Younger is referred to as '*commentarii*', 'memoirs' and 'autobiography'. His division into autobiographic writings and comprehensive autobiography proves artificial when it comes to Agrippina's *commentarii*.[79] Despite its title, Tacitus' description makes it clear that Agrippina aimed for a life account, or at least as Lewis points out, could not follow the military content of the previously discussed *commentarii*.[80] Lewis is thus forced to discuss Agrippina in an individual subsection, as with her title and imperial connections, she evidently transgresses both his categories.[81]

Pausch also looks at imperial autobiography by considering the imperial adoption and monopolization of autobiography as an important part of the emperor's public self-representation, which in turn inhibited potential 'private' authors of autobiography from writing.[82] In contrast to Scholz, Pausch highlights the paucity of confirmed examples of Roman Republican autobiographies; while Scholz calculates a much higher number of non-extant tests, Pausch limits their number to six.[83] He suggests that although the Roman aristocracy recognized a genre ('Gattung') of autobiography, it was not well received as a strategy aimed at acquiring peer approval. He dismisses Tacitus' comment that in earlier times, such literary strategies had been common and well accepted (see *Agricola* 1.3-4) as highly idealized and argumentative.[84] Autobiography in Republican times constituted a literary strategy for preserving the *memoria* of the author but was written only by men already on the far side of controversial, men such as

78 Lewis, 'Imperial Autobiography', 630–1.
79 Tacitus, *Ann.* 4.53: *Id ego, a scriptoribus annalium non traditum, repperi in commentariis Agrippinae filiae, quae Neronis principis mater vitam suam et casus suorum posteris memoravit.* – 'This incident, not noticed by the professed historians, I found in the commentaries of her daughter Agrippina, mother of the emperor Nero, who recorded for posterity her life and the vicissitudes of her house.' Unless otherwise mentioned, all longer translation are taken from the Loeb Classical Library.
80 Lewis, 'Imperial Autobiography', 652.
81 Further discussions, Chapters 2 and 7, will highlight the importance of understanding the dynamics within a fluid genre and the benefits of understanding their inherent structure and various sub-genres.
82 Dennis Pausch, 'Formen Literarischer Selbstdarstellung in Der Kaiserzeit: Die Von Römischen Herrschern Verfassten Autobiographischen Schriften Und Ihr Literarisches Umfeld', *Rheinisches Museum für Philologie* 147 (2004): 303–36. Malitz, 'Autobiographien', 237, also notes the sudden imperial prerogative of writing autobiography, as does Mellor, *Roman Historians*, 177.
83 Pausch, 'Formen', 304. Scholz, 'Autobiographien', above.
84 Pausch, 'Formen', 305n.8.

Aemilius Scaurus (died 89 BCE) or Sulla.[85] Controversially, ironically (?), the same genre that had previously not been accepted in Roman literary circles in turn became an integral literary part of imperial self-presentation. Unfortunately, the progression remains unclear in Pausch's argument. Beginning with Augustus, Pausch traces the history of the 'Herrscherautobiographie' through to Hadrian (ruled 117–138 CE), suggesting that as with many other aspects of the imperial institution, Augustus was the first to adopt and adapt a previously 'problembehaftete[s]' literary genre, to become socially acceptable, even an imperial tradition.[86] Consequently, any author writing a proper autobiography would, so Pausch, set themselves up as serious competition to the emperor. He suggests that potential authors looked to other, politically less-problematic genres they could fill with their own autobiographical content – other genres such as 'geographische Fachliteratur' were used as an 'Ausweichbewegung', taking on autobiographical functions. He dismisses Nicolaus of Damascus and Josephus; given their alternative social status, there was no danger of them competing with imperial autobiographies.[87] Pausch does not further consider these authors' choice of genre and its implications. As foreigners, of course, they presented no threat to the imperial position or reputation. However, I suggest that choosing a genre so closely associated with the imperial tradition must surely carry implications of its own. Displaying considerable literary *chuzpa* by choosing a genre so closely associated with the emperors, Josephus especially must have had good reason to feel comfortable in his literary choices.[88] The prestige afforded the (imperial) authors of autobiography may similarly have affected the prestige afforded the genre itself.[89]

To prove his theory of literary evasive strategies, Pausch looks at a range of writings which may at first glance seem unrelated but based on their sociocultural autobiographical functions all interact – Pausch transcends generic boundaries to look for the autobiographical content in other genres, or the

---

85 Cf. here Uwe Walter, 'Annales and Analysis', in *The Oxford History of Historical Writing. Volume 1: Beginnings to 600 AD*, ed. by Andrew Feldherr and Grant Hardy (Oxford: Oxford University Press, 2011), 270, who argues that in the competitive atmosphere of Republican Rome, it was the defeated men who turned to autobiography to restore their reputations.
86 Pausch, 'Formen', 311–23, for the quote, 313.
87 Ibid., 324–5. He similarly dismisses Agrippina based on gender, an attitude criticized by Malitz, 'Autobiographien', 237–8, who asks why Agrippina's autobiography had received so little public recognition given her position as Nero's mother and her evident imperial self-confidence.
88 Other scholars have similarly argued that Josephus, being a foreigner, posed no threat to the imperial position and could thus have easily written an autobiography without fear of repercussions: Mason, *Life*, xliii; Eelco Glas, 'Flavius Josephus' Self–Characterization in First-Century Rome' (PhD diss., University of Groningen, Groningen, 2020), 156. Mellor, *Roman Historians*, 183, makes no mention of Josephus in his chapter 'Autobiography at Rome'.
89 See Adams, *Greek Genres*, 12, on genres acquiring prestige.

autobiographical mode (see Chapter 2). References to the concepts of genre, sub-genre and mode, which allow for the transference of individual generic features and functions onto other genres, would surely have helped Pausch streamline his discussion even more, grounding his insightful arguments in a theory-based methodology, and clarify more specifically how far certain works could be understood as taking on functions and features of other genres.[90]

Lastly, several edited collections have recently been published concerned only with autobiography in antiquity. The German contribution must be commended for including two chapters on the literary theory and psychoanalytical view of autobiography.[91] However, the editor is well aware of his limitations and clarifies that rather than portraying ancient autobiography as a whole ('die antike Autobiographie völlig darzustellen'), the volume offers a representative cross-section through various periods and genres ('Gattungen'), in which autobiographical texts ('autobiographische Schriften') were composed and published, from the seventh century BCE to the fifth century CE.[92] This introduction alone, in combination with the subtitle *Werke–Epochen–Gattungen*, should alert us to the fact that we will not find the definition of the genre autobiography in these contributions, but rather a learned view of the different ancient literary genres in which works were published that allow us to extrapolate personal information about the author. We thus learn much about portraits of the author, direct or indirect, in early Greek poetry, Xenophon's *Anabasis*, daily life as reflected in papyri, Josephus' self-presentation in *War*, or Augustine's *Confessions*, but little about the continuous existence, development or features of the genre, even though its existence is accepted.[93]

Overall, scholars have approached the genre discussion in different ways without rejecting either the concept of autobiography or the notion of genre as a whole, using varied terminology that may lead to some confusion given the various definitions of terms such as 'autobiography' and 'memoir'.[94] It

---

90 See, Chapter 2, for a discussion of these terms and their importance in genre theory.
91 Michael Reichel, *Antike Autobiographien. Werke-Epochen-Gattungen* (Köln, Weimar, Wien: Böhlau Verlag, 2005).
92 Ibid., vii.
93 Chronological anthologies offer a detailed diachronic view, whose drawback, despite the ability to offer great detail on individual periods, is the potential omission of cross-generational features and boundaries of the genre – the development appears seamless and gradual, and generic features and their implications cannot easily be recognised. Candau sees only a possible lack of style in autobiographies written during the Republic, but does not recognize this as a transcending feature of autobiography: José M. Candau, 'Republican Rome: Autobiography and Political Struggles', in *Political Autobiographies and Memoirs in Antiquity: A Brill Companion*, ed. by Gabriele Marasco (Leiden, Boston: Brill, 2011). For style as a generic feature, see Chapter 6.
94 The loose interchange or lack of distinguishing explanations between different generic terms (autobiography, memoir, autobiographical etc.) is also evident in *The Lost Memoirs of Augustus*

has also become clear that the many individual discussions, especially in the edited collections, outline a development of literary history as opposed to an overview of the variety of features which made up the genre in all its differences. Several scholars have noted the issue of fluid boundaries and the fact that there appears not to have been a fully encoded literary genre of autobiography; these statements carry with them questions about generic features, audience reception and genre-expectations, yet despite using genre terminology and concepts based on genre theory, scholars have not yet fully brought the two discussions together.

On the other hand, other scholars have recently voiced their doubts and instead employ modal terms such as 'autobiographical', or see only precursors of what we today understand as autobiography. Whitmarsh unfavourably compares ancient biography, *bios*, with autobiography, arguing for the lack of a specific genre title and 'sharply defined concepts'.[95] It would be meaningless, so Whitmarsh, to ask whether texts that include 'a substantial amount' of personal narrative (e.g. Plato's *Seventh Letter,* Xenophon's *Anabasis,* Augustus' *RGDA,* Marcus Aurelius' *Meditations,* or St. Augustine's *Confessions*) should be counted as autobiography, an inherently modern construct.[96] Instead, Whitmarsh argues that what we call autobiography was in fact a rhetorical *apologia* (defence speech) modelled on Socrates' speech in court. While autobiography, in Whitmarsh's estimation, did not yet exist in antiquity, he sees a strong link with *apologia*; referring to Plutarch's advice that self-praise was acceptable mainly in a self-defensive framework, Whitmarsh concludes that authors inserted their autobiographical contents into rhetorical defence speeches.[97] However, without wanting to anticipate discussions further, attributing any genre to a text based on one feature alone is untenable from a literary critical point of view. An apologetic

---

and the Development of Roman Autobiography, ed. by Christopher Smith and Anton Powell (Swansea: The Classical Press of Wales, 2009); Gabriele Marasco, *Political Autobiographies and Memoirs in Antiquity: A Brill Companion* (Leiden: Brill, 2011); Ben Zion Wacholder, *Nicolaus of Damascus* (Berkeley, Los Angeles: University of California Press, 1962); Momigliano, *Development,* 14, categorizes the works of Aemilius Scaurus and Rutilius Rufus as memoirs despite stating that the title (*vita*) corresponds to the Greek equivalent for autobiography. Cf. also ibid., 93-4. Dilke inexplicably switches from 'imperial autobiography' to 'memoirs' when discussing Vespasian: O. A. W. Dilke, 'The Literary Output of the Roman Emperors', *Greece & Rome* 4 (1957): 78-97 (87); also Joseph Geiger, 'The Augustan Age', in *Political Autobiographies and Memoirs in Antiquity,* ed. by Gabriele Marasco (Leiden, Boston: Brill, 2011).

95 Whitmarsh, *Second Sophistic,* 79.
96 This attitude towards genre correlates with his earlier statement that defining genres amounts to an 'uninteresting' endeavour: Whitmarsh, *Second Sophistic,* 5.
97 To contradict Whitmarsh's argument at this stage would require me to anticipate several lines of argument. An aim of this study is to demonstrate that a consistent terminology existed in ancient literature that authors and audiences used to introduce and interpret the group of texts discussed in the literary analysis in Part 2 of this study. Writing about one's own cause had an immediate urgency to it that required authors and audiences to be very clear in their intentions and interpretations; I would submit that the inherent messages were too important to hide in a separate, distinct genre.

purpose does not mandate the genre of *apologia*, and it is unfortunate that scholars have not made this distinction clearer. Simultaneously, the existence of the genre of *apologia* itself is not undisputed in classical scholarship – especially prior to the second-century Christian apologists such as Tertullian, Tatian or Justin Martyr.[98]

Pelling discusses Plutarch's method of quoting from Augustus' lost *De vita sua*.[99] Prior to his detailed discussion on his undisputed area of expertise, the Plutarchan corpus, Pelling argues that the genre of autobiography did in fact not exist in antiquity, at least not in a form that suggests firm expectations on behalf of both author and audience.[100] Pelling does not reject the notion of genre in general but does warn that perhaps generic expectations and features were not as 'firmly or widely' held as others may suppose. Pelling merely appreciates that 'quarter-expectations' existed which would have been a sufficiently clear starting point for author and audience, before citing the evident differences between the works composed by Sulla and Caesar respectively to warn of any possible reconstructions for Augustus' lost autobiography or generic expectations as a whole. For example, to expect a childhood account by Augustus, based on modern expectations and the evidence thereof in some other ancient texts, is problematic.[101] However, the suggestion that Sulla influenced Augustus'

---

98 Wolfram Kinzig, 'Apologists, Christian', in *OCD*³, 128–9. In Mark Edwards et al., *Apologetics in the Roman Empire: Pagans, Jews, and Christians* (Oxford, New York: Oxford University Press, 1999), 1, a recent compilation on apologetic literature spanning the period of the Roman Empire, the editors define apologetic as 'the defence of a cause of a party supposed to be of paramount importance to the speaker', and attempt to unearth the dynamics of ancient apologetics. However, as David Noy, 'Apologetics', *The Classical Review (New Series)* 52 (2002): 138–40, correctly noted, the overall impression the reader takes away is that the majority of contributors in fact argue that there was no genre of apologia. *Apology* for Young is not a genre, but 'a defence or excuses offered in a less precise context or genre': Frances Young, 'Greek Apologists of the Second Century', in *Apologetics in the Roman Empire: Pagans, Jews, and Christians*, ed. by Mark Edwards, et al. (Oxford, New York: Oxford University Press, 1999), 91. Loveday Alexander speaks of a 'wide range and fuzzy definition', which is complemented by Rajak's 'nebulous genre': Loveday Alexander, 'The Acts of the Apostles as an Apologetic Text', in *Apologetics in the Roman Empire*, ed. by Mark Edwards, Martin Goodman, Simon Price and Christopher Rowland (Oxford, New York: Oxford University Press, 1999), 16; Tessa Rajak, 'Talking at Trypho: Christian Apologetic as Anti-Judaism in Justin's Dialogue with Trypho', in *Apologetics in the Roman Empire: Pagans, Jews, and Christians*, ed. by Mark Edwards, et al. (Oxford, New York: Oxford University Press, 1999), 61.
99 Pelling, 'Ancient Genre'.
100 Ibid., 41, for example 43n.7: 'It would be misleading to think of any firmly demarcated "autobiographical genre".' Cf. Martin Hinterberger, *Autobiographische Traditionen in Byzanz* (Wien: Verlag der Österreichischen Akademie der Wissenschaften, 1999), 383, who concludes that autobiography is not an independent genre ('keine selbstständige Gattung') but rather a manner of narration ('Form des Erzählens') – rather than a genre, he finds autobiographical sections in other genres.
101 Pelling, 'Ancient Genre', 44. See Chapter 3 for more details on the individual works. For the similarities between Sulla and Augustus, see most recently Alexander Thein, 'Felicitas and the Memoirs of Sulla and Augustus', in *The Lost Memoirs of Augustus and the Development of Roman Autobiography*, ed. by Christopher Smith and Anton Powell (Swansea: The Classical Press of Wales, 2009); T. P. Wiseman, 'Augustus, Sulla and the Supernatural', in *The Lost Memoirs of*

autobiography, and perhaps also Caesar's *commentarii* by constituting the opposite of what Caesar wanted to achieve, contradicts Pelling's argument, suggesting the existence of a more sophisticated genre awareness, cultural competence and generic expectations than 'quarter-expectations' might imply.

Pelling argues that there was no fully acknowledged genre of autobiography in antiquity, yet at the same time discusses how Plutarch knowingly and masterfully quoted from Augustus' lost autobiography, making it clear that both author and transmitter knew exactly what they were doing. He also argues, quoting Lewis (see earlier discussion) that Cicero consciously avoided writing an autobiography, preferring to publish instead works Pelling classifies as 'autobiographic' – for example the ὑπόμνημα on his consulship or *Brutus*.[102] However, while Pelling is certainly right to caution the application of modern expectations on to ancient literature, his arguments suggest that autobiography must have existed as a genre sufficiently defined and recognized by ancient authors to allow Cicero to avoid writing one, to allow Augustus consciously to adapt and reposition one, and to allow Plutarch to quote one. Furthermore, Tacitus and Cicero refer to the alleged and preferred avoidance of writing autobiography, further demonstrating the genre's actual existence, showing us that the ancient authors quoted by Pelling knew exactly what they were or were not writing.[103] Ultimately, even Pelling admits to a generic framework for expectations, even if in his opinion it was rather vague.

Aims and structure of this study

Scholars have debated the question whether the *Life* really is an autobiography (in terms of an expectation-generating literary framework) and the issue has been reflected upon both in the positive and in the negative. Neither answer has prevented scholars from further interaction with the text. Many recent opinions are rather favourable, accepting readily that ancient literature cannot and must not be judged according to the standards of modern literary expectations.

Augustus and the Development of Roman Autobiography, ed. by Anton Powell and Christopher Smith (Swansea: The Classical Press of Wales, 2009). For Caesar distancing himself from Sulla in terms of literature, see Christopher Smith, 'Sulla's *Memoirs*', in *The Lost Memoirs of Augustus and the Development of Roman Autobiography*, ed. by Christopher Smith and Anton Powell (Swansea: The Classical Press of Wales, 2009), 79.

102 Pelling, 'Ancient Genre', 46. See also Andrew M. Riggsby, 'Memoir and Autobiography in Republican Rome', in *Companion to Greek and Roman Historiography Vol.1*, ed. by John Marincola (Malden; Oxford: Blackwell, 2007), 272, who argues that Cicero consciously employed various strategic tactics to avoid writing an autobiography, but that nevertheless recognition on behalf of the audience would have been immediate.

103 Quotes cited by Pelling, 'Ancient Genre', 42–6.

Nevertheless, recent contributions to *Life*'s genre feel comfortable enough to pursue different avenues. Scholarship in the wider classical literary field has similarly debated the issue, with varying outcomes; there is a considerable amount of interaction with the ancient texts which has not resulted in a clear outlook. Some scholars preface their discussions by positing the lack of a firmly encoded genre, others find sufficient evidence to speak of standardized forms, while again other scholars acknowledge that some ancient texts merely constitute important precursors to modern autobiography. How is it possible that academic opinions diverge so significantly? Most scholars do not discuss in detail how far, or whether at all, autobiography created audience expectations or overreaching, generically recognizable features, and if so, how they were communicated. The question is further eclipsed by the dual task of recreating the mostly fragmentary texts and discussing the historical reliability of the authors and the corresponding content. However, prior to discussing truth or untruth, understanding the genre of a text is important; I aim to show that we need to adopt an interdisciplinary approach combining knowledge of Josephus with classical literary history as well as with genre theory and literary criticism. A nuanced study using genre theory can bring out the particulars of the ancient genre of autobiography, thereby facilitating the identification and interpretation of literary works as autobiography. Thereafter, Josephus' *Life* may be examined whether it can appropriately be classified as autobiography; the genre of *Life* has not yet been discussed based on an approach informed by genre theory, and now becomes the focus of a diachronic and cross-cultural literary study.

This book comprises the following components: this first chapter has presented us with a review of previous commentaries on *Life*'s genre and autobiography in antiquity. Chapter 2 will expand on the importance of genre by introducing the pertinent aspects of modern genre theory, based on the fundamental question, what is a genre? Using a methodological approach to ancient literature based on genre theory is justified by a closer look at the ancient literary understanding of genres, which allows for the overlay of modern concepts and combines to produce a fruitful and valid methodology that has previously been applied successfully in the fields of Classics and New Testament study: a literary analysis, comparing a range of texts and their features. These features include size, structure, literary units, scale, topoi, style, time of composition, and opening features (e.g. title, subject, preface). It is proposed that such a methodological examination will result in a better understanding of the literary boundaries of autobiography in antiquity and will illustrate Josephus' thought process during the composition of *Life*.

In order to generate a framework of literary practices, other texts within Josephus' literary spheres, all associated with autobiography, will be introduced in Chapter 3. The discussion includes a more detailed examination of the ancient discourse on writing about oneself and simultaneously praising oneself inoffensively. Advice and guides on how-to-write-an autobiography did not exist in antiquity, with the prominent exception of Plutarch's *How to praise inoffensively*, and even this treaty does not supply specific generic help. We must therefore consider how a passive education can supplement active educational essays and guides on other, more prominent genres in classical literature, that is, one's cultural competence, a literary sensibility to a social and literary environment. A brief view of the status quo of genre-related discussions will highlight that many texts do not necessarily fit neatly into scholars' current genre understanding but instead hover uncomfortably in a rather grey area with fuzzy generic boundaries. The comparative texts will include, *inter alia*, Caesar's *Gallic War*, Xenophon's *Anabasis* and Libanius' *Oration 1*. Other texts in a fragmentary state will be included as and when reasonable discussion is permissible given their partially limited extant status, such as the lost works of Sulla, Augustus or Nicolaus of Damascus. The wide range of texts will be considered because of their potential direct and indirect influence on Josephus and on the literary and social milieus that he was dialoguing with.

The main part of this book, the practical, genre-based literary analysis of Josephus' *Life* and other ancient autobiographies has been divided into Chapters 4–6. Chapter 7 will summarize the results of the detailed literary analysis of Josephus' *Life* and the comparanda introduced in Chapter 3. A notable contribution lies in the conclusions arising out of this analysis based firmly on genre theory: the conclusions demonstrate the existence of autobiography as a literary genre based on genre-generating features and family resemblance, as well as the division into two distinct sub-genres. Based on these conclusions, I argue that the analysis allows us to track the development of the genre and to situate Josephus' *Life* within the genre. I further argue that Josephus was expertly aware of the generic and literary details during his composition of *Life*. Chapter 8 adds new facets and angles to our understanding of *Life* by discussing the hermeneutic benefits of understanding *Life*'s genre in context and offering new readings of the text in light of a better understanding of Josephus' literary skills and his cultural awareness.

The question of *Life*'s genre will be the focal point of this analysis in order to round off our knowledge of Josephus and should not be marginalized by discussions of *Life*'s content, reliability, purpose or dating. Drawing the circle a bit wider, this book also aims to supplement the current discussion on genre and autobiography in the wider classical world.

2

Genre theory

This chapter has several aims: to introduce the genre understanding which constitutes the foundation of this study; to introduce the methodology of the literary analysis to be applied to Josephus' *Life* and a variety of other texts in the search for ancient autobiography; to demonstrate that modern genre theory can successfully be set into dialogue with an ancient understanding of genre; to discuss the ancient mindset of writing about oneself. This is very much a theoretical chapter, and readers with a confident knowledge of genre theory are welcome to skip around the chapter or move on to Chapter 3. Its usefulness will hopefully become evident in the subsequent literary analysis. For ease of reference, where relevant, I shall briefly break up the narrative and endeavour to explain how the individual sections of the chapter are relevant for the subsequent discussion and analysis of *Life* and the other comparative literature.

Modern genre theory

What is genre and how do we recognize it when we see it?

Genre is commonly understood as a concept of literary conventions. For Tzvetan Todorov, genres function as 'horizons of expectations' for readers and as 'models of writing' for authors.[1] Genres affect authors and readers; in the words of Heather Dubrow, they act as a means of communication between these levels. She speaks of a 'generic contract' between author and reader, constructed out of signals (e.g. title, metre, familiar topoi) which the author includes. Effectively,

---

1 Tzvetan Todorov, *Genres in Discourse*. Translated by By Catherine Porter (Cambridge: Cambridge University Press, 1990), 18–19.

the author agrees to follow patterns and conventions associated with the genre, while in turn, the audience agrees to pay sufficient attention to recognize them.[2]

Genres are recognized by means of features, which when understood as a tool and strategy of communication can be employed and recognized efficiently. References to conventions and patterns that build up the framework abound, for example in Dubrow's notion of a contract requesting that the author include certain features and the audience pay sufficient attention to them; as such, the responsibility for the recognition of genre is shared by both sides.[3] The selection of both a genre and features becomes a further act of communication between the author and his audience.[4]

The combination of formal, structural and content-related features is a foundational tenet for the present study; specific features will be presented further in theory and will be applied in practice to a selection of ancient texts in Chapters 4, 5 and 6. Adams reiterates that while external features provide 'structural cues' to the readers, internal or content-related features 'affirm and support' the external features; identifying the genre of a text consists of identifying and evaluating the constellation of external and internal features in comparison to other texts and other genres.[5]

Works may share any number of features with other, related genres – the *genera proxima* – and the more features are shared, the more blurry or fuzzy the boundaries may appear and generic associations become uncertain, if not contradictory. Xenophon's *Anabasis* was written by the author about a significant episode of his life, but the direct association between author/narrator is not given, nor does the author offer an account of his entire life. As will be shown in Chapter 3, the text – as well as others – hovers uncomfortably on the boundaries intersecting several genres (e.g. autobiography, historiography). Understanding,

---

2 Heather Dubrow, *Genre* (London: Methuen, 1982), 31. For Conte, they are procedures that imply a response: Gian Biagio Conte, *The Rhetoric of Imitation: Genre and Poetic Memory in Virgil and Other Latin Poets. Translated from the Italian with a Foreword by Charles Segal* (Ithaca and London: Cornell University Press, 1986), 112.
3 Cf. also Alastair Fowler, *Kinds of Literature: An Introduction to the Theory of Genres and Modes* (Oxford: Clarendon Press, 1982), 257, who insists on the responsibility of the author to learn the conventions necessary to ensure interpretation.
4 Eric Donald Hirsch Jr., *Validity in Interpretation* (New Haven, London: Yale University Press, 1967), 93.
5 Adams, *Genre of Acts*, 58; cf. Todorov, *Genres*, 18. See also John Frow, *Genre* (London and New York: Routledge, 2006), 76, and Rene Wellek and Austin Warren, *Theory of Literature*, 3rd edn (Harmondsworth: Penguin, Pelican, 1982 reprint of 1963 edn), 231, who refer to 'a grouping of literary works based, theoretically, upon both outer form (specific metre or structure) and also upon the inner form (attitude, tone, purpose – more crudely, subject and audience). The ostensible basis may be one or the other . . . but the critical problem will then be to find the other dimension, to complete the diagram'.

or being able to visualize, a genre system may well prove helpful in approaching these texts and their generic association with more confidence.

A work may be classified as participating in a genre even without presenting certain features – while we are able to evaluate single features individually, Burridge emphasizes that not all features need appear to the same extent in every work, otherwise each specimen of any given genre would be identical to the next.[6] Ultimately, while there may be some features more immediately or more easily recognizable, it is the combination of features that creates an overwhelming similarity between works, a relationship the philosopher Ludwig Wittgenstein has nominated a 'family resemblance'.[7] The selection of texts presented in Chapter 3 and discussed in the literary analysis in Chapters 4, 5 ,6 all evidence a variety of features, some of which they share, some of which they do not; perhaps without actively appreciating the importance of Wittgenstein's family resemblance, these texts have consistently been grouped together somehow as participating in autobiography.

A 'cluster' develops in which those works that exhibit many recognizable features are more easily recognizable in terms of genre affiliation and family resemblance, while those displaying fewer characteristic features are placed at the periphery, resulting in a subjective, and misplaced, hierarchy.[8] We see such judgements directed at *Life* suggesting that as an autobiography, it had not quite succeeded (attributing *Life* with a rather low hierarchical status).

As part of the recognition process, Hirsch understands the concept of genre as a 'system of expectations'; these expectations could have arisen only from a previously established notion of genre: 'in this type of utterance, we expect these types of traits'.[9] Expectations arise out of literary competence and the experience of previous, similar or different types of genres. These are based on contemporaneous culture and literary experiences, which highlights the importance of understanding the milieu of the text we are reading. A brief overview of the ancient genre system will round off this discussion.

---

6 Individual features can appear in different genres; importantly, it is the combination which constitutes the genre: for example Richard Burridge, *What Are the Gospels? A Comparison with Graeco-Roman Biography*, 2nd edn (Michigan: William B. Eerdmans Pub. Co., 2004), 41, 107; Hirsch, *Validity*, 110; Fowler, *Kinds of Literature*, 74.
7 Ludwig Wittgenstein, *Philosophical Investigations* (Oxford: Basil Blackwell, 1968), 31–2. All examples from a given genre, based on their demonstration of generic features, share a certain resemblance, or pattern, which identifies them as participating in the same genre, without necessarily having to share one feature common to them all. Cf. Alastair Fowler, 'The Life and Death of Literary Forms', *New Literary History* 2 (1971): 199–216 (202): 'Recognition of genre depends on associating a complex of elements, which need not all appear in one work', or Gian Biagio Conte, *Latin Literature: A History*, Rev. edn (Baltimore: John Hopkins University Press, 1994), 108.
8 Dubrow, *Genre*, 106–7.
9 Hirsch, *Validity*, 83, 73.

Generic expectations can be either confirmed during the reading process, or they can be challenged, depending on the presence or omission of aforementioned internal or external features. The process of recognition can be immediate, based on overt signalling features such as a title or the opening words of a text; readers begin their recognition process and adaptation of expectations differently depending for example on the introductory words 'Once upon a time' or a title such as 'Cooking for Beginners'.[10] Next, the reader embarks on the process of confirming or realigning their expectations of the genre based on the presence or lack of features. When something unexpected happens, we are challenged in our conception and must decide whether to continue down the same genre route or change genres.[11] Our expectations form the way we read a text and the way in which we can change our minds and build new expectations based on what we are reading.[12] These changing expectations and the challenging of our expectations do not imply a breakdown of the genre system itself, but energize it, helping the system develop and reinvent itself. As Todorov points out, in order for transgression to take place, there has to be something to transgress in the first place.[13]

Genre and its recognition, then, can be understood to lie at the intersection of authorial intent and reader response.[14] The author can include as many or as few features as desired to aid in, or confuse, his readers' recognition and interpretative process; the reader need not acknowledge them, although he will be conditioned by his own literary knowledgebase and his context to note the presence or omission of features in his thought process.[15]

---

10 Burridge, *Gospels*, 108–13, on signalling features. Also Adams, *Genre of Acts*, 48.
11 John Sturrock, *Structuralism: With a New Introduction by Jean-Michel Rabaté*, 2nd edn (Oxford: Blackwell, 2003), 111.
12 Cf. Frow, *Genre*, 28.
13 Todorov, *Genres*, 14. Expectations, norms, and conventions become visible when they are transgressed and positively challenge us to consider and reconsider our genre expectations.
14 Texts can of course be read and interpreted without knowledge of the text's genre as intended by the author, even contrary to generic conventions. Anti-authorialist theories such as those advanced by Roland Barthes deny the author any relevance once the text leaves his responsibility and reaches a readership, for example Roland Barthes, 'Death of an Author', *Aspen* 5–6 (1967). Post-modern theories have advocated approaching texts from various perspectives, with much success and interesting ensuing interpretation. Without wishing to discredit these reader-response approaches, which can offer fruitful counter-impulses to authorial-intent theories, this study approaches *Life* and ancient autobiography with the basic understanding that knowing the genre of a text, as intended by the author, provides an important interpretive framework for readers.
15 Cf. Terry Eagleton, *Literary Theory: An Introduction*, 2nd edn (London: Blackwell Publishers, 1996), 60, who refers to the lack of coercive features in the text in relation to the interpretive process, positing that if, as readers, we do not respect the author's meaning, we are left with no norms of interpretation.

The relationships and developments of genres

This play with expectations affects the fluidity and development of genres, suggesting an organic, rather than a rigid, system, maintaining its own momentum in a state of fluidity in which genres arise, change, develop, mix with other genres and are overtaken. According to Fowler, the *primary stage* of a genre begins when an oral, or proto, tradition assumes a literary shape and forms a recognizable group, made up of previously independent features. Often this stage is unconscious on the part of the author, and the recognition of this primary stage must be retroactive – the author may not necessarily be aware of his actions or any literary parallels.[16] Isocrates however was aware of the novelty that his *Antidosis* represented, as evidenced in his preface.[17] During the *secondary stage*, others compose their works using the primary model consciously as their literary base.[18] The final, *tertiary stage*, redirects the secondary models towards a new direction, incorporating radically new features.[19]

Frow argues that the continuity of a generic name can disguise discontinuities in terms of content, as it passes from one system to another.[20] As Fowler terms it, a 'radix' is necessary which signifies the specific time period within the life of a genre.[21] Fowler deliberates on the transformation of generic labels, explaining that while the label, that is name, of a respective genre remains the same, the content can change dramatically.[22] Using the genre designation autobiography in our current discussions remains appropriate, thusly, as long as we understand that modern conceptions of autobiography will present us with a different content to the ancient version.

---

16 Burridge, *Gospels*, 44; Fowler, *Kinds of Literature*, 149–69. Cf. Todorov's concept of the origins of genre arising out of other genres: Todorov, *Genres*, 15, 21–6: a new genre is the transformation of one or several existing genres by means of inversion, displacement, combination.
17 Arguing the other side of this coin, Reichel suggests that the lack of a preface implies that Isocrates' contemporary Xenophon was equally, if more self-consciously, aware of the 'Neuartigkeit' of his *Anabasis*: Michael Reichel, 'Ist Xenophons Anabasis eine Autobiographie?', in *Antike Autobiographien. Werke-Epochen-Gattungen*, ed. by Michael Reichel (Köln, Weimar, Wien: Böhlau Verlag, 2005), 46.
18 Fowler, *Kinds of Literature*, 160–2. Burridge, *Gospels*, 44, in this context mentions the classical notion of μίμησις/imitatio, discussed as follows, which encourages the modelling process.
19 Fowler, *Kinds of Literature*, 162–4.
20 Frow, *Genre*, 131, cf. 133. Wellek and Warren, *Theory*, 246–7, discuss in how far generic continuity can even exist despite or because of generic development. Cf. also Burridge, *Gospels*, 43, and Fowler, *Kinds of Literature*, 130–48, who talks of 'generic labels'.
21 Fowler, *Kinds of Literature*, 134.
22 Ibid., 106–29. He also mentions the need for a 'chronological frame of reference': Fowler, 'Life and Death', 208.

Modes and sub-genres

At the same time as borrowing features, texts relate to other genres by adopting the respective mode for individual passages, or even the entire text. The mode of work, according to genre theory, can be used to categorize literary works in relation to their genre. According to Fowler, *mode* is expressed in the adjectival form, in contrast to the genre and sub-genre given as a noun.[23] Working on a level above genre, the mode of a text describes its linguistic and stylistic features and consequently does not imply generic affiliation or an external form; on the contrary, any text within a genre can exhibit different linguistic features in addition to (or instead of) its genre-defining features. We have already seen that scholars discussing autobiography in ancient literature prefer the terms 'autobiographical' or 'autobiographic', unaware that categorizing a text only by its mode causes confusion 'as if they were separate entities capable of existing on their own'.[24] Any text, or parts of it, can of course be written in the autobiographical mode, but simultaneously requires a generic affiliation.[25] Specifically, while autobiography is the genre, the autobiographical mode can manifest itself in other genres, demonstrating only a selection of internal features. Josephus' *War* undoubtedly belongs to historiography; in his preface, Josephus clearly announces his historiographical intentions and even apologizes for transgressing generic decorum.[26] Subsequently, Josephus expertly weaves passages participating in a different generic mode into his narrative. In *War* 2.568–3.408, Josephus features himself and his experiences as the main character. However, this narrative is a seamlessly integrated part of a much longer historiographical narrative and serves these historiographical purposes. While in this storyline, author equals character and Josephus as character certainly features most prominently (see further, allocation of space as a feature of autobiography), the narrative is not an autobiography, but written in the autobiographical mode, offering the reader autobiographical information as part of a larger, historiographical narrative.[27]

---

23 Fowler, *Kinds of Literature*, 106–29.
24 Ibid., 108.
25 Burridge, *Gospels*, 40, offers the more popular example of tragedy as a genre with all its conventions as opposed to other works written in the tragic mode.
26 See Glas, 'Self-Characterization' for a recent interpretation of the emotionally charged preface; on *War*'s historiographical character, see exemplary Steve Mason, 'Josephus's Judean War', in *A Companion to Josephus*, ed. by Honora Howell Chapman and Zuleika Rodgers (Chichester: Wiley Blackwell, 2016) and Jonathan Price, 'Josephus', in *The Oxford History of Historical Writing. Beginnings to AD 600*, ed. by Andrew Feldherr and Grant Hardy (Oxford: Oxford University Press, 2011).
27 For an in-depth analysis of the autobiographical passages in *War*, see Glas, 'Self-Characterization'.

The various sub-genres in contrast operate on a different level, as described by Fowler as divisions of genre by 'subject matter and motif'.[28] Sub-genres share among themselves the various features of their genre but are usually divided by content. As the history of scholarship in Chapter 1 has highlighted, several scholars had struggled with the different temporal boundaries ancient authors had set in their respective narratives – some authors endeavoured to incorporate as much of a life-to-point of writing narrative as possible, whereas other authors preferred to narrate a much shorter period.[29] Employing genre theory and understanding the concepts of sub-genres would surely have helped these scholars streamline their discussions and avoid having to come up with artificial groupings or headings. We will come across the concepts again in the final chapters which will clarify how ancient authors, and Josephus especially, employed temporal boundaries to participate in autobiography's sub-genres.

The importance of genre

Echoing Hirsch's often-quoted 'all verbal meaning is genre-bound', Frow asks why genre matters, pointing to the centrality of genre to meaning-making and to the social struggle over meanings.[30] An underlying premise of this analysis of *Life* is that determining the genre of a literary text is fundamentally important for interpretation. Various interpretations have been attributed to *Life* in the history of scholarship, as outlined in Chapter 1, and they all rest on the respective genre affiliations attributed to *Life* – which remain debated and debatable. The concept of genre helps in the interpretation of literature by allowing the reader a conceptual starting point from which to embark on his process of understanding and interpretation. Thus, genre as a construct, a system, allows for the recognition, categorization and interpretation of literature by means of a comparative approach during the reading process: 'All along the way we construe this meaning instead of that because this meaning belongs to the type of meaning we are interpreting while that does not.'[31]

---

28 Fowler, *Kinds of Literature,* 112. On the sub-genres of biography and the Gospels, see Justin M. Smith, 'Genre, Sub-Genre and Questions of Audience: A Proposed Typology for Greco-Roman Biography', *Journal of Greco-Roman Christianity and Judaism* 4 (2007): 184–216.
29 See for more detail, Chapters 3 and 5.
30 Hirsch, *Validity*, 76; Frow, *Genre*, 10.
31 Hirsch, *Validity*, 76. Cf. Frow, *Genre*, 8, arguing that based on the different genre conceptions formulated by the reader, with which he approaches a text, different aspects and features of the text will stand out or be ignored and be interpreted accordingly.

Genres can also function on a social level, reflecting contemporaneous values and ideologies.[32] The choice or identification of a genre transmits the expectations of authority and truthfulness, social and moral features which are part of society's expectations. Take for example the scandal surrounding the Latvian holocaust survivor Binjamin Wilkormiski and his autobiography, describing his experiences as a child-survivor of the war.[33] The book was initially received to great critical acclaim. However, a Swiss journalist began to question the veracity of Wilkormiski's autobiography, suggesting the author was in fact born Bruno Grosjean from Switzerland.[34] Wilkormiski's publisher reacted and commissioned the historian Stefan Maechler to investigate both the accusations and Wilkormiski's background; the inquest confirmed Wilkormiski's fake persona and fake history.[35]

The reaction to the allegations reflects the importance of the social expectations a genre and its subsequent interpretations carry with it. As Maechler himself stated, 'Once the professed interrelationship between the first-person narrator, the death-camp story he narrates, and historical reality are proved palpably false, what was a masterpiece becomes kitsch.'[36] The genre of the book, autobiography, allowed a certain social process of interpretation that, once the genre had changed, had to be rejected.

Methodological case studies

An integral aspect of recognizing the genre in which a given text participates is the combination of generic features an author inserts into or omits from the text and the extent to which these features (or their omission) are recognizable to an audience. A variety of factors must come together for a text to be associated with a genre. As noted in Chapter 1, the instability of *Life*'s association with autobiography rests in part on the insecurity of the ancient literary landscape

---

32 As noted in the previous chapter, Roman societal values appreciated a certain level of self-promotion which included inscriptions, statues and also literature. Yarrow's comment that the motivation for autobiography in antiquity was closely tied with self-glorification and thus presented an 'obvious problem' adds unnecessary value judgements onto ancient values: Liv Mariah Yarrow, *Historiography at the End of the Republic* (Oxford: Oxford University Press, 2006), 67.
33 Binjamin Wilkomirski, *Bruchstücke. Aus Einer Kindheit 1939-1948* (Frankfurt: Jüdischer Verlag, 1995).
34 Daniel Ganzfried, 'Die Geliehene Holocaust-Biographie', *Weltwoche* Nr. 35, 27 (September 1998): S. 45f.
35 Stefan Mächler, *Der Fall Wilkomirski. Über Die Wahrheit Einer Biografie* (Zürich: Pendo Verlag, 2000).
36 Ibid., 281.

and the question of whether autobiography existed as a recognizable, and writeable, genre. A genre-oriented detailed literary analysis as proposed in this book will substantially contribute to the ongoing discussion by offering a methodological framework within which to set *Life* and comparative texts in the search for autobiography.

Genre-based analyses of ancient literature are not new, but have been used successfully in the past to settle issues of genre association. Often, what may be perceived as a simple approach can challenge us and our perspectives, and can alter the way that we approach ancient texts. Burridge sets out to compare the canonical gospels to Greco-Roman biography, in an attempt to determine the genre of the Gospels.[37] Building on genre theory as outlined earlier, Burridge bases his approach on the main tenet that a text cannot exist *sui generis*.[38]

Aiming to set up a framework with which to compare the Gospels, Burridge analyses biographies by Isocrates, Philo (first century CE), Plutarch (before 50 and after 120 CE) and Suetonius (*c.* 70–*c.* 130 CE), composed before, contemporaneous with and after the Gospels. Burridge compiled a list of features 'as comprehensive as possible', by means of which he organizes his analysis to identify the generic features of biography in antiquity, with which to compare the Gospels.[39] These include:

- Opening features (title, opening words, prologue/preface);
- Subject (analysis of verb subjects, allocation of space);
- External features (mode of representation, metre, size/length, structure, scale, literary units, sources, method of characterization);
- Internal features (setting, topics, style, tone, mood, attitude, values, the quality of characterization, social setting and authorial intention).[40]

---

37 Burridge, *Gospels*. Burridge reacts to a century of scholarship that has alternated between claiming the gospels are biography and asserting they are texts sui generis. The book has now been publlished in its third edition.
38 Burridge reacts to the previous popular theories advanced by Rudolph Bultmann, who had rejected any relationship between the Gospels and biography and suggested that they were a unique literary creation, that is *sui generis*: Rudolf Bultmann, *Die Geschichte der synoptischen Tradition. Zweite neubearbeitete Auflage* (Göttingen: Vandenhoeck und Ruprecht, 1931), 411. See also Burridge, *Gospels*, 9–11, for a review.
39 Burridge, *Gospels*, 105.
40 Ibid., 107, cf. 105–23 for a more detailed description of the individual features. Admittedly, a few features in this list may appear redundant once the results of the analysis have been compiled – Burridge's conclusions in regard to 'atmosphere', for example, cover the range of possibilities which for Burridge demonstrate the flexibility inherent in genre: 'This is a further reminder of the flexibility of *bios*, with the contrast between this lighter atmosphere and the more serious tone of the others.' (144); 'Thus we may conclude that although the atmosphere of *bioi* . . . tends to be mostly serious and respectful . . . in some, it can be much lighter in others' (177). Also ibid., 204, 227.

Because of the inherent flexibility and dynamic nature of genres, Burridge emphasizes that some borrowing of generic features must be expected, and we must anticipate that throughout the literary analysis we will see that texts can relate to features from other genres such as history or *commentarii*.[41] In addition, some of the individual comparisons and conclusions might seem obvious and unnecessary; however, setting these seemingly obvious observations into context within a systematic study will allow us to compare trends and developments.

Burridge subsequently applies this range of features, which make up the generic parameters of Greco-Roman biography, to the Gospels, separated into Synoptic and John, and he successfully integrates them into the genre, or the system, of *bioi*. His results and solution, based on the data collected by his analysis, demonstrate and explain the Gospels' generic categorization as examples of Greco-Roman biography.[42] The interpretative benefits of Burridge's results are now being used as the basis for future scholars, and the basic methodology has subsequently been successfully applied by Burridge to the genre of Acts as a biography of the Church; in a full-length study based on the same principles of genre theory, Adams further develops his understanding of Acts as a collective biography of the Church, and Justin Smith, similarly stimulated by Burridge's approach, analyses the Gospels in the search for potential sub-genres of biography.[43]

In this study, Burridge's list of features will be retained as far as possible, although some changes are necessary to account both for the fact that the authors are writing about themselves, and for the fragmentary nature of several comparative texts.[44] The fragmentary nature of some texts proves more challenging to circumvent, as features such as allocation of space or atmosphere cannot be determined from a handful of fragments and references by other authors; our knowledge remains hypothetical. Passages are usually quoted by the transmitting author for one purpose or another, and with a bias; for example,

---

41 Ibid., 63. For the encomium, see earlier and Neyrey, 'Josephus' *Vita*'.

42 The results of Burridge's methodology are widely accepted and evident in the perception change, initiated by the works of Aune and Talbert, that occurred as a result of his study: scholars call it a 'sea-change', convinced that his study 'ought to end any legitimate denials of the canonical Gospels' biographical character. It has made its case'. Christopher Tuckett, 'Book Review: *What Are the Gospels? A Comparison with Graeco-Roman Biography*', *Theology* 96 (1993): 74–5; Charles H. Talbert, '*What Are the Gospels? A Comparison with Graeco-Roman Biography*', *JBL* 112 (1993): 714–15. For a collection of positive reviews and responses, see Burridge, *Gospels*, 252–88. See also more recently, Smith, 'Genre', 200–3.

43 Richard Burridge, 'The Genre of Acts: Revisited', in *Reading Acts Today: Essays in Honour of Loveday C. A. Alexander*, ed. by Steve Walton, Thomas E. Phillips, et al. (London, New York: T & T Clark, 2011), 3–28; Adams, *Genre of Acts*; Smith, 'Genre'.

44 For example, while Burridge discusses the depiction of the biographee's death scenes, this analysis will consider reference to the author's retirement or end of career. The time of composition and publication has been added as an additional internal feature as it reflects directly on to the authorial intention and the social setting.

they may be preserved for grammatical interest or to transmit a certain image of the subject. Therefore, at times it is advisable either to remain silent or advance estimated guesses at best. As Andrew Riggsby has pointed out, the fragmentary nature of the evidence suggests a more marginal place for autobiography in the Roman world; this need not be disputed, and Riggsby remains confident that despite these caveats, patterns are discernible and that the genre of autobiography existed to a sufficiently recognizable degree for these patterns, expectations and conventions to emerge and be recognized.[45]

Ancient genre theory

The previous section has explained how this study intends to apply insights from modern genre theory to ancient literature. To ward off cries of anachronism, the following section aims – briefly – to outline ancient perspectives on genre directly relevant to the proposed literary analysis.[46] Ancient literary critics had developed a comprehensive genre system which can be strengthened and more fully explored by the application of modern genre theory. Our sources are not comprehensive, nor are they systematic studies of genre or literary criticism; instead, we derive our information from explicit statements of principles or theory, criticism of other authors, and from practice, creating a composite picture of ancient genre theory.

Distinctions between genres

We find a variety of comments suggesting the formulation of genre categories/labels or a genre system. Plutarch's statement, for example, that he was writing lives (βίους), not history (οὔτε γὰρ ἱστορίας, *Alex.* 1.2) functions to alert the audience to generic relationships or differences, allowing audiences to adjust their expectations for a better interpretation.[47] Centuries earlier, Isocrates

---

45 Riggsby 'Memoir and Autobiography', 266. Riggsby's approach also considers features and similarities between the same selection of texts as introduced in Chapter 3, although his approach is by necessity much briefer and more superficial than the present study, considering only the political trajectories of authors, their genealogy and social standing, and the era they were all writing in.
46 Others have admirably gathered together wider evidence pertaining to concepts of ancient genre theory as a whole, which need not be repeated here. See more fully Adams, *Genre of Acts* and idem., *Greek Genres*.
47 For a more detailed discussion of this passage in Plutarch, see Burridge, *Gospels*, 61–2, who picks up earlier suggestions that Plutarch had too much material for his *Alexander* and was explaining his omissions based on genre choice. For Stephen J. Harrison, *Generic Enrichment in Vergil and Horace* (Oxford: Oxford University Press, 2007), 12, in an ancient context, this sort of generic label

already had recognized that there are as many varieties of prose (τρόποι τῶν λόγων) as there were of poetry (ποιημάτων, *Antid.* 45), and Cicero provides us with a list of poetic genres including tragedy, comedy or epic, which according to Cicero can be distinguished from the others: *diversum a reliquis* (Cicero, *Opt. gen.* 1). Cicero also testifies to the distinctions between prose genres:

> 'Thucydidem' inquit 'imitamur.' optume, si historiam scribere, non si causas dicere cogitatis. Thucydides enim rerum gestarum pronuntiator sincerus et grandis etiam fuit; hoc forense concertatorium iudiciale non tractavit genus.
>
> Thucydides, you say, we strive to imitate. Very good, if you are thinking of writing history, but not if you contemplate pleading cases. Thucydides was a herald of deeds, faithful and even grand, but our forensic speech with its wrangling, its atmosphere of the courtroom, he never used. (*Brut.* 287)

Features

This distinction between genres was achieved by the use of textual components, generic features. Ancient critics related specific features with specific genres, considering them appropriate or not for the respective subject matter. Decorum, *to prepon,* was a fundamental value in ancient society and literature. As Horace (65–8 BCE) warns us, 'let each style keep the singular place for which it is suited' (*Ars P.* 92). The fundamental division is based on the use of metre: poetry or prose. As Dionysius of Halicarnassus (first century BCE) claims, ἔστι τοίνυν πᾶσα λέξις ᾗ σημαίνομεν τὰς νοήσεις ἢ μὲν ἔμμετρος, ἢ δὲ ἄμετρος – 'every utterance, then, by which we express our thoughts is either in metre or not in metre' (*Comp.* 3). Dionysius discusses examples taken from poets (ποιηταί) such as Sophocles and prose authors (συγγραφεῖς) such as Demosthenes (*Comp.* 9). Maintaining decorum, Aelius Aristides (117–181 CE), in praising both prose and poetry, understands prose as the more natural medium for men to use, holding the capacity to 'propound an appropriate subject, the well-thought-out arrangement of details'.[48]

Poetry is further subdivided into poetic genres paired with metres (e.g. hexameter, iambic, trochaic tetrameter), allowing the audience a genre

---

is informative and helps to generate part of the text's interpretation by creating generic norms and expectations for the audience, in parallel to Hirsch's understanding, earlier, of how generic boundaries allow a critical reading by providing a framework against which to set the reader's interpretation.

48 Transl. Donald Andrew Russell and Michael Winterbottom, *Ancient Literary Criticism: The Principal Texts in New Translations* (Oxford: Clarendon Press, 1972), 559. See also Philo, *Abr.* 4.23, who distinguishes between poetry (ποιημάτων) and prose (συγγραμμάτων).

identification based partially on metre. As Farrell notes, ancient critics did not recognize generic ambiguity as an issue, instead sharing the confidence that poems belonged to one genre or another; there was a stable relationship between genre and metrical form.[49] Narrative prose did not have this instant recognition based on metre; instead, ancients could evaluate and categorize prose narratives in terms of style (low, middle, high), although the fluidity of genre allowed for trends and fashions; Cicero bemoaned the fact that people no longer read Cato because the trends in what styles were considered acceptable kept changing (*Brut.* 65–8, cf. 78).[50] At the same time, considering that prose authors could easily write different prose genres, sometimes these authors might (un)consciously confuse the appropriate style for the respective subject matter, such as Demochares (Demosthenes' nephew), who according to Cicero wrote both history and oratory: 'the history of Athens during his lifetime was less in the style of a historian but more of an orator'. (*Brut.* 286).

Closely related to metre and style was the subject matter; Harrison sees a 'fundamental connection' between topic and metre.[51] In poetry, metres were lyrical representations of certain subjects, and each subject had to be paired with the appropriate metre.[52] Epic, according to Aristotle, requires 'heroic verse' (μέτρον τὸ ἡρωικὸν, *Poet.* 24, 1459b) and substantial/exalted characters, (μίμησις . . . σπουδαίων, *Poet.* 1449b) while comedy deals with low characters (μίμησις φαυλοτέρων, *Poet.* 1449a). Similarly, we read in Aristophanes (d. 386 BCE) how Euripides is criticized by Aeschylus for staging people and subjects inappropriate for tragedy (*Ran.* 1010–98), again demonstrating an early example of genre awareness and associations. According to Aristotle, prose was reserved for themes that were less grand, for the roles of slaves or low characters (*Rhet.* 3.2.3, 1404b), and the subject matter was not as explicitly tied to the style as for poetry, although some pairings, such as history with a high style, were more appropriate than others (e.g. Dion. Hal., *Ant. rom.* 1.1.2).[53] Quintilian emphasizes the ultimate importance (*maxime necessaria*, *Inst.* 11.1.1) of appropriate speech and style, while Horace succinctly summarizes ancient

---

49 Joseph Farrell, 'Classical Genre in Theory and Practice', *New Literary History* 34 (2003): 383–408 (386).
50 For high, middle or low styles and their application, see, for example, Cicero, *Orat.* 75–121; Quintilian, *Inst.* 12.10.58–72, 11.1.3.
51 Harrison, *Generic Enrichment*, 3.
52 Cf. [Demetrius] *On style* 190. Horace, *Ars P.* 89, states that a comic theme cannot be expressed (*exponi non volt*) in tragic verse.
53 See also Joseph Farrell, 'Literary Criticism', in *The Oxford Handbook of Roman Studies*, ed. by Alessandro Barchiese and Walter Scheidel (Oxford: Oxford University Press, 2010), 183; Geiger, *Cornelius Nepos*, 17.

thought: *Singula quaeque locum teneant sortita decentem.* – 'Let each style keep the becoming place allotted it.' (*Ars P.* 92)⁵⁴

A further feature mentioned by ancient authors was length; epic, for example, was defined by Aristotle in terms of length (Aristotle, *Poet.* 14, 1459b), and he also understood tragedy as being short enough for several works to be presented at the same occasion (Aristotle, *Poet.* 14, 1459b). While for prose works, lengths varied considerably, nevertheless we see that ancient authors were aware of the feature and did on occasion comment on the length of their texts (e.g. Josephus, *Ant.* 20.267; cf. *War* 1.30; *Ag. Ap.* 1.320).⁵⁵ Cicero mentions a speech by Crassus given during his consulship in 95 BCE whose length would be considered short if understood as an oration but was acceptable in terms of length if read as panegyric (*Brut.* 162); Appian notes that the Illyrian affairs in written form would not have been long enough to make up a book by themselves, hence his decision to include them with the Macedonian Wars (*B Civ.* 5.14.145). Similarly, literary studies such as those by Burridge or Lawrence Wills, who have attempted to clarify the generic affiliation of different works, have regarded the size of the respective works as an important feature.⁵⁶ Burridge, following Fowler, distinguishes three different general lengths (short, medium, long) for ancient literature. Burridge classifies books as medium length if they fit onto one standard scroll and can be read aloud comfortably in one sitting; he calculates the length to lie between 10,000–25,000 words depending on the handwriting. Short books accordingly are shorter than 10,000 words and can fit several onto a single scroll, whereas longer works measure more than 25,000 and require several scrolls and sittings.⁵⁷

For Horace, the preface sets the stage for the entire work, preparing the audience for what is to come and offering a framework for their expectations and subsequent interpretation (*Ars P.* 136–52). According to Lucian of Samosata (b. *c.* 120 CE), the preface is especially important for narrative works as it allows

---

54 Quintilian agrees, citing Cicero, 'One single style of oratory is not suited to every case, nor to every audience, nor every speaker, nor every occasion.' (*Inst.* 11.1.4).
55 From earliest times, ancient authors had recourse to the art of stichometry, an ancient system of numbering the lines of a text: P. J. Parsons, 'Stichometry', in *OCD³*, 1443. According to Galen, the standard line measured 15–16 syllables (*De Placitis Hippocrats et Platonis* 8.1.23). See also Jay B. Kennedy, 'Plato's Forms, Pythagorean Mathematics, and Stichometry', *APEIRON* (2010): 1–32 (4), who refers to this as a 'routine job' in antiquity.
56 Burridge, *Gospels*, 114–15. Wills discusses the genre of the Jewish novel in the ancient world and uses the comparative size of his examples to affirm the existence of such a genre: Lawrence M. Wills, *The Jewish Novel in the Ancient World* (Ithaca and London: Cornell University Press, 1995), 27.
57 Burridge, *Gospels*, 114; Fowler, *Kinds of Literature*, 63. Burridge bases his calculations on the following measurements for scrolls: 8–12 inches high, 30–35 feet long. Malitz, 'Autobiographien', 229, considers Caesar's *Civil War* 1 or Tacitus' *Annals* 1 short books, coming in at just under fifty Oxford pages.

the author to outline his methodology and purpose, directing and preparing the receiving audience (*Hist. conscr.* 23). The preface also introduces the subject matter, earlier, which itself can impact on the structure of a text. History, according to Dionysius of Halicarnassus (*Thuc.* 9) can be structured either topographically or chronologically (ἢ κατὰ τόπους . . . ἢ κατὰ χρόνους cf. Dio Siculus 17.1.2), and Thucydides' experiment to structure his history differently failed (οὐκ ὀρθὸς), whereas biography is structured around the life (and death) of the subject.

The preface can also introduce the purpose of writing, and we see authors commenting on the generic relationship between the function or purpose of a text and the appropriate genre. Isocrates differentiates between an encomium (ἐγκώμιον) and a defence (ἀπολογίαν) based on the author's purpose (*Hel. enc.* 14), and Aristotle distinguished between Homer and Empedocles based on their intentions (*Poet.* 1447b). Similarly, for Lucian, history and poetry have different aims (*Hist. conscr.* 8); he sees a firm distinction between encomium and history: the encomiast is concerned only with praise, to gladden his subject, even if he has to lie, while history does not tolerate untruth. Dionysius of Halicarnassus, *Ant. Rom.* 1.1.2–3, directly pairs the subject matter of a work with the author's purpose.

We see how ancient literature had developed a set of features considered appropriate for respective genres and how these features offered authors and audiences a framework for composition and comprehension. We also see that even though the ancient authors singled out in this discussion range in time and space, nevertheless the overall tenor and trend of their comments have held fast over the course of the intervening centuries. These features, along with a selection of additional features as discussed earlier (methodological case studies) will form the foundation for a literary analysis (as follows) applied to a range of ancient texts, focused on the question whether and in how far a set of features had been established for autobiography.

Mixing/Theory versus practice

While in theory, the overall tenor of comments offers the impression of a rather restrictive set of features, we need not accept that every author adhered to them. In fact, breaking these conventions was as much the norm as adhering to them. The aforementioned fluidity of genre was true in antiquity as much as it applies today. In theory, the mixing of features was not considered appropriate, given the ancient emphasis on decorum. While Horace admits that sometimes mixing can be done legitimately (*Ars P.* 93–4), others including Plato (*Resp* III 397d), Cicero (*Opt. gen.* 1), Quintilian (*Inst.* 10.2.22), and Demetrius (*On style* 5) comment on the importance of firm boundaries between the various genres, and discourage mixing in their rather prescriptive theory.[58] Lucian complains about authors of history who do not research facts and instead praise rulers and generals; they praise too strongly the merits of their own men and disparage the enemy, crossing over the boundary between encomium and history (*Hist. conscr.* 6–13). He also considers it a grave mistake not to be able to distinguish between poetry and history (εἰ μὴ εἰδείη τις χωρίζειν τὰ ἱστορίας καὶ τὰ ποιητικῆς), but to want to mix features from one into the other (τὰ τῆς ἑτέρας κομμώματα; *Hist. consr.* 8). He compares the process as wanting to take an athlete and dress him in pink as a prostitute.

The emphasis on the importance of maintaining decorum suggests that practice did not follow theory.[59] Isocrates alerts his audience to generic transgressions in the preface of *Evagoras* (esp. vv. 9–11), emphasizing that he was about to breach genre conventions by praising a man in prose, not verse, thereby alerting his audience and allowing them to prepare and understand the work more easily – giving them the opportunity to adjust their genre expectations. Dionysius of Halicarnassus advises his audience that he also planned to transgress genre boundaries by not following previous historiographical patterns (*Rom. Ant.* 1.8.3). Roy Kenneth Hack, looking at ancient literary theory in his criticisms of the traditional approaches to Horace's poetry, shows that despite what Horace says about the importance of propriety and the balanced relationship between content and metre (*Ars P.* 73–98), Horace himself does not always stick to his own rules.[60] The best of Horace's poems, according to Hack, were in fact those which broke his own rules, and Hack finds a contradiction where 'the laws of the lyric genre upheld by Horace the critic are definitely annulled by Horace the poet.'[61] When discussing the genre of a given text, critics must recognize the relevant conventions but also the author's ability to bend or break them – theoretical

---

58 Cf. Harrison, *Generic Enrichment*, 6.
59 Gian Biagio Conte, *Genres and Readers: Lucretius, Love Elegy, Pliny's Encyclopedia. Transl. By Glenn W. Most. With a Foreword by Charles Segal* (Baltimore and London: John Hopkins University Press, 1994), suggests that a theory of genre was absent in antiquity, and that it would be more fruitful to look at practice rather than theoretical pronouncements; Cf. Farrell, 'Literary Criticism', 183 on ancient theory versus practice. Harrison, *Generic Enrichment*, 1, understands the term 'generic enrichment' as the way in which generically identifiable texts gain literary depth and texture from confrontation with or inclusion of elements from texts of other genres.
60 Roy Kenneth Hack, 'The Doctrine of Literary Forms', *Harvard Studies in Classical Philology* 27 (1916): 1–65 (27). For Horace's rules, see ibid., 15–27.
61 Ibid., 31.

genre conventions existed, but authors retained a measure of flexibility in their application.

Nevertheless, mixing can create tension; as Pelling has noted, some genres may not be hospitable for other elements (e.g. comic elements in serious history), and he credits the reader sensing that in these passages, the generic relationship is strained.[62] As Pelling notes, this sensitivity to mismatches can generate an interpretative effect (e.g. something feels wrong here – why?), further highlighting the importance of genre for the interpretation process. The mixing of generic features in practice required a sophisticated genre understanding.[63] The practice also suggests an awareness that different features could behave differently without impacting genre recognition. Ancient authors, critics and audiences had constructed for themselves a working system of genres that were recognizable enough and fluid enough to allow for development and innovation alongside the classic value of imitation; we can see both literary theory and literary practice in action and in a dynamic relationship.

This mixing of features and the discrepancy between theory and practice will become relevant in the next chapter and the subsequent literary analysis, as we shall see that features could be employed across generic boundaries; when taken for themselves, these result in an uncertainty regarding a work's generic affiliation.

Development

As we have seen so far, ancients had developed a catalogue of features appropriate for various genres but were also aware that practice did not always support the theory. Accepting an inherent fluidity of genre encouraged them to realize that genres go through a cycle of development. They frequently noted the importance of individual authors who created a genre (e.g. Aristotle, *Poet.* 1449a38; Polybius 5.33.2; Horace, *Ars P.* 74–82; Quintilian, *Inst.* 10.1.46). Quintilian claims satire as an entirely Roman creation (Quintilian, *Inst.* 10.1.85, 93: *Satura quidem tota*

---

62 Christopher Pelling, 'Epilogue', in *The Limits of Historiography: Genre and Narrative in Ancient Historical Texts*, ed. by Christina Shuttleworth Kraus (Leiden: Brill, 1999), 338.
63 Harrison, in his study of Augustan literature, relies on a clear notion of literary genres and how these genres and their constitutive elements could and were manipulated and perceived, implying a high level of genre awareness and sophistication in antiquity. Similarly, John Marincola, 'Genre, Convention, and Innovation in Greco-Roman Historiography', in *The Limits of Historiography: Genre and Narrative in Ancient Historical Texts*, ed. by Christina Shuttleworth Kraus (Leiden, Boston, Cologne: Brill, 1999), 281, states that we need to appreciate the complex role that generic tradition and individual innovation play within ancient literary composition, rejecting any strict or formalistic taxonomies in favour of a more balanced view of theory, practice, innovation, literary action and reaction.

nostra est); Cicero's thoughts on the invention of the epistolary genre (*Fam.* 2.4.1) suggest that the process of developing genres was not a thing of past literature and he also praised M. Cornelius Cethegus as the first man to have been called an orator (*Brut.* 58).

Authors could also praise themselves for their inventiveness. Isocrates did so during the composition of his *Evagoras*; Polybius explains to his audience how he was the first to write universal history as previous authors, focusing on individual wars or cities, could not hope to represent Fortune's achievements in their totality (1.4.1-7);[64] we also note Pliny's generic posturing preface of his *Natural History*:[65]

> Nemo apud now qui idem temptaverit, nemo apud Grecos qui unis omnia ea tractaverit.
>
> There is not one person to be found among us who has made the same venture, nor yet one among the Greeks who has tackled single-handed all departments of the subject. (*HN* pr. 14)

These authorial claims at generic innovation are credited by Conte with a sophisticated genre awareness, attempts to fill in the literary or generic gaps that authors noticed when confronted by something new, in an attempt to be just different enough within established generic expectations.[66]

Alongside the awareness of generic development, ancient authors also appreciated the finished product at the end of the development cycle; Aristotle sees tragedy as having stopped evolving once it had reached its perfected form (*Poet.* 1449a). According to Dionysius of Halicarnassus, *Dem.* 16, Isocrates and Plato had developed a style further than anyone else without perfecting it (οὐ μὴν καὶ τελειῶσαι) allowing Demosthenes to complete the task. Ancients understood clearly that genres had a point of origin, changed over time and could reach a final stage in their development, all influenced by individual authors.

Imitatio

This section aims to act simply as a brief reminder of the importance of *imitatio* in ancient literature. The reminder is important because authors actively reacted

---

64 Although subsequently, Polybius does admit that generations earlier, Ephorus had written a universal history (5.33.2).
65 Cf. Harrison, *Generic Enrichment*, 6.
66 Conte's 'empty slots': Conte, *Genres and Readers*, 117; cf. Marincola, 'Genre', 300. Pelling 'Epilogue', 344-8, also admits that audiences will find a story more plausible if they at least recognize the pattern.

to their literary milieu when composing literature. We have seen that authors commented on how certain features were more or less appropriate for certain genres, facilitating the composition process of younger generations by offering a framework and suggestive guidelines. However, as we will see in the next chapter, we can find only a few references on how best to write about oneself. Might we surmise that the level of literary sensitivity, the exposure to one's literary milieu, based on the foundations of the ancient education system, was sufficiently high to be able to extract and abstract which features were and were not appropriate in the development of ancient autobiography? The ease with which authors interacted with the aforementioned genre conventions, theories and practices suggests a very high level of ancient literary skill.

Imitatio/μίμησις has aptly been defined as 'the study and conspicuous deployment of features recognizably characteristic of a canonical author's style or content, so as to define one's own generic affiliation'.[67] The study and imitation of central works was a firm fixture in education and by the first century CE 'fundamental to Latin literature', pupils being tasked with copying and imitating literature as school exercises.[68] Authors including Horace, Longinus, Dionysius of Halicarnassus and Quintilian discussed the relevance and qualities of *imitatio* and understood the concept as a natural literary process not to be undertaken lightly:

> Quapropter exactissimo iudicio circa hanc partem studiorum examinanda sunt omnia.
>
> Consequently the nicest judgement is required in the examination of everything connected with this department of study. (Quintilian, *Inst.* 10.2.14)

Quintilian explains that first one must carefully choose who to imitate and subsequently decide what to imitate (*Inst.* 10.2.14–15, but see the entire section 10.2 on *imitatio*). Pliny Minor (*c*. 61–*c*. 112 CE) suggests that the imitation of the best models can lead to original composition and healthy literary competition (*Ep.* 7.9), a notion echoed by Quintilian:

> Cedendum vero in hoc, quod et prior fuit et ex magna parte Ciceronem, quantus est, fecit. Nam mihi videtur M. Tullius, cum se totum ad imitationem Graecorum contulisset, effinxisse vim Demosthenis, copiam Platonis, iucunditatem Isocratis.

---

67 Gian Biagio Conte and Glenn W. Most, '*Imitatio* (Μίμησις)', in *OCD*³, 749.
68 David West and Tony Woodman, *Creative Imitation and Latin Literature* (Cambridge: Cambridge University Press, 1979), ix. See also other contributions in the same volume. For the use of imitation in education, see, for example, Quintilian, *Inst.* 10.2.2,20–21.

> But, on the other hand, there is one point in which the Greek has the undoubted superiority: he comes first in point of time, and it was largely due to him that Cicero was able to attain greatness. For it seems to me that Cicero, who devoted himself heard and soul to the imitation of the Greeks, succeeded in reproducing the force of Demosthenes, the copious flow of Plato, and the charm of Isocrates. (*Inst.* 10.1.108)

Cicero, thusly praised by Quintilian, himself emphasized the importance of *imitatio* during the composition of speeches. He admits that despite his literary abilities, Cato 'indeed, that he is not sufficiently polished, and that recourse must be had to a more perfect model for imitation' (*Brut.* 69); for Cicero's own education, he praises Crassus' oration in defence and praise of Q. Caepio as an oration which had strongly influenced his own, 'my pattern, and my instructor, from my very childhood'. (*Brut.* 164) Cicero praises others for actively choosing good literary models to imitate: Sulpicius imitated Crassus, Cotta preferred Antonius as a model (*Brut.* 203; cf. 286). Libanius, several centuries later, provides us with evidence that ancient appreciation for and use of *imitatio* remained largely stable; he claims that his original plan had been to become an imitator of his preferred teacher (prior actually to studying with him in Athens, *Oration* 1.23). Had his plan come to fruition, he would have reminded the audience of some hack instead of, as he does now, reminding them of the great classical authors.

Simultaneously, these critics have preserved for us the understanding that slavish imitation was not the aim, word-for-word imitation (plagiarism) should be avoided, *imitatio per se ipsa non sufficit* (Quintilian, *Inst.* 10.2.4).[69] Instead, authors should strive to create a literary connection with their models, which simultaneously created a generic connection as well. Authors have their faults and the imitators must take care to improve on their chosen authors rather than imitating their faults. *Imitatio* of this type, then, as we can see in Quintilian's praise of Cicero, was a more complex process of composition, requiring a certain level of literary and generic awareness as well as rhetoric ability.[70]

The composition of literature entailed the knowledge of what had come before and working that knowledge into one's own composition, it involved

---

69 Cf. Horace, *Ars P.* 132.
70 Donald Andrew Russell, 'De Imitatione', in *Creative Imitation and Latin Literature*, ed. by David West and Tony Woodman (Cambridge: Cambridge University Press, 1979), 5, summarizes the way that this understanding of imitation and combination is expressed in antiquity: 'the true object of imitation is not a single author, but the good qualities abstracted from many ... the second point, related to the first, is that the imitator must always penetrate below the superficial, verbal features of his exemplar to its spirit and significance'.

recreating past sources in new texts.⁷¹ Literature in the Greco-Roman world was inherently bound up with the recognition of features, resemblances, and generic relationships and strived both to enhance and combine relationships; the imitation and adaptation of previous works required skill as well as literary sensitivity and rhetorical ability. Authors had to be aware which features, which style was suited or appropriate, what was not and how audiences would react. They also had to be aware of their limitations. This was especially important if they did not have a genre cut out for what they wanted to express, encouraging authors to experiment with features and genres – as was definitely the case for Isocrates' composition process writing his *Antidosis*. Simultaneously, the audience, well-educated and experienced, fully expected to be reminded of past authors and would have been ready to recognize and appreciate good *imitatio*. We shall see in the next chapter how authors applied their skills and sensitivities to writing about themselves; they used a variety of forms and formats and relied on their skills of literary *imitatio* to ensure that their audiences would receive and interpret the works in accordance with the author's expectations.

Ancient comments on writing about oneself

In Isocrates' *Antidosis*, we find one of the earliest explicit deliberations of how to present one's character and life. Isocrates knows that with his *Antidosis*, a recapitulation of his character and life events (*Antid.* 7), he is attempting a novelty which requires an explanation:

> νῦν δὲ διὰ τὴν καινότητα καὶ τὴν διαφορὰν ἀναγκαῖόν ἐστι προειπεῖν τὰς αἰτίας, δι' ἃς οὕτως ἀνόμοιον αὐτὸν ὄντα τοῖς ἄλλοις γράφειν προειλόμην· μὴ γὰρ τούτων δηλωθεισῶν πολλοῖς ἂν ἴσως ἄτοπος εἶναι δόξειεν.
>
> Since, however, it is novel and different in character, it is necessary to begin by setting forth the reasons why I chose to write a discourse so different from any other; for if I neglected to make this clear, my speech would no doubt impress many as curious and strange. (*Antid.* 1)

Isocrates alerts his audience to expect something different from his speech. He expresses concern that his audience would not know how to categorize – generically speaking – his speech without this explanation and justification.⁷²

---

71 Cf. Conte, *Rhetoric*, 26, who speaks of a 'competition with and improvement over the original'.
72 Compare interestingly his comments about inventing a novel eulogy in the form of his *Evagoras*, where he praises himself for being the first to eulogize a living person, esp. *Evag.* 6–8.

Hence his decision, for want of a more suitable genre, to frame his account as a defence speech admissible at court (*Antid.* 8).⁷³ Similarly, Plato (*Seventh Epistle*) and Demosthenes (*De corona*) claim underlying defensive motives. Plato wrote to justify his actions during his second trip to Sicily, suggesting that an account of his actions would be appropriate given the strange and illogical rumours in circulation (352a). Demosthenes in turn delivered his speech a few decades later (about 330 BCE), defending himself against Aeschines. Demosthenes suggests he cannot be blamed for writing about himself; rather, his adversary and the attacks on Demosthenes' character had forced him to justify himself (*De cor.* 3–4).

Later authors evidently felt more confident writing about themselves without portraying the illusion of self-defence as strongly as their predecessors.⁷⁴ As the next chapter will show, several authors took to writing about themselves, with many references dating to the later Roman Republic. In the mid-second century, Appian (*c.* 95–165 CE) proudly concludes his preface to his *Roman History* with a reference to a (lost) work about himself (*pref.* 15); he suggests that any audience members interested in learning more about himself and his career, which he briefly summarizes, should consult the book separately. This rise in self-promotion is usually interpreted as part of a wider societal shift towards a more competitive public atmosphere.⁷⁵

Two passages are frequently used in arguments against ancient autobiography. First, Cicero's letter to the popular historian Lucceius (*Fam.* 5.12). Scholars typically interpret Cicero as reluctant to offer a publication about himself, despite insisting that he would be in good company in doing so, *multorum tamen exemplo et clarorum virorum* (*Fam.* 5.12.8); hence his request of Lucceius to publish on his behalf.⁷⁶ Such a theory, however, overlooks both Cicero's copious compositions about his past achievements for which he clearly expected

---

73 In Hellenistic oratory, both Aristotle (*Rhet.* 2.1.2) and Demosthenes (*De cor.* 4, 8) demonstrate the importance of self-praise: the orator had to present himself in as good a light as possible to convince the audience of his case.
74 Contra Whitmarsh, *Second Sophistic* (2005), 79, who argues that authors inserted their autobiographical contents (he argues against the existence of autobiography in antiquity) into defence speeches (*apologia*) in line with the assumption that self-praise (*periautologia*) was palatable to an audience only in a defensive setting. Whitmarsh however focuses only on Greek literature in relation to the Second Sophistic, thereby disregarding contemporaneous Latin authors.
75 For example, Mellor, *Roman Historians*, 167; Whitmarsh, *Second Sophistic*, 12. Malitz, 'Autobiographien', 228, suggests that autobiography in the Roman Republic arose out of the tradition that political/military officials had to submit reports of their actions at the end of their year in office/military campaign.
76 See most recently Thomas Baier, 'Autobiographie in der späten Römischen Republik', in *Antike Autobiographien: Werke-Epochen-Gattungen*, ed. by Michael Reichel (Köln, Weimar, Wien: Böhlau Verlag, 2005). See the following for a more detailed discussion of the *commentarius*.

a welcoming audience, and his background and the political situation in Rome; Cicero was even able to joke about his various literary attempts: *tertium poema expectato ne quod genus a me ipso laudis meae praetermittatur* – 'As a third item you may expect a poem, not to leave any form of singing my own praises unattempted' (*Att.* 1.19.10).[77]

Following his successful consulship in 63 BCE, forces gathered against Cicero and he was exiled in 58 BCE. Reintegration into Roman society after his speedy return in 57 BCE proved difficult, as contemporary letters to Atticus demonstrate (e.g. *Att.* 1.19, 1.20, 2.4, 2.5, 2.6, 2.11). A historical monograph by Lucceius, Cicero reasoned, would allow him to return to his previous position of power and influence: his name would gain celebrity through Lucceius and the support of his testimony and evidence of his goodwill (*Fam.* 5.12.1; cf. Plutarch, *Comp. Dem. Cic.* 2); Lucceius' name would confer onto Cicero public approval (*Fam.* 5.12.7). Cicero contrasts these advantages with the consequences of writing about himself. Both sides know that an author writing about himself alternatively elevates or conceals deeds, events and character qualities and, more importantly, that such a man displays a lack of modesty.[78] Some of Cicero's apparent humility can be attributed to rhetoric, yet we find similar references to omissions in narratives by authors of other genres; we should not attribute omissions only to such authors who wished to publish their own version of events.[79] Cicero, perhaps aware of the limited success of his own publications and similar ones such as the account of Quintus Lutatius Catulus, was desperate

---

77 See also his joke in *Brutus* 318 on his literary output. For Cicero's numerous publications about his consulship, we have references to a public account to Pompey (Plutarch, *Caes.* 8.3), a poem (*Att.* 2.3, 1.19.10), Greek and Latin versions for publication in Athens (*Att.* 2.1.1), and different versions to different authors, for example *Att.* 1.16.15: *Archias nihil de me scripserit*. Cf. also Tatum, 'Late Republic', 162n.4.

78 For example, Plutarch, *Sull.* 5.2: ἔοικε δὲ τὴν ἀληθῆ τῆς ἀποτεύξεως αἰτίαν οὐχ ὁμολογῶν ὁ Σύλλας ἐλέγχεσθαι τοῖς πράγμασιν. – 'But subsequent events would seem to show that Sulla does not confess the real reason for his failure.' Cf. also Plutarch, *Caes.* 8.3: τοῦτο μὲν οὖν οὐκ οἶδα ὅπως ὁ Κικέρων εἴπερ ἦν ἀληθές, ἐν τῷ περὶ τῆς ὑπατείας οὐκ ἔγραψεν . . . – 'Now, if this is true, I do not see why Cicero did not mention it in the treatise on his consulship . . . '

79 For example, Ammianus Marcellinus, writing historiography and justifying his decision to omit historical events (29.3.1): *Quisquis igitur dicta considerat, perpendat etiam cetera, quae tacentur, veniam daturus, ut prudens, si non cuncta complectimur, quae consiliorum pravitas crimina in maius exaggerando commisit.* – 'Therefore, whoever ponders what I have told, should also carefully weigh the rest which are passed over in silence; and, like a reasonable person, he will pardon me for not including everything which deliberate wickedness committed by exaggerating the importance of the charges.' See also Josephus, *Life* 339; Herodotus, *Hist.* 3.125.3, 4.36; Jn 21:25. Aristotle, *Poet.* 1451a, praises Homer for recognizing that, during the composition of the *Odyssey*, it was not necessary to report on everything Odysseus had done or experienced. See also Burridge, *Gospels*, 61–2, discussing Plutarch, *Alex.* 1.2.

for the wide dissemination that the historian could offer that he himself had failed to reach.[80]

Simultaneously, both Plutarch and Quintilian imply that the adverse reaction Cicero received was not because he spoke about himself and his achievements (tacitly implying that this was an accepted topic), but rather because in his writings he praised his own eloquence and oratorical ability, an unseemly topic in the eyes of Quintilian (*Inst.* 11.1.25). Perhaps such accusations had already been directed at Cicero during his lifetime, since he specifically states that he did not want to parade his talent or eloquence (*ingenium et eloquentiam meam*, *Brut.* 318). Quintilian notes how Cicero had been criticized even though (*quamquam*) he spoke more (*maior*) about his deeds than about his oratory (*quam eloquentiae*, *Inst.* 11.1.17). Plutarch clearly sees the problem in the fact that Cicero praises his speeches and elevates oratory over military triumphs, and that he advances the notion that fame should stem from eloquence:

βοῶντος ὡς τὰ ὅπλα ἔδει τῇ τηβέννῳ καὶ τῇ γλώττῃ τὴν θριαμβικὴν ὑπείκειν δάφνην.

> His cry being that arms must give place to the toga and the laurel of triumph to the tongue. (Plutarch, *Comp. Dem. Cic.* 2.)

> Καὶ μέγιστον μὲν ἴσχυσεν ἐν τῇ πόλει τότε πολλοῖς δ' ἐπίφθονον ἑαυτὸν ποίησεν ἀπ' οὐδενὸς ἔργου πονηροῦ, τῷ δ' ἐπαινεῖν ἀεὶ καὶ μεγαλύνειν αὐτὸς ἑαυτὸν ὑπὸ πολλῶν δυσχεραινόμενος.

> So at this time Cicero had the greatest power in the state but he made himself generally odious, not by any base action but by continually praising and magnifying himself, which made him hateful to many. (Plutarch, *Cic.* 24.1)

Second, Tacitus' remark in his *Agricola* is a favourite passage cited by detractors of autobiography in antiquity:[81]

> Sed apud priores ut agere digna memoratu pronum magisque in aperto erat, ita celeberrimus quisque ingenio ad prodendam virtutis memoriam sine gratia aut ambitione bonae tantum conscientiae pretio ducebatur. ac plerique suam ipsi vitam narrare fiduciam potius morum quam adrogantiam arbitrati sunt, nec id Rutilio et Scauro citra fidem aut obtrectationi fuit: adeo virtutes isdem

---

80 For example, his remark that no one was reading Catulus, *Brut.* 132–33. Stephanie Kurczyk, *Cicero und die Inszenierung der eigenen Vergangenheit* (Köln, Weimar, Wien: Böhlau Verlag, 2006), 62, offers an alternative theory for Lucceius' involvement, which need not be mutually exclusive to mine. She posits that Cicero pressured Lucceius to influence actively what posterity would think of him. However, Cicero's frequent insistence in the same letter that he was pressuring Lucceius so that he could still enjoy fame and praise during his lifetime contradicts Kurczyk's theory.
81 For example, Pelling, 'Ancient Genre', 46, who is extremely doubtful regarding the historicity of Tacitus' comment.

temporibus optime aestimantur, quibus facillime gignuntur. at nunc narraturo mihi vitam defuncti hominis venia opus fuit, quam non petissem incusaturus: tam saeva et infesta virtutibus tempora.

But in our fathers' times, just as it was easy, and there was more scope, to do deeds worth recording, so also there was inducement then to the most distinguished men of ability to publish such records of virtue. Partisanship or self-seeking was not the motive: a good conscience was its own reward; indeed, many men even counted it not presumption but self-respect, to narrate their own lives. A Rutilius, a Scaurus could do so without being disbelieved or provoking a sneer; so true is it that virtues are best appreciated in those ages which most readily give them birth; but in these times, even though I was about to write the life of a man who was already dead, I had to seek permission which I should not have needed, had invective been my purpose; so harsh was the spirit of the age, so cynical towards virtue. (*Agr.* 1.2–4.)

The passage has been used to argue that presenting a life's narrative was frowned upon and used only as a last resort for those men already on the defensive.[82] Scholars habitually suggest that Tacitus is referring to a period of literary darkness under the Emperor Domitian (ruled 81–96 CE).[83] In the glorious days of their forefathers, so Tacitus, virtuous men were appreciated – they were praised by having lives, *vitae*, written about their character and achievements which highlight their virtues, or could even narrate their own lives without anyone having to fear retribution based on jealousy or envy. These times Tacitus contrasts with literary life under Domitian.

Be that as it may, I suggest that this passage offers us more detailed, valuable insight into Tacitus' view of autobiography and that of his audience. For our immediate purposes, it is important to note that Tacitus clearly expected his audience to understand exactly what he meant, which genre he was referencing, and the role of Aemilius Scaurus and Rutilius Rufus in this context. Tacitus was confident that referencing two authors from earlier centuries would not result

---

82 For example, Lewis, 'Imperial Autobiography', 660. Similarly, Scholz, 'Sulla's *Commentarii*', 187 suggests that authors wrote mostly in exile or isolation as opposed to during the daily political struggles.
83 For example, John Marincola, *Authority and Tradition in Ancient Historiography* (Cambridge: Cambridge University Press, 1997), 308. The literary testimony of Tacitus, Suetonius, Cassius Dio and Juvenal has evoked the notion of an oppressive reign under Domitian which severely curtailed literary development, and has in the past been taken on by modern scholars. See recently Marcus Wilson, 'After the Silence: Tacitus, Suetonius, Juvenal', in *Flavian Rome: Culture, Image, Text*, ed. by Anthony James Boyle and William Dominik (Leiden, Boston: Brill, 2003) for an overview and the new revisionist view which reads the accounts in the light of hindsight under a new imperial regime. See also Frédéric Hurlet, 'Sources and Evidence' and Alessandro Galimberti, 'The Emperor Domitian', both in *A Companion to the Flavian Age of Rome*, ed. by Andrew Zissos (Chicester; Malden, MA: John Wiley & Sons, 2016).

in any misunderstandings. Even if, as Pausch and much of the literary evidence suggests, autobiography had become an imperial prerogative, it must still have been sufficiently present in a 'private' that is non-imperial, audience's literary milieu. Further, even if Tacitus here presents an idealized view of the former, Republican literary landscape, I would offer the suggestion that he also includes a distinctly passive-aggressive undernote, implying that both audience and author would have wished it differently. By invoking bygone times and genres, Tacitus builds up literary suspense. The passage also contains implicit information about Tacitus' generic perception of writing about others or oneself. The aim was a written record of the subject's virtue, exemplified in Roman thought by his actions and achievements, and in the mind of Tacitus the two concepts of biography and autobiography were closely related but distinct.

At the same time, there was a literary discourse on self-praise in antiquity which goes hand in hand with a discourse on autobiographical literature. Authors clearly associated writing about oneself with the rather complicated issue of praising oneself. Demosthenes says περὶ ἐμαυτοῦ λέγειν (*De cor.* 4, 321), to separate self-praise from self-mention, as does Plutarch several centuries later (*De laude* 539A), distinguishing the term from the self-praise he uses in the title, περὶ ἑαυτόν ἐπαίνειν.

> Καὶ μέγιστον μὲν ἴσχυσεν ἐν τῇ πόλει τότε πολλοῖς δ' ἐπίφθονον ἑαυτὸν ποίησεν ἀπ' οὐδενὸς ἔργου πονηροῦ, τῷ δ' ἐπαινεῖν ἀεὶ καὶ μεγαλύνειν αὐτὸς ἑαυτον ὑπὸ πολλῶν δυσχεραινόμενος.
>
> So at this time Cicero had the greatest power in the state but he made himself generally odious, not by any base action but by continually praising and magnifying himself, which made him hateful to many. (Plutarch, *Cic.* 24.1)

Pliny deliberates on how closely self-mention is related to self-praise (*Ep.* 1.8.4–7) and Cassius Dio has Caesar ask 'why is it necessary for me to go into details and become offensive by praising myself?' (ὡς καὶ ἐμαυτὸν ἐπαινοῦντα, 43.15.6).[84] An awareness existed among ancient authors that to speak about oneself was inevitably understood as praising oneself, and not always positively so:

> ὁ δὲ Κάτων ἀεὶ μέν τις ἦν, ὡς ἔοικε, τῶν ἰδίων ἐγκωμίων ἀφειδὴς καί τὴν ἄντικρυς μεγαλαυχίαν ὡς ἐπακολούθημα τῆς μεγαλουργίας οὐκ ἔφευγε, πλεῖστον δὲ ταῖς πράξεσι ταύταις ὄγκον περιτέθεικε,

---

84 Cf. Dion. Hal., *Rom. Ant.* 1, who claims he does not want to dwell too long on self-praise, it being distasteful to the reader.

Cato, who was ever rather generous, it would seem, in his own praises, and did not hesitate to follow up his great achievements with boastings equally great, is very pompous in his account of this exploit, (Plutarch, *Cato Mai.* 14.2)

Ancient critics realized that any kind of personal narrative could very easily descend into self-praise, which in theory should be avoided, because, as Herodotus tells us, 'from birth, envy is rooted in men' (3.80.3). The author must be aware of his audience, which instinctively tends to react negatively and jealously when confronted with self-praise.[85]

Yet they also understood that there were appropriate ways of praising oneself as much as there were inappropriate ways, comparable to any other mode of writing; Polybius notes that in a fit of passion, Hermias began singing his own praises 'in the worst taste', as opposed to in a beneficial, expedient way (5.49.4). Thus, rather than offering critiques, ancient authors devised and collated a set of acceptable conventions: Quintilian (*Inst.* 11.15) and Plutarch (*De laude* 539E) agree that if a positive purpose is evident, self-mention in the form of self-praise can be acceptable, even expedient. This includes self-defence and didactic intentions as the most common situations in which an author can fall back on περιαυτολόγια (Plutarch, *De laude* 539D). As an example, both Plutarch (*De laude* 514F) and Quintilian (*Inst.* 11.22) mention Demosthenes' *De corona*. Plutarch also refers to Pericles and others, who likewise defended themselves by emphasizing their achievements (*De laude* 540C). Such an emphasis on one's own deeds has the positive effect of encouraging imitation if the audience recognizes the author's intentions and offers a good reception of the comments (Plutarch, *De laude* 539F, 544D-F). A further example of such exemplary intentions includes the now fragmentary work by the multi-faceted Nicolaus of Damascus, who extols his virtues as philosopher to encourage imitation.[86]

This collection of τὰ φάρμακα καὶ τὰ παρηγορήματα, 'medicines and palliatives' (Plutarch, *De laude* 543A), with which to soothe the audience, is largely based on common sense and visible long before critics such as Quintilian or Plutarch took it upon themselves to compile literary manuals.[87] Speaking of

---

85 Aristotle, *Rhet.* 1.9.30; Isocrates, *Antid.* 8; Quintilian, *Inst.* 11.15-17, 21; Plutarch, *De laude* 539E. For the prevalence of envy in ancient thought, we note Sallust, *Cat.* 2. See most prominently Peter Walcot, *Envy and the Greeks: A Study of Human Behaviour* (Warminster: Aris & Phillips, 1978), and more recently, Ed Sanders, *Envy and Jealousy in Classical Athens: A Socio-Psychological Approach* (New York: Oxford University Press, 2014).
86 *FGrH* 90 FF 131-39.
87 Pnina Stern, 'Josephus and Justus: The Place of Chapter 65 (336-367) in *Life*, the Autobiography of Flavius Josephus', in *Flavius Josephus: Interpretation and History*, ed. by Jack Pastor, Pnina Stern and Menahem Mor (Leiden, Boston: Brill, 2011), 395, speaks of 'literary conventions'. See also Vivien J. Gray, 'Classical Greece', in *Political Autobiographies and Memoirs in Antiquity: A Brill Companion*,

oneself in the third person singular, or placing praise into the mouth of other actors was a common feature, yet we must consider Aristotle's qualification 'sometimes' (ἔνια, *Rhet.* 3.17.16); no rule was universal, nor any convention mandatory. Ancient literature was fully aware of the habit of speaking and writing about oneself and its do's and don'ts, and on a whole, did not reject the notion, nor the person doing so.[88]

We are faced with a conflicting situation: surviving ancient texts do not provide detailed how-to-write-an-autobiography guidelines. While Cicero surely over-dramatizes for added effect, note his reference to the laws of history he is asking Lucceius to bend, *leges historiae neglegas* (*Fam.* 5.12.2). The ancient literary landscape differentiated between genres, accepted that some features were more appropriate for certain genres than for others, and understood the fluidity of genres, to the point that we have a range of manuals or useful comments on how to compose which genre. However, we find little evidence pertaining to autobiography. Authors occasionally reflected on some specifics involved, but this does not amount to wider generic guidelines. nevertheless, autobiographical practices are frequently attested. We must admit that authors did not simply wake up one morning with an exact roadmap of how to structure and formulate their compositions. The scholarly debate regarding the existence of ancient autobiography rests partly on the apparent lack of clear-cut rules and conventions on how best to do so.

Summary

The first part of this chapter aimed to introduce readers to the basic concepts of genre theory. Genres are understood as conventions that facilitate communication and understanding on different levels between author, reader, text and society at large. They are made up of features and family resemblance (form and content), whose acquisition is often unconscious and an inherent part of the social, literary and ideological milieu. The importance of genre is evident in the inherent human need to categorize and to eliminate communication errors that can arise

---

ed. by Gabriele Marasco (Leiden, Boston: Brill, 2011), 34, who points out that Xenophon and Isocrates had already adopted these stratagems to disarm the audience.

88 These guidelines and conventions focus on internal features, techniques and strategies, offering valuable rhetorical advice. It will be a fruitful endeavour, having established the generic blueprint for ancient autobiography and the position of Josephus' *Life*, to determine in how far Josephus heeds his colleagues' advice. For a similar analysis of Josephus' attempts to minimize giving offence in the course of his autobiographical account in *War*, see Glas, 'Self-Characterization'.

out of mistaken expectations. The function of genre is understood as a code of social behaviour, a manner of communication between author and reader. The expectation of the author and his choice of genre (social code) is embedded in the genre contract. As a result, a reader's genre assumption frames their reading of a text, their approach to individual aspects of the text, and ultimately their interpretation. From this understanding derives the importance of appreciating the cultural context, as genre identification becomes more difficult if the reader is removed from the text by culture and time. Here we arrive back at our starting point and the genre of Josephus' *Life*; genre theory emphasizes the importance of understanding the genre of a text in order to begin the process of interpretation.

Subsequently, the chapter introduced the methodological foundations of literary analysis which forms the main part of this book (Chapters 4–6). The application of genre theory allows scholars a basis and terminology for the investigation of the nature of genre in ancient literature and has previously been successfully applied to both classical and Biblical literature. While Pelling may point to some concerns in using generic labels or terms unfamiliar to the author or original audience of a text, Todorov justifies these perceived anachronisms as heuristic tools.[89] Based on a selection of generic features, Josephus' *Life* and a range of comparanda will be subject to a detailed, genre-based literary analysis to establish a generic framework for ancient autobiography.

The second part of this chapter moved us closer to the ancient literary world, to discuss contemporaneous genre understanding. The two concepts, modern and ancient, can be mapped onto each other and a firm foundation in genre theory can illuminate and further our understanding of the function of ancient genres. We see the sophistication of ancient understanding in terms of the life cycles of genres, their recognition and distinction, as well as their ability to mix and relate to each other.

---

89 Pelling, 'Epilogue', 337; Todorov, *Genres*, 17n.9. See also Bolin, *Freedom*, 46–53, on the control procedure. Further, John Patrick Sullivan and Irene de Jong, *Modern Critical Theory and Classical Literature* (Leiden: Brill, 1994), 14, comment on the continuity between ancient and modern literary criticism and theory, stating that the concept of genre was 'adumbrated, even regulated' by Aristotle and that it remained a 'systematic concern' later on, adapted by Quintilian and others for their purposes. Sullivan also sees analogies and resemblances between ancient and contemporary literary and cultural theories, ibid., 21. Their book is a testament to the fruitful engagement of modern critical theory and Greco-Roman literature, and genre theory features alongside narratology, intertextuality, exemplarity and reader response.

3

Josephus' literary milieu

The purpose of this final theoretical chapter is to re-immerse ourselves into the ancient literary scene for an overview of texts and opinions on writing about oneself, thereby establishing the literary milieu with which Josephus and his audiences were dialoguing.

No literary text can exist *sui generis*, since it relies on a construct of precedents, parallels, similarities, innovations, author and audience.[1] The comparative texts will be briefly introduced, along with the relevant state of research that has attempted to set the texts into a dialogue with autobiography. The following texts are a diverse group, although the majority of references and texts date to late Republican/early imperial times, a politically and socially tumultuous period, including works by Sulla, Augustus, Nicolaus of Damascus, Q. Lutatius Catulus, Cicero and Caesar.[2] The latest text under consideration is Libanius' *Oration 1*, written 374 CE.[3] It was not necessary for Josephus to have known all texts, and perhaps he knew texts now lost to us; their relevance lies in the wider literary milieu, guiding audience expectations as much as authorial intentions.[4]

---

1   Cf. Conte, *Genres and Readers*, 29, who argues that any text can only be read in combination with other texts which together form a pattern against which the text is perceived.
2   Riggsby, 'Memoir and Autobiography', 268, recently argued that he feels confident gathering together a similar group of texts and projecting and retrojecting attitudes as over the course of the wider period, ancient values did not change too drastically. Riggsby gathers together texts by Aemilius Scaurus, Rutilius Rufus, Q. Lutatius Catulus, Sulla, Cicero and Caesar to discuss autobiography in antiquity. Raffaella Cribiore, *Libanius the Sophist: Rhetoric, Reality, and Religion in the Fourth Century* (Ithaca; London: Cornell University Press, 2013), 27, states that although considerations of genre were neither 'constant or identical' in different periods, they did remain sufficiently stable throughout antiquity to compare texts over a larger period of time. Cf. Glas, 'Self–Characterization', 188, 192–3.
3   Texts by Christian authors such as Gregory of Nazianzus or St. Augustine are not considered in this study, as there is general consensus that with the introduction of the introspective self-evaluation evident in these texts, a paradigm-shifting break has occurred that sees a new stage in the development of autobiography. Within the framework of the present thesis, this period cannot be considered.
4   This study is also based on the expectation that Josephus had a sufficient command of the Latin language to engage with contemporaneous literature. Several scholars have denied Josephus any substantial knowledge of Latin, including Thackeray, *Josephus*, 118; Seth Schwartz, *Josephus and Judaean Politics, Columbia Studies in the Classical Tradition* (Leiden, New York, København, Köln:

The overviews in this chapter are not meant to replicate more comprehensive discussions into the individual texts, but rather act as an introduction and historiographical survey to highlight the range of opinions on genre and autobiography; further details in terms of both content and context will, where relevant, be presented in the course of the analysis. It will become apparent that many texts do not neatly fit into genre categories and discussions can easily remain inconclusive. Texts are situated in a grey area with fuzzy boundaries, which proves rather unsatisfactory given our inherent need to categorize. The present aim is to discuss and clarify the respective nomenclatures (*vita/bios/commentarius/res gestae* etc) and we ask what genre considerations have been applied to the texts under discussion, what connections have been made between them, and how it can be, and has been, decided which text does, and which text does not, participate in the genre of ancient autobiography. The length of the following individual discussions will vary, as some texts are and have been more easily categorized than others.

Res Gestae

Consul alongside Gaius Marius in 102 BCE, Quintus Lutatius Catulus (149–87 BCE) fought against the Cimbri and Teutones (Plutarch, *Mar.* 23–7). Despite their collaboration, Marius received the larger part of the praise and recognition for their military victories (*Mar.* 27). Catulus' attempts at clarification and recognition failed, and he eventually sided with Marius' opponent Cornelius Sulla Felix during the Roman civil wars.[5] Plutarch notes Catulus' efforts to justify his demands for recognition (*Mar.* 25), including his *Liber de consulate et de rebus gestis*

E.J.Brill, 1990), 35, 37n.48; Günther Christian Hansen, 'Einige Anmerkungen Zum Sprachgebrauch Des Josephus', in *Internationales Josephus-Kolloquium, Brüssel 1998*, ed. by Jürgen U. Kalms and Folker Siegert (Münster: LIT Verlag, 1999). Paul's suggestion that Vespasian and Titus wrote their *commentarii* (whose contents Josephus prominently claims to know well, *Life*, 358) in Greek, rather than Latin, is an unlikely theory: G. M. Paul, 'The Presentation of Titus in the Jewish War of Josephus: Two Aspects', *Phoenix* 47 (1993): 56–66. However, their individual arguments have proven largely untenable, and recent scholars have argued strongly for Josephus' proficiency in Latin. See here Mason, *Life*, xlvii, cf. Steve Mason, 'Of Audience and Meaning: Reading Josephus' Bellum Judaicum in the Context of a Flavian Audience', in *Josephus and Jewish History in Flavian Rome and Beyond*, ed. Josephus Sievers and Gaia Lembi (Leiden: Brill, 2005), 94n.2; Timothy David Barnes, 'The Sack of the Temple in Josephus and Tacitus', in *Flavius Josephus and Flavian Rome*, ed. by Jonathan Edmondson, Steve Mason and James Rives (Oxford: Oxford University Press, 2005), 137, 140–2; Rajak, *Josephus*, 235. See further Steve Mason, 'Flavius Josephus in Flavian Rome: Reading on and between the Lines', in *Flavian Rome: Culture, Image, Text*, ed. by Anthony James Boyle and William Dominik (Leiden, Boston: Brill, 2003), 559–90.

5   For more detailed information about Catulus' background and the wars, see F. Münzer, 'Lutatius (4)', in *Pauly's Realenzyklopädie der classischen Altertumswissenschaft. Neue Bearbeitung*, ed. by Wilhelm Kroll (Stuttgart: J.B. Metzlersche Verlagsbuchhandlung, 1927).

suis (Cicero, *Brut.* 132).⁶ Plutarch's fragments cover military events and topics highlighting Catulus' involvement in the wars.⁷ This military content has led José Candau to conclude that 'his autobiography took . . . the form of *commentarii*'.⁸ Candau's terminology is slightly confusing, as he groups Catulus with 'his two contemporaries in the field of autobiography, Aemilius Scaurus and Rutilius Rufus', reading together three authors whose literary differences Candau had previously set out – the latter two had written longer works referred to as *vitae* (see the following) covering their entire lives as opposed to Catulus' short and brief *liber*.⁹

Cicero's comparison of Catulus' style to that of Xenophon (*Brut.* 132) has led some scholars to suggest that Cicero was alluding to their respective autobiographical aspects, positing a generic relationship between the two.¹⁰ We see the genre relationship postulated between texts as varied as Catulus' *RG*, Scaurus' *Vita* or Xenophon's *Anabasis*, varied in terms of date, length, content and purpose. Nevertheless, despite these differences, scholars have confidently discussed and compared them within the framework of a genre autobiography, based on the similarity of the author writing about himself. Part of the present literary analysis aims to use an approach based more comprehensively on genre theory to analyse whether these texts had further features in common and to account for their differences, to justify their being grouped together so consistently in scholarship.

Vita/βίος

The examples discussed in this section are those by Nicolaus of Damascus (b. 64 BCE), Augustus and Libanius, given their seemingly straightforward

---

6 Fragments in *HRR* vol. 1, 191–2. See also Cicero, *De or.* 3.9, *Tusc.* 5.5, *Brut.* 397; Plutarch, *Mar.* 44.8. Cicero uses a different terminology when he mentions Scaurus' *Vita* (*Brut.* 112) or his own *Commentarius* (Att. 2.1).
7 Whether or not Plutarch knew the book directly or via a third party is unclear; Baier, 'Autobiographie', 136, argues, based on his phrasings, that Plutarch did not know it first-hand.
8 Candau, 'Republican Rome', 151. Candau makes assumptions similar to Werner Suerbaum, *Die Archaische Literatur von den Anfängen bis Sullas Tod: Die vorliterarische Periode und die Zeit von 240 bis 78 V.Chr.* (München: C.H. Beck, 2002), 448. Candau's decision to group Catulus with the *vitae* of Scaurus and Rufus is exemplary for most scholarship, grouping these texts together based on their obvious shared feature, writing about themselves, without offering an explanation for the differences between the texts.
9 Ibid.
10 Baier, 'Autobiographie', 135. Reichel, 'Xenophons *Anabasis*', 45n.6, suggests it but also considers the possibility that Cicero only meant the verbal style. I would note that despite the undeniable commonality, Cicero does not mention the *Anabasis* and he is distinct in his terminology when referring to his own *commentarius* and Catulus' *RG*, as well as when referring to other authors and their works.

association with autobiography in scholarship; Sulla's work (shown further, also referred to as *vita*) and its conflicting relationship with historiography demonstrates that a discussion of ancient autobiography cannot be solved with a straightforward terminological study or any other singular strand of comparative analysis, but instead requires a multi-faceted approach.[11] A brief overview of the reasons why biography will not be considered in this study complements the section.

While the βίος of Nicolaus is lost, Josephus' writings contain much information about him.[12] Jacoby's collection of fragments offers us a helpful guide to the content, including Nicolaus' genealogy and education (F131–32), his interest in philosophy (F133, F137), his diplomatic career at Herod's court (F134, F136), his close relationship to Herod himself (F135) and his interest in philosophy (F133, F137).[13]

Nicolaus is praised by some for writing the first (extant) full autobiography in antiquity.[14] However, confusingly, and emblematically for the debate surrounding autobiography in antiquity, other scholars have confidently awarded the same distinction to other texts.[15] This (passive) debate exemplifies the state of the question and reinforces the importance of determining the genre of autobiography in antiquity. Simultaneously, assumptions as to what an autobiography might include as opposed to a historiography lead to insecurities.

---

11 Other (non-extant/fragmentary) texts referred to as *vita* include those written by: Aemilius Scaurus (Sallust, *Iug.* 15.4), M. Vipsanius Agrippa (Servius Auctus, *Ad Verg. Geor.* 2.162), the emperor Claudius (Suetonius, *Claud.* 41), and Agrippina the Younger (Tacitus, *Ann.* 4.53.3).

12 Nicolaus was the tutor of Anthony and Cleopatra's children, before relocating to Herod's court where he became one of the king's closest advisors. After Herod's death in 4 BCE, it seems that Nicolaus settled in Rome. For a full discussion of Nicolaus' history, see comprehensively Wacholder, *Nicolaus*, and Yarrow, *Historiography*, 67–76.

13 Jacoby, *FGrH*. See also *Fragmente der Historiker: Nikolaus von Damaskus*. Übersetzt, eingeleitet und erläutert von Tino Sahin (Anton Hiersemann: Stuttgart, 2018); Mark Toher, *Nicolaus of Damascus: The Life of Augustus and the Autobiography: Texts, Translations and Historical Commentary* (Cambridge: Cambridge University Press, 2016).

14 Mark Toher, 'On the Use of Nicolaus' Historical Fragments', *CA* 8 (1989): 159–72 (159); A. Sizoo, 'Autobiographie', in *Reallexikon für Antike und Christentum*, ed. by Theodor Klauser (Stuttgart: Hiersemann Verlags-GmbH, 1950); Yarrow, *Historiography*, 70n.117 declares Nicolaus the author of the earliest known Greek autobiography.

15 Dormeyer, 'Vita', 15–16 and Villalba Varneda, 'Early Empire', 327, suggest Josephus as the author of the first full autobiography, while Ernst Badian, 'Aemilius Scaurus, Marucs', in OCD^3, 22, nominates Scaurus. Scholars frequently consider Augustine to be the author of the first autobiography, based mainly on his ability to present an inner self-awareness and self-knowledge. Gusdorf, 'Conditions'; Roy Pascal, *Die Autobiographie; Gehalt und Gestalt* (Stuttgart, Berlin: W. Kohlhammer Verlag, 1965), 22–3; Karl Joachim Weintraub, *The Value of the Individual – Self and Circumstance in Autobiography* (Chicago: University of Chicago Press, 1976), 1, 45. John Sturrock, *The Language of Autobiography: Studies in the First Person Singular* (Cambridge: Cambridge University Press, 1993), begins his discussion of autobiography with Augustine. See also Sidonie Smith and Julia Watson, *Reading Autobiography: A Guide for Interpreting Life Narratives*. 2nd edn (Minneapolis: University of Minnesota Press, 2010), 105.

Strabo claims that Nicolaus had met members of the Indian delegation sent to Augustus, then residing at Antioch (90 F 100 = Strabo, *Geography*, XV 1.73). While originally Jacoby attributed the fragment to Nicolaus' *Universal History*, he admitted to hesitance as given the nature of the fragment, it might also have originated in his autobiography.[16]

Augustus wrote his autobiography in the mid-20s BCE in Rome, ending the thirteen-book-long narrative with his participation in the Cantabrian War (Suetonius, *Aug.* 85.1).[17] He honoured Agrippa and Maecenas by addressing the autobiography to them (F5), emphasizing his relationship with his adoptive father, Julius Caesar, and includes several references to supernatural (a comet, F1–2) or metaphysical events (prophetic dreams, F4, F7; superstition, F18) to reinforce his political status and justify his actions.[18] Aside from his political and military experiences, Augustus also included some private information relating to his ancestors (F11) and his marriages (F15, F19). Latin authors consistently refer to the text as *vita*, hence the decision to introduce the text in this section; however, Greek-speaking authors prefer the term ὑπόμνημα.[19] This largely unnoticed discrepancy contradicts the correlation of the terms '*vita*' and 'βίος' and complicates the correlation of *commentarius* and ὑπόμνημα, a relationship which scholars have strongly advocated.[20]

Generations after Nicolaus and Augustus, Libanius of Antioch (b. 314 CE) was born into a wealthy local family. He studied and eventually taught rhetoric in Athens, Constantinople and Nicomedia before settling again in Antioch. A pagan, he corresponded frequently with the emperor Julian (331–363 CE), after whose death Libanius' own career suffered sharply.[21] A vast amount of Libanius' literary corpus has been preserved, including his *Oration 1*, generally referred

---

16 Jacoby, *FGrH* IIc 255 line 26. Wacholder, *Nicolaus*, 3 reinforces his final conclusion (attributing the fragment to Nicolaus' *Universal History*) by arguing that Strabo could not have used Nicolaus' autobiography because it was written too late. See also Yarrow, *Historiography*, 70.
17 John Rich, 'Cantabrian Closure: Augustus' Spanish War and the Ending of His Memoirs', in *The Lost Memoirs of Augustus and the Development of Roman Autobiography*, ed. by Anton Powell and Christopher Smith (Swansea: The Classical Press of Wales, 2009). For further discussion of dating and references, see Dobesch, 'Nikolaos von Damaskus', who after weighing the evidence also suggests a composition date after the Cantabrian war.
18 Fragments are listed according to Christopher Smith, 'The Memoirs of Augustus: *testimonia* and fragments', in *The Lost Memoirs of Augustus and the Development of Roman Autobiography*, ed. by Christopher Smith and Anton Powell (Swansea: The Classical Press of Wales, 2009).
19 Smith, 'Memoirs', does not notice the discrepancy of title-designations across the languages.
20 For example, Engels, 'Hypomnemata–Schriften'; Franz Boemer, 'Der Commentarius: Zur Vorgeschichte und Literarischen Form der Schriften Caesars', *Hermes* 81 (1953): 210–50. To add to the confusion, Wacholder, *Nicolaus*, 37n.6 lumps together the writings of Caesar (as follows) and Augustus under the heading 'commentarii'. See also the discussion.
21 For a more detailed biography of Libanius, see Jorit Wintjes, *Das Leben Des Libanius*, (Radhen/Westf.: Verlag Marie Leidorf GmbH, 2005).

to as his *Autobiography*: βίος ἢ πέρι τῆς ἑαυτοῦ τύχης. The text consists of two distinct parts, a more polished first half (verses 1–155) written by 374 CE, and a second half consisting of individual, unconnected elements written and added at a later stage. The first half covers Libanius' life to the date of writing, including childhood, education, career and the various stages of his life, while the second part consists of less polished and largely unconnected thoughts and narratives, darker topics such as memory and death. Because of the disparate styles, structures and contents, this second half has been referred to as private musings in contrast to the more polished autobiography of the first half.[22]

Scholars discussing the genre of the text, especially A. F. Norman and Raffaella Cribiore, have both argued that *Oration 1* must have been more than 'merely' an autobiography.[23] Both scholars see deeper implications than an account of Libanius' life; for Norman, the relevance lies in the role of Fortune (τύχη) and the sophistic exercise Libanius incorporated into his narrative, while Cribiore understands Libanius as attempting to set himself into the literary tradition of the 'lives of holy men'.[24] Both scholars are comfortable using the term 'autobiography', although they understand it differently. Norman understands autobiography as a genre with the relevant audience expectations.[25] Cribiore, however, despite referring to the text as Libanius' autobiography, does not see a distinct genre of autobiography, but instead accepts only that authors from Hesiod onwards used autobiography in parts of their works.[26] Instead, for Cribiore, the text must belong to biography as she continues her analysis by comparing *Oration 1* to other roughly contemporary biographies.[27] She admits, adhering to genre theory, that no text can exist in a vacuum, suggesting Libanius had been influenced by other biographies of holy men but does not explain how both Gregory of Nazianzus and St. Augustine published their *De vita sua* and

---

22 Libanius and A. F. Norman, *Autobiography and Selected Letters*. Loeb Classical Library (Cambridge, MA: Harvard University Press, 1992), 9; A. F. Norman, *Libanius' Autobiography (Oration 1): The Greek Text/ Edited, with Introduction, Translation and Notes* (London, New York: Published for the University of Hull by the Oxford University Press, University of Hull, 1965), xiii; Cribiore, *Libanius the Sophist*, 17–19. It appears as though Libanius had occasionally added passages to the original *Oration*, perhaps planning to streamline and incorporate them better at a later stage, allowing us a measure of insight into his composition process.
23 Libanius and Norman, *Autobiography and Selected Letters*, 11.
24 Ibid.; Cribiore, *Libanius the Sophist*, 20.
25 Norman, *Libanius' Autobiography*, xv. According to Norman, the overt use of rhetoric by Libanius restricted his opportunities of deviating elsewhere from the classic panegyric structure Norman claims for the text, as this 'overly rhetorical form' was already unfamiliar enough for an audience expecting autobiography.
26 Cribiore, *Libanius the Sophist*, 42.
27 Ibid., 49–72. Unfortunately, Cribiore offers little supporting documentation or evidence for her rather bald statements, nor does she offer further information about the genre of biography, looking only for common themes and motifs in her analysis.

Confessions respectively roughly contemporaneously with Libanius, from where their inspiration came, or the implications for genre development.

At this point, it is prudent to explain why biography will be excluded from the ensuing literary analysis, despite the apparent similarities of title and theme.[28] Autobiography and biography contain similar features, sharing their aim to narrate the life, or forming periods, of their main character; biography, however, had established itself as a more talked-about genre early in Greek History and continued on to become highly popular in Roman literature.[29]

The events the subject has become renowned for, which merit the biography, determine what the author selects to interpret for his biography, in terms of both sources and topics.[30] Simultaneously, the biographer must rely on external sources and evaluate them in hindsight, whereas the author of autobiography relies on personal memories and employs other sources crucial to the biographer merely as support to persuade the audience of his narratives and recollections.[31] Thomas Hägg, despite applying as 'inclusive' a definition of biography as possible, excludes autobiography as 'something basically different' based on the fact that ultimately, biographies are replaceable; he points to the multitude of Pythagorean biographies in circulation in antiquity.[32] The object of a biography has little to no influence on the final product, which can result in polemical tones or biographies written with a deterring aim in mind, as pointed out by Plutarch. He defends his choice of writing about Demetrius and Anthony, both considered negative examples in Roman history:

> οὕτω μοι δοκοῦμεν καὶ ἡμεῖς προθυμότεροι τῶν βελτιόνων ἔσεσθαι καὶ θεαταὶ καὶ μιμηταὶ βίων εἰ μηδὲ τῶν φαύλων καὶ ψεγομένων ἀνιστορήτως ἔχοιμεν.
>
> In this manner it seems to me that we should be more eager to observe and to imitate the better lives if we are not left uninformed about the thoughtless and blameworthy ones. (Plutarch, *Demetr.* 1.6)

---

28 Biographies in antiquity were also entitled *vitae*; the collections by Plutarch and Suetonius speak for themselves, as does Nicolaus' biography of Augustus or Tacitus' *De vita et moribus Iulii Agricolae*. For biography, see the still relevant Momigliano, *Development*, and for an overall view of the general development of the genre, its reception in scholarship, its features and generic relationships, see Burridge, *Gospels*; Thomas Hägg, *The Art of Biography in Antiquity* (Cambridge: Cambridge University Press, 2012). Scholars combining the two genres include Momigliano, *Development*, 12; Engels, 'Hypomnemata–Schriften', 19; Cohen, *Josephus*, 101. Cf. Baier, 'Autobiographie', 26: 'die Biographie und deren besondere Ausprägung, die Autobiographie'; Stern, 'Life of Josephus', 67.
29 Momigliano, *Development*, 12.
30 Smith and Watson, *Reading Autobiography*, 6. They see 'crucial distinctions', as authors of biographies document and interpret their subjects' lives from an external and retrospective point of view.
31 Ibid., 7.
32 Hägg, *Biography*, ix, 69. For Pythagoras, see ibid., 69–77, 352–68. See also Smith and Watson, *Reading Autobiography*, 6, arguing that biographies of certain historical figures appear continuously with differing interpretations.

Given these differences, this study will not consider biographical material. While biography was a critical aspect of the contemporaneous literary milieu, and arguably related to autobiography, ancient authors themselves have made it clear that writing and reading an autobiography was fundamentally different from writing or reading a biography, as is evident in the aforementioned discourse on how to speak and write about oneself.[33]

Commentarius

Ancient and modern authors have applied the term *commentarius* to a large selection of texts. This section begins with a brief overview of the range of texts referred to as *commentarius* and some problematic debates before introducing Caesar's *Gallic Wars*.[34]

Ancient authors frequently refer to *commentarii*, very few of which have survived due to their inherent short-term relevance.[35] Summing up scholarly definition of the term is Gian Biagio Conte's explanation of a *commentarius* during the Late Republic; he understands *commentarii* as distinct from traditional annals, as 'more personal and not necessarily public writings'.[36] For Conte, the *commentarius* can be widely applied, and by itself can 'denote nothing more than "notes", "memoirs", "observations" of a private character'. These *commentarii*, for Conte, present themselves as non-professional texts, supposedly supplying information and 'personal recollections', and can be traced back to bureaucratic processes such as a magistrate's running diary. For Conte, the practice of writing *commentarii* likely influenced the composition of 'proper' memoirs. [37]

---

33 See Chapter 2. See further Wacholder, *Nicolaus*, 40. See here also Misch, *Geschichte*, 43–4, who insists that biography had become a 'feste Literaturform' among the Greeks, in contrast to the 'geistige Schranke' that he claims inhibited autobiography. For the purposes of this book, excluding biographical material on the one hand, one might argue, limits the comparative material necessary to formulate a genre pattern; on the other hand, the comparatively large number of biographies would overshadow the extent autobiographical material which contains many details and information which will prove useful in our subsequent analysis of the genre.
34 For a detailed historical study of the *commentarius*, see best most recently Andrew M. Riggsby, *Caesar in Gaul and Rome: War in Words* (Austin: University of Texas Press, 2006); Christopher Pelling, '*Commentarii*', in *OCD*,[3] 373. Boemer, 'Der Commentarius', remains relevant.
35 Riggsby, *Caesar*, 133n.1, does not see a difference between the masculine form *commentarius* or the neuter *commentarium*.
36 The following paragraph is a summary of Conte, *Latin Literature*, 18.
37 Conte, *Latin Literature*, 18. See the shorter, more succinct definition of Riggsby, *Caesar*, 140: '*commentarii* must be simply 'notes' on some topic or other.' Mellor, *Roman Historians*, 167, similarly understands the *commentaries* as a private aide-memoir or notes for later usage, or a (supposedly) private journal. Many scholars concur with this comprehensive description, offering similar ones themselves and frequently connect the *commentarius* with the development of autobiography in antiquity, for example Pelling, '*Commentarii*'; Boemer, 'Der Commentarius'; A. H.

It remains a fact that a multitude of texts is referred to as *commentarii*, yet only few can be described as autobiographical. The majority refers to a (historical) sketch or *Vorlage* (e.g. Livy 42.6.3; Quintilian, *Inst.* 2.11.7, 3.8.58,67; Tacitus, *Ann.* 6.47 but see Cicero, *Att.* 21.2, who mentions Atticus' *commentarius* on Cicero's consulship that required no further embellishment), personal notebooks and documents (e.g. Suetonius, *Aug.* 64; Plutarch, *Ant.* 15.2,5), official and magisterial archives and notes (e.g. Livy 1.31.8, 1.32.2; Tacitus, *Hist.* 4.40; Cicero, *Verr.* 2.5.54), or as a commentary or professional manual for a specialized audience such as the *commentarii* by Frontinus (*De aquae ductu urbis Romae*) or Q. Cicero's *Commentariolum petitionis*.[38] A single term was easily capable of representing a wide range of texts and respective purposes; the majority of these texts were not meant for wide-scale distribution but were kept for administrative/professional or personal reasons.

From this basic understanding of the *commentarius* constituting a rather straightforward literary vehicle for maintaining notes, some scholars have seen a trend of skilled authors using the *commentarius* genre to convey their own achievements and successes for more wide-spread publication; it has been suggested, based partly on Cicero's own words, that Caesar consciously entitled his works *commentarius* to convey an air of honesty and simplicity.[39] The understanding of a *commentarius* as the literary stage between source material and a polished text is usually ascribed to both Lucian's advice to employ it prior to publication, scholars equating Lucian's Greek term ὑπόμνημα with *commentarius* (as does Cicero, *Att.* 21.2) and the fact that several authors in their prefaces refer to a third person to whom the author entrusts the ostensible stylistic improvement and publication of his *Vorlage*.[40]

McDonald, 'Theme and Style in Roman Historiography', *JRS* 65 (1975): 1–10; Lindsay Hall, '*Ratio* and *Romanitas* in the *Bellum Gallicum*', in *Julius Caesar as Artful Reporter: The War Commentaries as Political Instruments,* ed. by Kathryn Welch and Anton Powell (London: Duckworth with The Classical Press of Wales, 1998), 15; Scholz, 'Sulla's *Commentarii*', 175.

38 Cf. also Aulus Gellius, *NA* 2.6.1: *commentarium in Vergilium*, or Pompey's request for a consular manual, *NA* 14.7.2. It seems that such manuals are referred to in the singular as opposed to the multitude of archival notes or documents referred to in the plural.

39 Cf. Plutarch, *De tranq. anim.* 464E–F. Lewis, 'Imperial Autobiography', 637; Tatum, 'Late Republic', 167. See also Conte, *Latin Literature,* 18.

40 Lucian, *Hist. conscr.* 48: καὶ ἐπειδὰν ἀθροίσῃ ἅπαντα ἢ τὰ πλεῖστα, πρῶτα μὲν ὑπόμνημά τι συνυφαινέτω αὐτῶν καὶ σῶμα ποιείτω ἀκαλλὲς ἔτι καὶ ἀδιάρθρωτον . . . – 'And whenever all the material, or the majority, has been collected, a short ὑπόμνημά must be put together from it, and then a whole body of work yet still without finish and not joined together.' Riggsby, *Caesar,* 147, suggests that Lucian was thinking of the same author for both the *Vorlage* and the finished history. For an equation of ὑπόμνημα with *commentarius* see the following, and Cicero's remarks in which he refers to his *commentarius* as a ὑπόμνημα: *Att.* 2.1.2, 15.23, 16.14.4, 5.11.6; *Fam.* 13.1.5. But note that Latin *vitae* were referred to as ὑπομνήμα by Greek authors, earlier. Augustus dedicates his ὑπόμνημά to Agrippa and Maecenas (Plutarch, *Comp. Dem. Cic.* 3.1); Sulla left a dedication to Lucullus (Plutarch, *Luc.* 4.5); Q. Cicero asks his brother to improve the literary qualities of his

Scholarly opinion is divided on whether or not Caesar was writing history, autobiography or a text intended as notes, a *commentarius*. Prior to turning to scholarship, however, a reminder of a Ciceronian passage further confounding the genre question and how Caesar's writings were received:

> Tum Brutus: orations quidem eius mihi vehementer probantur. Compluris autem legi atque etiam commentarios, quos idem scripsit rerum suarum.
>
> At this point Brutus broke in: 'His orations certainly seem to me very admirable; I have read a number of them, as well as the *Commentaries* which he wrote about his own deeds.' (*Brut.* 262.)

Caesar's contemporaries understood his *Commentaries* to focus on Caesar and his own deeds (*rerum suarum*); Cicero uses the same terminology to refer to the contents of his own *commentarius nostris rebus* (*Att.* 2.1.2), leaving no doubt as to how they were to be received by an audience.[41] However, Cicero goes on to suggest that Caesar's aim was to supply other authors with material for their histories (*qui vellent scribere historiam*). In contrast, Caesar's long-term officer Aulus Hirtius (consul 43 BCE), who wrote the eighth book of the *Gallic Wars* after Caesar's murder, emphasizes their *elegantia* and claims that they had been published for the historian's benefit in terms of knowledge but that simultaneously, historians had been robbed of an opportunity to publish themselves (*B Gall.* 8 preface).

Scholarly assessment of *Gallic War*'s genre participation remains inconclusive. Answers or suggestions to the question as to how Caesar would have understood his work are diametrically opposed. While Gelzer argues that Caesar understood his works as history, Scholz insists that Caesar chose the designation *commentarius* to distance himself from historiography.[42] Roland Mellor tries to sit on both sides of the fence, suggesting that Caesar had created a new genre between *commentarius* and history.[43]

Caesar's *Gallic War* seems to be resting uncomfortably between distinct genres, and in 2006, Riggsby stated that the search for *Gallic War*'s genre has

---

commentarius (*Comment. pet.* 58); for further discussion of these dedications in the preface, see the following.

41 Cicero's words, both in regard to his own *commentarius* and Caesar's, suggest that while most texts can be reused or refigured as history, they could also be understood and interpreted within a different genre.

42 Gelzer, *Kleine Schriften*, II, 308–10; Scholz, 'Sulla's *Commentarii*', 180.

43 Mellor, *Roman Historians*, 174. He discusses *Gallic War* under the 'autobiography' heading. Unfortunately, Mellor does not consider the important implications of such a statement in terms of genre development, audience reception or generic guidelines.

shown only 'unsatisfactory results'.⁴⁴ This notion was more recently reiterated by Marc Mayer, who also claims that *Gallic War* distances itself from autobiography but simultaneously could not be considered as a straightforward historical narrative either.⁴⁵ It appears that the lack of more detailed knowledge of which, if any, generic conventions for autobiography existed in antiquity has complicated generic associations for the *Gallic War*, a shortcoming this study aims to alleviate. It remains a fact that the meticulous detail and thoughtfulness that shines through Caesar's narrative should alert us to the fact that he did not want his audience to misunderstand or misinterpret his narrative but to recognize his importance and contributions to the events narrated. This would have been hard to achieve if the audience were still puzzled as to the *Gallic War*'s genre participation. A better understanding of the range of conventions associated with autobiography will surely allow for a more foundational understanding of the *Gallic War*'s genre.

Ὑπομνήματα

Like the *commentarius*, a ὑπόμνημα can fulfil several roles in Greek literature, described by Engels as an 'aide-memoire', a 'scientific commentary', and as 'autobiographical texts'.⁴⁶ Recent trends frequently equate the Greek term with the English 'memoir', understood as a text focusing on a short period of the author's life; this association is based on a variety of early Hellenistic texts though, to contribute to the early stages of the development of autobiography in Greek literature.⁴⁷ However, scholars largely fail to take into consideration that

---

44 Riggsby, *Caesar*, 133, 142. He understands Caesar as experimenting with genre to avoid the instant recognition that a title such as *vita* would have supplied, with all the inherent expectations built up around it, but nevertheless still suggests that Caesar aimed to convey an account of his success. Riggsby understands autobiography in antiquity as a work whose central purpose was 'to narrate a significant portion of the author's life', 266, accepting the existence of a genre on this basis for the period under discussion, in contrast to the later requirement of an introspective point of view, exemplified by St. Augustine. Cf. also Mellor, *Roman Historians*, 165, for whom the paradigm of personal self-revelation was unknown in antiquity, but who instead understands autobiography as a narrative of one's past life with a historical dimension.
45 Marc Mayer, 'Caesar and the *Corpus Caesarianum*', in *Political Autobiographies and Memoirs in Antiquity*, ed. by Gabriele Marasco (Leiden, Boston: Brill, 2011), 192.
46 Johannes Engels, *Augusteische Oikumenegeographie und Universalhistorie im Werk Strabons von Amaseia* (Stuttgart: Franz Steiner Verlag GmbH, 1999), 60–1. Cf. Engels, 'Hypomnemata–Schriften', 26–7, and the distinct category of 'Autobiographien, Memoiren, und Memoirenhaftes', in *FGrH*, 227–38.
47 For the early usage of ὑπόμνημα in Hellenistic literature, see Engels, 'Hypomnemata–Schriften'; Marasco, 'Hellenistic Age'; Cinzia Bearzot, 'Autobiography in the Hellenistic Age', in *Political Autobiographies and Memoirs in Antiquity: A Brill Companion*, ed. by Gabriele Marasco (Leiden,

Augustus' *Vita*, earlier, was routinely referred to as ὑπόμνημα in Greek, and that Josephus uses the same terminology to introduce *Life* (*Ant.* 20.267).

The development of ὑπομνήματα has been admirably charted by Boemer and Engels, both in agreement that while the Latin *commentarius*-tradition was the longer, the development of both ὑπόμνημα and *commentarius* was independent of each other in its origins, and only through a rapprochement of Greek and Roman culture, language, and literature did the two terms become (roughly) equated.[48] The equation becomes visible in Cicero's distinctive language; he uses both terms, the Greek and the Latin, to refer to one text, the *commentarius* on his consulship (*Att.* 11.1.2, 2.1, 21.2).[49] However, the equation is not consistent. Plutarch refers to Caesar's *Gallic War* as ἐφημερίς, translated as diary or journal (*Caes.* 22.2) but uses ὑπομνήματα to refer to Caesar's private documents (*Ant.* 15.2), and the Latin *vita* of Augustus is understood as ὑπόμνημα in Greek (Plutarch, *Comp. Dem. Cic.* 3.1).[50] As mentioned earlier, Plutarch also uses the term to refer to the works by Sulla (*Mar.* 35.5; *Sull.* 23.2) and Demosthenes (*Dem.* 5.5.).

Josephus' usage

In this discussion of ὑπομνήματα, I therefore propose to analyse the usage of the term in Josephus, especially in light of Richard Laqueur's theory that Josephus wrote his *Life* on the basis of such a ὑπόμνημα – 'Rechenschaftsbericht', a theory which has shaped so much of Josephus-scholarship.[51] It will be illuminating to consider how Josephus understood the term itself, an analysis omitted by Laqueur and subsequent scholarship.

Several times Josephus understands ὑπόμνημα to contain an autobiographical, literary aspect: the imperial ὑπομνήματα of Vespasian and Titus (*Life* 342, 358;

Boston: Brill, 2011), 37–87. For equation with the memoir, see recently ibid., 79; Marasco, 'Hellenistic Age', 104–5; Geiger, *Cornelius Nepos*, 79; Tatum, 'Late Republic', 166.

48 Boemer, 'Der Commentarius'; Engels, 'Hypomnemata–Schriften', esp. 34. For an overview of a cultural Greco-Roman symbiosis, see Elaine Fantham, *Roman Literary Culture from Cicero to Apuleius* (Baltimore and London: Johns Hopkins University Press, 1999). Fowler, *Kinds of Literature,* 133–4, however warns of directly transferring genre labels due to shifting expectations, boundaries and socio-cultural contexts.

49 However, as Boemer, 'Der Commentarius', 235, correctly warns, 'die Korrelate schwanken'. To my knowledge no scholar discussing the correlation of the two terms has referred to the letter of Cicero's son to Tiro (*Fam.* 16.21), in which Junior refers to his notes using the Latin term *hypomnematis*.

50 See the earlier discussion. To my knowledge, Riggsby, *Caesar*, 137, is the only voice to have also noted the discrepancy and problems between the various titles associated with the works discussed here, but has omitted any further discussion into the consequences of such discrepancies. See further as follows.

51 Laqueur, *Josephus*.

Ag.Ap. 1.56) and those of King Herod (*Ant.* 15.174). He refers to them to defend his veracity and superiority as historian, indicating that all his information could be checked against these ὑπομνήματα, which any good historian should have consulted.[52]

In his biblical narrative (*Antiquities* 1–11), where we can more easily trace his source's language, Josephus frequently uses ὑπόμνημα to refer to archival records or royal archives (*Ant.* 7.110, 293; 10.5, 55; 11.94, 98, 104, 208, 249).[53] That he uses the term consistently and consciously is evident when we compare his source's terminology. A lack of continuity in both the Hebrew and Greek *Vorlagen* indicates that Josephus, regardless of whether he was using the Hebrew or Greek version, streamlined his account by using one term only where his sources used many, confident not only in his own understanding but also in the ability of his audience to comprehend and appreciate the uniformity of his expression.[54]

The other contexts in which Josephus uses ὑπόμνημα refer to an act, deed or custom of remembrance, be it the consumption of unleavened bread (*Ant.* 17.213, *War* 2.10), Agrippa's golden chain, a gift of the emperor Caligula (*Ant.* 19.294), or their religious customs themselves (*Ant.* 16.43).

Excursus – Ἀπομνημονεύματα

The linguistic and conceptual relationship between ὑπόμνημα and ἀπομνημονεύματα warrants a brief look at what seems to be an independent,

---

52 Imperial writings about campaigns in which they partook personally are a frequent occurrence especially among Roman generals and emperors: Engels, *Oikumenegeographie*, 361: 'Alle berühmten Feldherren ... verfassten *commentarii* über ihre Kriegszüge.'
53 In how far Josephus used the Hebrew Bible or the Septuagint for his biblical narratives in *Ant.* 1–11 remains unclear. See Louis Feldman and Gohei Hata, *Josephus, the Bible and History* (Detroit: Wayne State University Press, 1989), for various treatises concerned with Josephus' biblical *Vorlage*, whereby the editors prefer the theory of a Greek *Vorlage* (e.g. 21, 25) which Josephus did not have to translate so much as interpret. Cf. also Louis Feldman, *Studies in Josephus' Rewritten Bible* (Leiden, New York: Brill, 1998), 539: 'Josephus is eclectic in the texts which he uses, generally preferring the Septuagint, but not infrequently using the Hebrew, the Aramaic Targumim, and the proto-Lucianic text; ... though, of course, it is possible that he had a text different from any of those that are extant.' See further: Thackeray, *Josephus*, 75–99; Bilde, *Josephus*, 80–1; Tessa Rajak, *Translation and Survival: the Greek Bible of the ancient Jewish Diaspora* (Oxford: Oxford University Press, 2011), 252–3; Daniel R. Schwartz, 'Many Sources but a Single Author: Josephus's *Jewish Antiquities*', and Paul Spilsbury, 'Josephus and the Bible', both in *A Companion to Josephus*, ed. by Honora Howell Chapman and Zuleika Rodgers (Chichester: John Wiley & Sons, 2016).
54 See, for example, *Ant.* 7.110 cf. 2 Sam. 8:16; *Ant.* 7.293 cf. 2 Sam. 20:24; *Ant.* 10.5 cf. 2 Kings 18:18; *Ant.* 10.55 cf. 2 Chron. 34:8; *Ant.* 11.94 cf Ezra 5:17/1 Esdras 6:21; *Ant.* 11.98 cf. Ezra 6:1; *Ant.* 11.208 cf. Esther 6:1.

if related, genre. In modern scholarship, the term and any texts referred to as ἀπομνημονεύματα are translated as memoirs or the sayings of famous men.⁵⁵

Hägg's treatment of Xenophon's ἀπομνημονεύματα of Socrates, traditionally translated into Latin as *Memorabilia*, demonstrates his at times inconsistent approach to ancient biography.⁵⁶ Hägg refers to the ἀπομνημονεύματα as 'a special kind of biographical composition' as well as a 'memoir' without noting the differences and also groups the work together with Plato's *Apologia* and *Phaedo* without pointing to the different titles of the three works.⁵⁷ In a detailed discussion, Hägg emphasizes that Xenophon's account of Socrates lacks many common biographical features (e.g. Socrates' ancestry, youth/childhood, family life/marriage) but nevertheless reads it as a 'key text' in the history of biography.⁵⁸ However, the majority of scholars translate ἀπομνημονεύματα as 'memoirs'.⁵⁹

Turning to ancient evidence, we find several authors using the term to refer to sayings or collections of sayings and deeds of notable figures, beginning of course with Xenophon's ἀπομνημονεύματα Σωκράτους, in which he narrates his own memories and knowledge of Socrates (e.g. 1.3.1: ὁπόσα ἂν διαμνημονεύσω. – 'as much as I can recall', 1.4.2: ἅ ποτε αὐτοῦ ἤκουσα – I heard from him). We further have testimonies of other ἀπομνημονεύματα by authors close to the object of their writings such as Zenon's ἀπομνημονεύματα Κράτητος (Diogenes Laertius 7.1.4) or Justin Martyr's understanding of the Gospels as the recollections of Jesus' apostles (1 *Apol.* 66.3, 67.3) as contrasted to τὰ συγγράμμ ατα τῶν προφητῶν, and also those of Peter (*Dial.* 106.3). Ancient understanding developed further to encompass a selection of famous and recorded sayings and recollections without the author having to be an eyewitness, as is demonstrated by Plutarch's use of the term (*Cato Mai.* 9.7; *Lyc.* 19.3; 20.2) or Favorinus' ἀπομνημονεύματα. Although the work is lost, Diogenes Laertius transmits several fragments and testimonies which indicate a range of anecdotes, sayings and other noteworthy events experienced by notable philosophers well in the

---

55 Ernst Köpke translates into the German 'Denkwürdigkeiten' and without doubt sees an independent genre, in distinction, but related to, the aforementioned ὑπόμνημα: Ernst Köpke, *Über die Gattung der Apomnemoneumata in der Griechischen Literatur* (Brandenburg, 1857), 3-4. For Köpke, the term refers to the recollection of something seen or experienced from memory – 'eine durch Errinnerung überlieferte, in Erzählsform mitgeteilte Rede oder Ausspruch (saying)' of a memorable person based on the author's memories of that person.
56 Hägg, *Biography*.
57 Ibid., 298, 226.
58 Ibid., 28-9.
59 For example, Gray, 'Classical Greece', 10; Loveday Alexander, 'What Is a Gospel', in *The Cambridge Companion to the Gospels*, ed. by Stephen C. Barton (Cambridge: Cambridge University Press, 2006), 21; Marius Reiser, *Sprache und literarischen Formen des Neuen Testaments: Eine Einführung* (Paderborn, München, Wien, Zürich: Ferdinand Schöningh, 2001), 101.

past, making it impossible for Favorinus, who wrote under Trajan (ruled 98–117 CE) and Hadrian (ruled 117–38 CE), to have known or heard them personally. Favorinus relates a trip to the Isthmus by Aristotle (Diogenes Laertius 2.5.23), how much Aristotle paid for a set of books (4.1.4) or gossips about Demetrius of Phalerum's marital situation (5.5.3).

Early examples such as Xenophon's or Zenon's ἀπομνημονεύματα involve the author as the eyewitness, adding an autobiographical element by being the author's personal recollections, a feature which ultimately goes towards explaining the original terminological relationship between ἀπομνημονεύματα and ὑπομνήματα. Subsequently, however, the concept of ἀπομνημονεύματα has expanded to encompass any recollections and noteworthy deeds and sayings which need not necessarily be witnessed by the author, adding instead a biographical element. We face some confusion searching for a Latin equivalent, especially given Aulus Gellius' terminology (c. 125 – after 180 CE). He refers to Xenophon's ἀπομνημονεύματα Σωκράτους with *dictorum atque factorum Socratis commentarios* (*NA* 14.3.5), while Cicero uses simply *dicta* (*Nat. d.* 1.13; cf. *Tusc.* 1.20). Gellius' use of the term *commentarius* reflects a generic connection across the languages (see earlier), yet again we are faced with a lack of titular consistency, both within the same language and across linguistic boundaries. While we see a connection between the ἀπομνημονεύματα, ὑπομνήματα, and *commentarii*, not one of the texts relevant for the present study are referred to as ἀπομνημονεύματα and there appears to be a clear generic distinction. Thus, despite the early connection and some misreadings, the ἀπομνημονεύματα do not impact significantly on our present line of enquiry.[60]

Historiography and autobiography

Lastly, we turn to texts which have created conceptual problems given their perceived proximity to historiography. This brings to mind Plutarch's quote insisting that he was writing lives, not history (*Alex.* 1.1–3), indicating a distinction between biography and historiography which might be extended to include a distinction autobiography/historiography. Generic definitions have proven complicated for Xenophon's *Anabasis,* paralleling some discussions

---

60 See Köpke, *Apomnemoneumata*, for scribal errors or misunderstandings between ἀπομνημονεύματα and ὑπόμνημα.

surrounding Caesar's *Gallic War*, earlier and the fragments of Sulla's literary life's work.

There are several parameters according to which we can try to separate: emic and etic understanding, how far the author extends his historical and geographical focus, statistics (how often does he mention himself compared to the whole corpus?), how far the text fulfils the generic markers of historiography. None of these features by themselves, of course, are determinative. Ammianus Marcellinus the author (330–95 CE) refers to himself as an actor in the first person (e.g. 18.6.10–11), Thucydides uses the third person (e.g. 1.112.2, 4.103.4), and yet both were consciously writing history (cf. Amm. Marc. 16.1.1–3; Thuc. 1.1). Meanwhile, Polybius switches from third- to first-person accounts (36.12.2).[61]

Equally disconcerting is the variety of terms signifying historiography in antiquity; *annals, historia and res gestae* are distinctive terms, yet all are applicable to historiography and part of a discourse.[62] The generic features of historiography are equally diverse; features such as a preface containing methodology and qualifications (e.g. Josephus, *War* 1.1–3, Herodotus, *Hist.* 1.1), a certain style (ornate, descriptive, simple), speeches, length, arrangement (topical or chronological) and digressions are not ubiquitous or even consistent. Although speeches were a common feature in Greek historiography, Cicero maintains that Fannius, writing his history in the late second century BCE, proved innovative by including speeches for his character (*Brut.* 81). Similarly, Velleius' two-book Roman history contrasts with Livy's multi-volume undertaking – and yet both works are considered historiography.[63] Genre categories were flexible entities yet they nevertheless offered the participants involved in the composition and interpretation processes a vital framework. The same problems confront us in our search for autobiography.

---

61 See Marincola, *Authority*, 188–92, for a detailed discussion of Polybius' narration technique. A brief reminder of the concepts of genre and mode might be helpful: all three authors ensured that their narratives would be interpreted as participating in the genre of historiography, and occasionally included autobiographical (mode) narratives (representing mainly internal genre features) within the larger genre-framework.

62 See Gellius, *NA* 5.18.1: *in quid et quantum differat historia ab annalibus; superque ea re verba posita ex libro Rerum Gestarum Sempronii Asellionis primo.* – 'In what and to what extent history differs from annals, and further the text cited about this issue from the first book of the *Res gestae* by Sempronius Asellius.'; Marincola, 'Genre', 289; Gerald P. Verbrugghe, 'On the Meaning of Annals', *Philologus* 133 (1989): 192–230.

63 Cf. Marincola, 'Genre', 311–12, who sets out to demonstrate that genre and generic requirements are fluid, evolving constantly. See also Lucian, *Hist. conscr.* 30, where he mentions an author who wrote 500 lines and called his oeuvre history.

Xenophon

From a genre perspective, Xenophon's *Anabasis* is consistently treated as a problematic text.⁶⁴ The text does not offer much information by way of title, preface, or any programmatic statements from which we can deduce the author's (explicit) aims. The title has been preserved by Dionysius of Halicarnassus (*Pomp.* 4.1):

> τήν τε Κύρου παιδείαν, εἰκόνα βασιλέως ἀγαθοῦ καὶ εὐδαίμονος· καὶ τὴν ἀνάβασιν τοῦ νεωτέρου Κύρου, ᾧ καὶ αὐτὸς συνανέβη, μέγιστον ἐγκώμιον ἔχουσαν τῶν συστρατευσαμένων Ἑλλήνων· καὶ τρίτην ἔτι τὴν Ἑλληνικήν.

The *Education of Cyrus,* the portrait of a good and successful king; *The Expedition of the Younger Cyrus,* in which Xenophon accompanied the prince, contains praises of the Greek auxiliaries in the highest terms; and thirdly the *Greek History*.⁶⁵

The fact that Xenophon wrote in the third-person singular and distinguishes consistently between author and actor carries little indication of his choice of genre – although perhaps his consistency itself might arouse suspicion should he have consciously wanted to avoid the first person. Thucydides (460–400 BCE), roughly contemporary with Xenophon, published his history of the Peloponnesian war (431–404 BCE) and included several passages with himself as actor, switching from the first to the third-person singular where necessary. Perhaps the fact that Xenophon does not is an indication of a disguise mentioned by Momigliano.⁶⁶

Many scholars have discussed the genre of the *Anabasis* from a variety of angles, although Misch had opted to exclude Xenophon from his detailed

---

64 Xenophon narrates a short, two-year period during which he had to lead the remainder of a mercenary Greek army back to Greece through Persia (401–399 BCE) following the death of Cyrus the Younger, son of Darius II, in 401 BCE. Upon his return to Greece, he was exiled by his fellow Athenians for cooperating with the Spartans and, with Spartan aid, settled in Scillus (near Olympia). Subsequent political disturbances forced him to resettle in Corinth. For a comprehensive biography, see Hans Rudolf Breitenbach, 'Xenophon S.V.', in *Paulys Real-Encyclopaedie der Classischen Altertumswissenschaft,* ed. by August Friedrich von Pauly and Georg Wissowa (Stuttgart: A. Druckenmüller, 1967).
65 See also Diogenes Laertius, *Xenophon,* 2.56-7; Reichel, 'Xenophons Anabasis', 46–7; Breitenbach, 'Xenophon'.
66 See Reichel, 'Xenophons Anabasis', for a detailed discussion of how Xenophon's use of the first and third person compares with other historians. Note that Isocrates, writing roughly contemporaneously, self-consciously wrote the *Antidosis* in the first person. Momigliano, *Development,* 57, suggests that Xenophon was trying to disguise the fact that the *Anabasis* was an autobiography, implying thereby that Xenophon was uncomfortable writing about himself. Momigliano cites the autobiographical character of the *Anabasis* as the reason for Xenophon publishing under a pseudonym and in the third person singular. Cf. also Marincola, 'Genre', 316.

discussion of autobiography;⁶⁷ they have concluded that somehow, Xenophon was not writing historiography, but not really autobiography either. Xenophon must have created something new, 'eine besondere Gattung'.⁶⁸ Reichel's recent acceptance of *Anabasis* as an autobiography offers a refreshing perspective.⁶⁹

Plutarch's statement that Xenophon became his own history (Ξενοφῶν μὲν γὰρ αὐτὸς ἑαυτοῦ γέγονεν ἱστορία, *Glor. Ath.* 345E) does not help the conundrum, and of the references by other ancient authors on Xenophon, not one refers to a possible autobiography, as Xenophon is understood either as philosopher or historian – the *Anabasis* itself is known as a work about Cyrus rather than Xenophon.⁷⁰ We might note, however, that given the range of Xenophon's publications (which included historiographical, philosophical and biographical writings, technical treatises and an encomium), it is likely that terms such as 'historian' or 'author' were used as a catch-all reference.⁷¹ We do however see that the *Anabasis* represents an author who wishes to write about himself, and uses the literary means available to him, at a time praised for its literary innovations.⁷²

---

67 Misch, *Geschichte*. He did, however, include Caesar's *Gallic War*, an equally problematic text in terms of genre participation.
68 Hans Rudolf Breitenbach, *Historiographische Anschauungsformen Xenophons* (Freiburg i.d. Schweiz: Paulusdruckerei, 1950), 43. Vivien J. Gray, *Xenophon* (Oxford, New York: Oxford University Press, 2010), includes the *Anabasis* in her 'historical writing' section of her book. Patrick J. Bradley, 'Irony and the Narrator in Xenophon's *Anabasis*', in *Xenophon*, ed. by Vivienne J. Gray (Oxford: Oxford University Press, 2010), 521 refers to a 'hybrid literary genre'.
69 Reichel, 'Xenophons *Anabasis*'. Reichel bases his understanding of autobiography on a definition found in literary theory, the 'lit. Darstellung des eigenen Lebens oder grösserer Abschnitte daraus; anders als das Tagebuch mit erklärtem Öffentlichkeitsbezug [. . .].' Based on this definition and modern critic Philip Lejeune's 'autobiographical pact', which allows for a third person narrative as long as the author, narrator and protagonist are identical, Reichel confidently states that 'die Anabasis erfüllt diese Kriterien im Wesentlichen' and that the Anabasis was 'eine . . . Selbstdarstellung . . . in einem der Geschichtschreibung nahestehenden Werk' by Xenophon owing to a lack of literary alternatives available to him at the time (ibid., 55, 69). Despite Reichel's laudable attempts to confirm autobiography as the determinative genre of the *Anabasis*, he omits a comparative approach with other texts and instead opts to distinguish the *Anabasis* from historiography. He bases his understanding of autobiography largely on the aforementioned definition which does not include internal or external characteristics but rather a loose, modern and general definition of the content.
70 Cf. Dionysius of Halicarnassus, *Pomp.* 4.1; Lucian, *Hist. conscr.* 39: δίκαιος συγγραφεύς – 'a just historian', cf. *Hist. conscr.* 23; Plyb 6.45.1: οἱ λογιώτατοι τῶν ἀρχαίων συγγραφέων, Ἔφορος, Ξενοφῶν, Καλλισθένης, Πλάτων, . . . – 'the most learned of the ancient writers, Ephorus, Xenophon, Callisthenes, Plato . . .'
71 In parallel, Nicolaus of Damascus wrote numerous works across a variety of genres but is generally referred to as 'philosopher'.
72 That Xenophon was writing in an adventurous and experimental literary age, and contributed greatly to the development of biography in particular, is emphasized by Momigliano, *Development*, 43–64. Hägg, *Biography*, 31–51, highlights the fact that both Isocrates and Xenophon stand at the beginning of new biographical traditions. It is noteworthy that simultaneously both authors also composed works that were to prove influential for the development of autobiography, the *Anabasis* and the *Antidosis*. The *Antidosis* will not be considered in the present analysis because of Isocrates'

Lucius Cornelius Sulla (138-78 BCE)

Sulla retired as dictator of Rome in 79 BCE and wrote a book described alternatively as ὑπόμνημα, *res gestae*, πράξεις or *historia*.[73] None of the extant fragments reflect Sulla's own terminology, but no commentators refer to it as *vita*, βίος, or *commentarius*. Some scholars, disregarding the lack of ancient references, carelessly include Sulla's work in the *commentarius* genre, because of the work's autobiographical aspect, and the Greek title ὑπόμνημα attributed to it.[74]

The length of the text (twenty-two books, F20), its expansive content, and the different titles and *Gattungsbezeichnungen* attributed to it indicate a certain measure of confusion in terms of generic affiliation.[75] The extant fragments offer us a glimpse into the content, including Sulla's genealogy, his reliance and trust in divination and dreams, Sulla's image as *felix*, military career and reforms for Rome; whether or not he included the contentious period 82-78 BCE during which he ruled Rome single-handedly has been much debated without a conclusive answer.[76] Sulla must have included much detailed information and perhaps some digressions on his ancestors, geographical landmarks (Plutarch, *Sull.* 16.1), military stories (*Sull.* 14.1-3), political discussions and perhaps even direct speech to make up twenty-two books worth of narrative.[77]

---

 own comments concerning his insecurities about his decision to frame the *Antidosis* as a defence speech (cf. *Antid.* 1 and above).
73 The fragments are collected in *HRR* vol. 1, 195-204. ὑπόμνημα: Plutarch, *Sull.* 6.5,6; 14.2,6; 17.1; Luc. 1.3; Mar. 35.2. RG: Aulus Gellius, *NA* 1.12.16, 20.6.3; πράξεις: Plutarch, *Luc.* 1.4. Historia: Cicero, *Div.* 1.72.
74 Thein, 'Felicitas', 89; Scholz, 'Sulla's *Commentarii*'; Holger Behr, *Die Selbstdarstellung Sullas: Ein Aristokratischer Politiker zwischen persönlichem Führungsanspruch und Standessolidarität* (Frankfurt am Main: Peter Lang, 1993); Pelling, '*Commentarii*'. Tatum, 'Late Republic', 166, also equates ὑπομνήμα with *commentarii*.
75 Aratus of Sicyon (271-213 BCE) is credited with writing a thirty-book-long ὑπόμνημα, whose fragments survive in Plutarch and Polybius (*FGrH* 231). It is noteworthy that despite the length and the overall historical narrative in which Aratus as leader of the Achaean League defends his decisions and actions, and despite the parallel features in Sulla's work, the text has not been subject to a similar debate concerning the relationship with historiography but appears to be accepted as either memoir or autobiography. See recently Marasco, 'Hellenistic Age', 104-17, with further references.
76 For a detailed discussion of the content, see Ernst Badian, *Lucius Sulla: The Deadly Reformer. The Seventh Todd Memorial Lecture Delivered in the University of Sydney, 11 September 1969* (Sydney: Sydney University Press, 1969); Arthur Keaveney, 'Sulla, the Marsi, and the Hirpini', *CP* 76 (1981): 292-6; idem., *Sulla. The Last Republican*, 2nd edn (London and New York: Routledge, 2005); Behr, *Selbstdarstellung Sullas*; Thein, 'Felicitas'; Tatum, 'Late Republic'; Geoffrey Lewis, 'Sulla's Autobiography: Scope and Economy', *Athenaeum* 79 (1991): 509-19. For a discussion of the period 82-78 BCE, see Ibid., 17-9; Behr, *Selbstdarstellung Sullas* 10-12; Keaveney, *Sulla*, 174.
77 For the suggestion that Sulla included direct speech, see Scholz, 'Sulla's *Commentarii*', 184.

Sulla himself never kept quiet about his wish to defend his actions publicly; Sulla's books were only one part of his express wish to justify his actions against Rome and the Roman people, along with speeches and letters.⁷⁸

> τοσοῦτον ἦν ἐν τῷδε τῷ ἀνδρὶ τόλμης καὶ τύχης: ὅν γέ φασιν ἐπειπεῖν ἐν ἀγορᾷ, τὴν ἀρχὴν ἀποτιθέμενον, ὅτι καὶ λόγον, εἴ τις αἰτοίη, τῶν γεγονότων ὑφέξει, [. . .]
> So great was this man's boldness and good fortune. It is said that he made a speech in the forum when he laid down his power, in which he offered to give the reasons for what he had done to anybody who should ask him. (Appian, *B Civ.* 1.104)

Ancient texts without any programmatic statements, multiple generic tags by third parties, and a lack of consistent generic markers are problematic, especially if one includes confusing modern terminology and an inconsistent approach, and acknowledges the fact that a large amount of literature has been lost to us.

Summary and conclusion

This chapter has introduced a variety of works that have previously all been associated with autobiography; some however have also been discussed within the framework of other genres. Differences and similarities have been noted between the texts, yet scholars who accept the existence of autobiography as a genre in antiquity tend to gather all the different texts discussed earlier, and more, together into one group (autobiography) despite, and without explaining, the differences between the individual works; Smith for example sees Caesar's *Gallic War* in the same genre as Sulla's autobiography despite what he terms 'sharper' differences.⁷⁹ Texts entitled *vita* or βίος can be accepted more easily within the framework of autobiography. Longer discussions, however, are necessary for texts not conforming to the life-to-death formula.

What is becoming clear is that ancient authors were experimenting with literary self-presentation, fully expecting their respective audiences to understand and appreciate their efforts. This aspect has been underestimated

---

78 Cf. also Appian, *B Civ.* 1.77,89,95; Plutarch, *Sull.* 34.2. It is also interesting to note the multitude of speeches and letters written by many of the authors discussed in this analysis, in their attempts to put across their messages and achievements: in addition to Cicero, Catulus, and Caesar (noted earlier), Augustus was also credited by Appian (*B Civ.* 5.13.130) with additional speeches given to the Senate which were subsequently transcribed and distributed. We must therefore also consider the relevant passages in Josephus' *War* 2.568–3.408 in this vein and consider the relationship and effect of the other publications in relation to the texts discussed in this analysis.
79 Smith, 'Sulla's *Memoirs*', 79.

in scholarship. Should an author wish to write about himself in the first century CE, he had several options available to him, implying that this was not an uncommon occurrence.[80] We see a period of active experimentation, ancient authors exhibiting an increasing impulse to write about themselves, as they searched for acceptable literary ways to express themselves: we perceive a lack of rigidity, the apparent variety indicates a measure of development and a sense of freedom in terms of authorial decisions and audience receptions. However, the subsequent literary analysis will help us determine whether this perceived range was in fact this diverse or whether authors and audiences had established a set of conventions.

Building on these previous discussions, collecting and analysing these works within a different approach and basing an analysis on genre theory, the present study rests on and aims to develop further previous scholarship in search of a genre of autobiography as a construct with conventions and expectations, by offering a contribution to scholarship in so far as such an in-depth, comprehensive genre theory-based approach has not yet been applied to a collection of texts consistently discussed together as a literary group. If these diverse but clearly related works, alongside Josephus' *Life,* show a similar pattern when analysed through the features discussed in Chapter 2, we can with greater confidence speak about a genre of autobiography in the sense of expectation-generating features, boundaries, conventions and we will be able to see in how far *Life* reflects the contemporary literary milieu. Authors cannot help being influenced by their literary milieu and knowledge base, both positively and negatively, consciously or subconsciously.

---

80 For example, Suetonius, *Iul.* 54.1, where he mentions the *commentarii* of anonymous men campaigning with Caesar in Spain. He uses these testimonies as credible sources for Caesar's actions, but what were they? We must ask ourselves whether Suetonius had access to unknown autobiographies lost to us or, considering that he does not offer specific authorship, whether he invented them, knowing that such testimonies were possible and credible. Similarly, Plutarch demonstrably relies on such accounts as source material for his books.

4

Opening features and subject

The literary analysis in the subsequent chapters will methodically examine individual elements and features in *Life*, followed by a comparison with the literature introduced in Chapter 3. For ease of reference, the analysis has been divided into the following three chapters (Chapters 4–6). Short summaries at the end of each chapter serve simply to tie together the respective set of features, before final, overarching conclusions in Chapter 7 can be drawn regarding the position of *Life* within its literary context. These conclusions will consider foremost whether a coherent pattern emerges into which individual texts can be integrated and whether any text consistently falls out of line or moves along the boundaries of an established pattern. The reliance on one shared common feature does not necessarily indicate a common genre, and some features, individually, will be present throughout a culture's literary corpus and thus by themselves will not be indicative; rather, we should focus on a combination of elements and an emerging pattern.[1] In order to determine the existence of a genre, this analysis is primarily focused on the range of features which are part of the contemporary literary milieu, identifying literary relationships on a broader level than that between individual texts only, searching for the possible existence of a family resemblance, a pattern emerging from the features used or avoided. The conclusions that will emerge from these analyses and discussions will contribute to our understanding and interpretation of *Life* and will increase our knowledge of Josephus' sensitivity to his literary surroundings, his literary thought processes and our understanding of autobiography as a genre in antiquity.

---

1 For a more detailed discussion of the fluidity of genres, and necessity of acknowledging common elements, see the discussion in Chapter 2.

Title

The text of Josephus' *Life* does not carry an individual title in its manuscripts, as it is usually appended to the text of the *Antiquities*.[2] However, this is not uncommon in ancient literature. If we consider that ancient manuscripts were written on scrolls, the first words visible upon unscrolling were either the opening or closing passages. Hence, authors, or subsequent librarians, inserted the titles and catchphrases into the preface or epilogue in order to alert the reader to the content of the respective scrolls.[3] Plato, for example, sums up the contents of his letter in the final sentence:

> But I deemed it necessary to explain the reasons why I undertook my second journey to Sicily because absurd and irrational stories are being told about it. If, therefore, the account I have now given appears to anyone more rational, and if anyone believes that it supplies sufficient excuses for what took place, then I shall regard that account as both reasonable and sufficient. (*Seventh Letter* 352a.)

Similarly, Josephus repeats the contents of *War* in the book's last sentence, repeating his promise to narrate the war between the Romans and the Judaeans (*War* 7.455). We can also infer a title from intra-textual comments or remarks from other authors. Josephus himself uses terminology that is highly indicative of how he himself would have referred to *Life*. Although Richard Laqueur originally based his ὑπόμνημα-hypothesis on the occurrence of the verb ὑπομήσω in *Ant.* 20.267, other indicators must be emphasized as well. In *Ant.* 20.266, Josephus introduces what follows as περὶ τῶν κατὰ τὸν βίον πράξεων – 'concerning the acts during my lifetime'. Similarly, he concludes the narrative with a mirroring phraseology: τῶν ἐν τῷ βίῳ μου πεπραγμένων – 'of the events in my life' (*Life* 413) and: τὰ πεπραγμένα μοι διὰ παντὸς τοῦ βίου – 'the events throughout my whole life' (430).[4] The repetition of the same, descriptive terminology at

---

2   For the manuscript tradition, see Schreckenberg, *Die Flavius-Josephus-Tradition*, 31.
3   Donald Earl, 'Prologue-Form in Ancient Historiography', in *Aufstieg und Niedergang der Römischen Welt*, ed. by Wolfgang Haase (Berlin: Walter de Gruyter, 1972), 842–56; Burridge, *Gospels*, 108; Revilo P. Oliver, 'The First Medicean Ms of Tacitus and the Titulature of Ancient Books', *Transactions and Proceedings of the American Philological Association* 82 (1951): 232–61 (243); Nicholas Horsfall, 'Some Problems of Titulature in Roman literary History', *BICS* 28 (1981): 103–14. Rajak, *Josephus*, 201–2, who also points out the lack of a consistent title for *War*; cf. Cohen, *Josephus*, 104. Q. Cicero gives the title of his work at the very end: *Volo enim hoc commentariolum petitionis haberi omni ratione perfectum.* – 'For I want this handbook of electioneering to be considered perfect in every way' (*Comment. pet.* 58.).
4   The mirror image is part of Josephus' deliberate concentric structure within *Life*. See Mason, *Life*, xxiii–xxvii.

the respective beginning and end indicates a stock catchphrase with which to capture the audience's attention and frame the work, generically speaking.

Comparanda

The works of Nicolaus of Damascus and Augustus carry titles or are referred to with terms that are almost identical with Josephan phraseology: Περὶ τοῦ ἰδίου βίου καὶ τῆς ἑαυτοῦ ἀγωγῆς – 'about his own life and his own education' (Nicolaus); Περὶ τοῦ ἰδίου βίου καὶ πράξεων – 'about his own life and acts' (Augustus).[5] Suetonius uses the Latin equivalent to πράξεις when referring to Sulla's lost work: *de rebus suis* (*Gram.* 12), a term which is repeated in Catulus' *De consulatu et de rebus gestis* and Caesar's *Commentarii rerum gestarum* (*B Gall.* 8 prf.).[6] Cicero uses the Latin *commentarius* to refer Catulus' work (Cicero, *Brut.* 132), and it is noteworthy that the title also parallels Cicero's own *De consulatu suo*.[7]

Josephus' use of ὑπομήσω/ὑπομιμνήσκω in *Ant.* 20.267 also corresponds both to his understanding of the term and to other Greek writers who know the word – family – to have autobiographic connotations and use it to refer to the works of Sulla (Plutarch, *Sull.* 6.7) and Augustus (Plutarch, *Comp. Dem. Cic.* 3.1).[8]

---

5   Wacholder, *Nicolaus*, 37, argues strongly that the transmitted title was Nicolaus' choice rather than a later attribution, suggesting it was the first instance of an author using the term 'bios' for an autobiography. It is unclear whether Wacholder focused only on Greek literature and therefore disregarded Latin works which he refers to as *commentarii de vita sua*. He suggests that Nicolaus chose the title to contrast his own βίος with 'the usual Greek memoirs (ὑπομνήματα)' or the Roman *commentarii*: rather than focusing on military events, Wacholder understands Nicolaus to de-emphasize the historical component and to focus on his personality, morals and philosophy.
6   For Vincent J. Cleary, 'Caesar's "Commentarii": Writings in Search of a Genre', *The Classical Journal* 80 (1985): 345–50 (345), the search for a genre comes down largely to the title Caesar chose for his text. Cleary insists that titles are helpful indicators as to how an author wanted his text to be received by the audience, and he reasonably argues that the genre perception built up by the audience, based on the title, would make an important difference in the meaning attributed to a text. Cleary follows the earlier analysis by Francis W. Kelsey, 'The Title of Caesar's Work on the Gallic and Civil Wars', *Transactions and Proceedings of the American Philological Association* 36 (1905): 211–38, who rejects the commonly adopted title of *Commentarii de bello gallico* in favour of *C. Iuli Caesaris commentarii rerum gestarum*. Such a title, so Cleary (ibid., 347), would prevent scholars from 'misjudging' the account by reading it too narrowly as a military account, as the terminology of *rerum gestarum* encompasses historical personal deeds in addition to the military. In contrast, Riggsby, 'Memoir and Autobiography', 272–3, postulates that Caesar composed his *Gallic War* to focus on his military campaigns in Gaul, arguing that in the original title no mention is made of Caesar's life or deed.
7   Suetonius refers to Claudius' autobiography as *De vita sua*, states its length (eight books) and adds a comment on its style (*Claud.* 41). However, in a passage Lewis, 'Imperial Autobiography', does not highlight, Suetonius also refers to the work as *historiis suis* (*Claud.* 21.2). See also Tacitus, *Ann.* 13.43, who has Nero refer to Claudius' *commentarii*, although it is not clear if both authors are referring to the same work. In general, Pausch, 'Formen', 310, refers to the interchangeability of titles, 'freie antike Zitierweise'.
8   Interestingly, the author of 2 Maccabees uses similar terminology to refer to the Book of Nehemiah (2 Macc 2:13).

Xenophon's *Anabasis* and Sulla's work stand out among these texts, the former carrying a specific title that has no related generic connotations, and the latter being referred to by a variety of titles including ὑπόμνημα, *rebus suis and historia*.⁹ Cicero, Aulus Gellius, and Plutarch refer to Sulla's books with titles frequently associated with historiography: *historiae, res gestae*, or πράξεις. Plutarch uses the terms interchangeably, alongside ὑπόμνημα (*Sull.* 6.9), and interestingly refers to the (Latin) *Vita* of Rutilius Rufus (Tacitus, *Agr.* 1.3) with ἱστορία as well (*Pomp.* 37.4; cf. *Mar.* 28.8).¹⁰ Lewis has suggested a title of *L. Sulla de rebus gestis*.¹¹ He is aware of Cicero's terminology (*et ut in Sullae scriptum historia videmus*) but explains this away in that Cicero used it for want of a better term, as Latin had no equivalent for the modern 'autobiography'. However, I would argue that Cicero had at his disposal the range of terms discussed in Chapter 2 (*commentarius, RG, vita*, ὑπόμνημα) and still he expressively chose a different term. We must consider the option that Cicero had adopted the title.¹²

Libanius' *Oration* 1 occupies a middle position; its title is traditionally referred to as βίος ἢ πέρι τῆς ἑαυτοῦ τύχης, or 'life, or concerning his fortune'. Thus, *we can conclude that Josephus availed himself of a phraseology that due to its familiarity would catch the audience's attention*. Josephus reacts to his literary predecessors and he reacts to an awareness of genre by framing *Life* with the range of terms available to him. Josephus evidently was acutely aware of his terminology and the contemporary use of these phrases. We see a consciousness at work that relates the texts to each other into an organic and

---

9   The fragments are collected in *HRR* vol.1, 195–204. ὑπόμνημα: Plutarch, *Sull.* 6.5,6; 14.2,6; 17.1; *Luc.* 1.3; *Mar.* 35.2. *RG*: Aulus Gellius, *Noct. att.* 1.12.16, 20.6.3; πράξεις: Plutarch, *Luc.* 1.4. *Historia*: Cicero, *Div.* 1.72.
10 Scholarship is engaged in a debate on the autobiography of Rutilius Rufus. Ancient authors mention both a *De vita sua* (Tacitus, *Agr.* 1; Charisius, *Ars grammatica* 154B,159B,166B,176B; Isidorus, *Etymologies* 20.11.4) and a ἱστορία (Plutarch, *Pomp.* 37.4; *Mar.* 28.8). Scholars have debated whether Rufus wrote two different texts, the same text in Greek and Latin, or an extended version of the original: Lewis, 'Imperial Autobiography', 665; G. L. Hendrickson, 'The Memoirs of Rutilius Rufus', *Classical Philology* 28 (1933): 153–75 (166); Hans Beck and Uwe Walter, *Die frühen Römischen Historiker. Band I von Fabius Pictor bis Cn. Gellius* (Darmstadt: Wissenschaftliche Buchgesellschaft, 2004), 101; Smith, 'Sulla's Memoirs', 73–4; Pelling, 'Ancient Genre', 42n.4. The discussion parallels the one regarding Sulla's title, and we could consider a parallel conclusion, that different authors referred to the same book with different terminology depending on their etic assessment of the book
11 Lewis, 'Sulla's Autobiography', 511n.10. Cf. *HRR* vol. 1, 195, and the title *L.Cornelii Sullae commentarii rerum gestarum*.
12 There are several instances in Cicero's corpus where he, rather than using his own words, reuses the original terminology. For example, Cicero uses the Greek term to refer to Athenodorus' work, *Att.* 16.14.4: *misit enim satis bellum* ὑπόμνημα. – 'for he [Athenodorus] has sent a good enough ὑπόμνημα of the war.' Cf. Randolph Richards, *Paul and First-Century Letter Writing: Secretaries, Composition and Collection* (Downers Grove: InterVarsity Press, 2004), 69, who points out that Cicero reused Tiro's original Greek term in a letter (angebar enim quod Tiro ἐνερευθέστερον te sibi esse visum dixerat. – 'For Tiro saying that he thought you looked heated had made me acutely uneasy.' *Att.* 12.4.1.E.

fluid generic state. The variety and mixing of catchphrases indicate that at the time of Josephus' publication of *Life,* a generic title had not been agreed upon in literary conventions, although as we have seen previously (Chapter 2), the genre had achieved a measure of distinction given the literary discourse of 'how to's'. Although Xenophon's title proves the exception to the other texts which all carry indicative, if not consistent, titles, it must be noted that the *Anabasis* precedes the others by several centuries, and what we see here is perhaps a transformation of a title for an evolving genre.

Opening formula/preface

Life lacks a prologue and immediately starts with ἐμοὶ δὲ γένος (*Life* 1) and Josephus' family history. Consequently, scholars have treated the epilogue of the *Antiquities* as a surrogate prologue:[13]

> Ἐπὶ τούτοις δὲ καταπαύσω τὴν ἀρχαιολογίαν βιβλίοις μὲν εἴκοσι περιειλημμένην, ἓξ δὲ μυριάσι στίχων κἂν τὸ θεῖον ἐπιτρέπῃ κατὰ περιδρομὴν ὑπομνήσω πάλιν τοῦ τε πολέμου καὶ τῶν συμβεβηκότων ἡμῖν μέχρι τῆς νῦν ἐνεστώσης ἡμέρας, ἥτις ἐστὶν τρισκαιδεκάτου μὲν ἔτους τῆς Δομετιανοῦ Καίσαρος ἀρχῆς, ἐμοὶ δ' ἀπὸ γενέσεως πεντηκοστοῦ τε καὶ ἕκτου.

> And with these I will conclude the *Antiquitates,* concentrated in these 20 books and 60.000 lines, and if God permits, I will cursorily note down in writing events from the war and things that we experienced up to the present day, which is in the 13th year of the reign of Domitian Caesar, and my 56th year. (*Ant.* 20.267)

The omission of any programmatic statements or introductions which accompany Josephus' other works (e.g. *War* 1.1–30; *Ant.* 1.1–9; *Ag.Ap.* 1.1–5) suggests a conscious authorial decision to use the epilogue of the *Antiquities* as a substitute for a preface and to use it as a conjunction between the two works. In this substitute preface, Josephus justifies his choices and reasoning for writing about himself and presenting his character, effectively indicating to his audience how to approach the subsequent *Life*. Previously, this justification has been understood defensively, although as mentioned earlier, Mason's interpretation of *Life* as a celebration has now been widely accepted – either way one wishes to interpret Josephus' reasoning, the fact remains that Josephus explains his literary decisions and choices. As in other prefaces, and in fact as most ancient authors

---

13 See Mason, *Life*, xiv.

were wont to do, Josephus uses both the (substitute) preface/transitionary passages and the conclusion of *Life* to introduce the topic of the book.¹⁴

Comparanda

Xenophon's *Anabasis* and Caesar's *Gallic War* open with a review of the respective local situation. Caesar describes the political situation in Gaul (*Gallia est omnis divisa in partes tres, B Gall.* 1.1), and Xenophon opens with the Persian king Darius, his wife and their progeny (*Anab.* 1.1; cf. Lucian, *Hist. conscr.* 23).¹⁵ Michael Reichel, without noting Xenophon's explicit programmatic statement in his *Cyropedia* (1.1.6), compares the lack of a preface in the *Anabasis* with the explicit historiographical prefaces of roughly contemporary writers Herodotus and Thucydides and suggests that Xenophon was aware of the novelty of his work.¹⁶

Libanius begins with a short preface and programmatic statement, claiming that he wishes to clear up any misapprehensions about his life (*Oration* 1.1). For the other texts we cannot determine the presence, or lack of, a prologue, due to their fragmentary state, or because the text has been too heavily embedded in a later framework. However, we do know that Sulla dedicated his work to Lucullus (Plutarch, *Luc.* 4.5).¹⁷ It is admittedly problematic that two of the fully extant texts (*Anabasis* and *Gallic War*) begin their narratives with historiographical or

---

14 The connection between *Life* and *Antiquities* has been briefly discussed in Chapter 1. It was not uncommon for contemporaneous authors to include short autobiographical sections into their larger works which participated in other genres (e.g. Cicero, *Brut.* 301–33, or Sallust, *Bell. Cat.* 3-4). Mason, *Life*, xlii, describes this custom as 'less conspicuous and threatening' as compared to the literature discussed in Chapter 3, stand-alone texts. At this initial stage of the analysis, I submit that Josephus consciously traversed from *Antiquities* to *Life* in adherence to the custom of incorporating autobiographical sections but expanding his text considerably (length-wise, see Chapter 5) to compose a work which his audiences would understand to participate in a separate genre from that of the foregoing *Antiquities*. See also Adams, *Greek Genres*, 252–4.
15 See Christina Shuttleworth Kraus, 'Bellum Gallicum', in *A Companion to Julius Caesar*, ed. by Miriam Griffin (Oxford: Wiley-Blackwell, 2009), 163–4, who also comments on the lack of a preface, but cannot offer a conclusive answer. Bradley, 'Irony', 529–33, suggests that Xenophon consciously omitted a preface to create narrative space. We can compare the omission of a preface with Xenophon's explicit programmatic statement in *Cyropedia* 1.1.6: ἡμεῖς μὲν δὴ ὡς ἄξιον ὄντα θ αυμάζεσθαι τοῦτον τὸν ἄνδρα ἐσκεψάμεθα τίς ποτ'ὢν γενεὰν καὶ ποίαν τινὰ φύσιν ἔχων καὶ ποίᾳ τινὶ παιδευθεὶς παιδείᾳ τοσοῦτον διήνεγκεν εἰς τὸ ἄρχειν ἀνθρώπων. ὅσα οὖν καὶ ἐπυθόμεθα καὶ ᾐσθῆσθαι δοκοῦμεν περὶ αὐτοῦ ταῦτα πειρασόμεθα διηγήσασθαι . . . – 'Believing this man to be deserving of all admiration, we have therefore investigated who he was in his origin, what natural endowments he possessed, and what sort of education he had enjoyed, that he so greatly excelled in governing men. According, what we have found out or think we know concerning him we shall no endeavour to present.'
16 Reichel, 'Xenophons *Anabasis*', 46.
17 Cf. Plutarch, *Comp. Dem. Cic.* 3.1: ὡς αὐτὸς ὁ Καῖσαρ ἐν τοῖς πρὸς Ἀγρίππαν καὶ Μαικήναν ὑπο μνήμασιν εἴρηκεν. – 'as the Emperor [Augustus] himself says in his autobiography addressed to Agrippa and Maecenas.'

geographical information, one of several factors conditioning their precarious position within the blurry boundary region of genres. Earlier works by Plato (*Seventh Epistle* 352a) and Demosthenes (*De cor.* 3–4), both considered to have contributed to the development of self-focused writing, used their respective opening and closing passages to explain their reasons for writing, thereby directing and guiding their audiences' expectations.

Analysis of verb subjects

A manual analysis of *Life* has revealed that Josephus uses himself as subject in roughly 250 sentences out of 630 sentences (39.7 per cent). He only uses his given name in speeches, and otherwise relies heavily on the use of the personal pronoun ἐγώ as opposed to merely the first-person singular verb form. He features in an additional 136 sentences (21.5 per cent) as object or matter of reference. In contrast, John of Gischala is used as the subject (whether directly by name or by means of a pronoun) in twenty-six sentences (4.1 per cent) and as an object in thirty-six additional sentences (5.7 per cent). Justus of Tiberias fares even worse, which reinforces the question how far the digression against him (*Life* 336–76) was included at a secondary stage; Josephus makes him the subject in fifteen sentences (2.4 per cent), excluding the digression, and he appears as object in a further eight sentences (1.2 per cent).[18] Within the digression, Justus is referred to as subject (either by his name or by pronoun) fifteen times (36.59 per cent), plus an additional four in the vocative (9.76 per cent); he features as an object in a further nine sentences (21.95 per cent).

Comparanda

Caesar similarly reigns supreme in his *Gallic War*, Books 1–7 (excluding the final book written by his legate Aulus Hirtius), although by a significantly lower margin. A computer analysis on the *Classical Latin Texts* by the Packard

---

18 For the digression, see Cohen, *Josephus*, 114–20, and Stern, 'Josephus and Justus'. Stern approaches the digression against Justus from a literary point of view and argues that the entire passage was not part of Josephus' original composition but rather included towards the end of the writing process. She compares the other passages in which Justus is mentioned with the digression and concludes that Justus was not the main focus of *Life* until Josephus realized that he had to defend himself against a recent publication, as Justus is consistently treated as if the digression did not exist. Josephus only subsequently inserted the digression (παρέκβασις, *Life*, 367) into a passage focusing on Tiberias.

Humanities Institute has revealed that Caesar, in the nominative case, is the subject of 212 sentences out of a total of 1,772 sentences for the entire work (11.96 per cent). He mentions himself in an additional 167 sentences (9.42 per cent) as a direct or indirect object in the other cases available to Latin writers.[19] In contrast, his fellow Romans and opponents feature only sparsely; the warrior Ariovistus appears twenty times (1.13 per cent) in the nominative case, and a further twenty-six times (1.47 per cent) in various other cases. Titus Labienus, Caesar's lieutenant, heads seventeen sentences (0.96 per cent), by name, and is referred to by name as object in thirty-four sentences (1.92 per cent). Surprisingly, Caesar's soldiers feature more heavily than any individual characters aside from Caesar himself: the *milites* – soldiers – appear in the nominative case in thirty-three sentences (1.86 per cent), and a staggering 126 times (7.11 per cent) in different cases. It is evident that just as Caesar stands out with over 21 per cent, and did not want to share centre stage in the narratives with any other individual, neither did Libanius. He features as a subject in 268 of 877 sentences (30.56 per cent), and as an object in a further 206 sentences (23.49 per cent). The fact that Libanius leaves other characters largely anonymous indicates that he does not want to share the attention but retains focus on himself consistently.

A computer search of Xenophon's *Anabasis*, with the help of the *Thesaurus Linguae Graecae*, has revealed that out of 2,271 sentences, Xenophon appears in the nominative case in 171 sentences (7.53 per cent), and as an object in other cases in a further seventy-eight sentences (3.43 per cent). In a direct parallel to the results from Caesar's *Gallic War*, Xenophon does not offer any other individual the opportunity to feature as strongly in his narrative; King Cyrus comes closest and is mentioned in the nominative case in ninety-one sentences (4 per cent), followed by Clearchus in the nominative case in sixty sentences (2.64 per cent) and in thirty-two sentences (1.4 per cent) in other cases. The Greeks as a group (Ἕλληνες) on the other hand actually overshadow Xenophon himself, if only statistically: they appear in the nominative case in 114 sentences (5 per cent), and in 256 sentences (11.27 per cent) in the other cases.[20]

---

19 As both Greek and Latin are inflected languages, it is possible to search for occurrences of a name in the nominative and other cases. Such a search cannot take into account those sentences where the subject is carried over from the previous (e.g. 'he said'), and thus we must expect the actual percentages to be higher than those computed here. This contradicts Riggsby's impression that Caesar himself was not present for much of what happens during the narrative: Riggsby, *Caesar*, 145.

20 This statistical evidence greatly enhances the notion of Panhellenism in the *Anabasis*; cf. Tim Rood, 'Panhellenism and Self-Presentation: Xenophon's Speeches', in *The Long March: Xenophon and the Ten Thousand*, ed. by Robin Lane Fox (New Haven, London: Yale University Press, 2004).

The other texts cannot be examined in a similar manner; for example, the extant narrative fragments of Nicolaus' autobiography amount to merely forty-six sentences. Of these, however, Nicolaus features as the subject in sixteen (34.78 per cent), and is referred to as an object in a further fourteen sentences (30.43 per cent), but we cannot determine how far these excerpts are exemplary for the entire text.

Josephus and Libanius dominate their respective narratives to the near exclusion of any other individual character, while Xenophon and Caesar, although still dominant, distribute the attention a little more evenly and especially Xenophon willingly shares the attention with his (generic) army.[21] *It is evident that all authors ensure that they are the focus of attention by making themselves the focus of sentences.*

Allocation of space

The allocation of space within a narrative to different events and time periods indicates what general topic or period the author focuses on, or wishes to communicate to the audience.

Josephus

It is immediately evident from Table 1 that the period of opposition and struggle that Josephus faces in Galilee (B) dominates the account, constituting roughly a third of the entire *Life*, followed by his victory narrative (C) and his life in Rome. The disproportionate allocation of space within *Life*, that is Josephus' single-minded focus on the events in Galilee in the spring of 67 CE, his omission of the events in Jotapata and as Roman prisoner including his interpretation of the prophecy, and his referral to the *War* for these events (*Life* 412) has been highlighted and discussed frequently, including the notion that Josephus purposefully framed the Galilee-narrative by including a 'cursory conclusion' with personal information

---

21 This realization in itself is an interesting detail, as it appears that both Caesar and Xenophon attempt to distribute the attention to their armies. The emphasis on the respective armies within the narrative suggests that both authors wished to be identified with their armies and by inference seen as another part of the state for which they were on campaign, thus rejecting any doubts as to the legality of their actions. As an avenue for further research, this may prove a fruitful topic for consideration, alongside the authors' literary-geographical context, considering how they place themselves in a context (geographical or otherwise) which is exemplary for their idealized social or political status. See as follows.

Table 1 Josephus

Section	Content	Passage	Sentences	Per cent sentences	Sentences total	Per cent total
A	Ancestry/early career	1–16	16	3.72	16	3.72
B	Josephus faces opposition in Galilee	17–303			287	66.74
B.1	Josephus asserts himself	17–63	47	10.93		
B.2	Opposition	64–203	140	32.56		
B.3	Dream sequence	204–12	9	2.09		
B.2	Opposition	213–44	32	7.44		
B.1	Josephus asserts himself	245–70	26	6.05		
B.2	Opposition	271–303	33	7.67		
C	Josephus achieves success in Galilee	304–406			103	23.95
C.1	Success	304–35	32	7.44		
C.2	Justus	336–67	32	7.44		
C.1	Success	368–89	22	5.12		
C.2	Justus	390–93	4	0.93		
C.1	Success	394–406	13	3.02		
D	Vespasian	407–13	7	1.63	7	1.63
E	Domestic/late career	414–29	16	3.72	16	3.72
F	Epilogue	430	1	0.23	1	0.23

to make it appear more like something of an autobiography, assuming that autobiography required such features.[22] For Shutt, *Life* thereby becomes 'not so much an autobiography in the ordinary sense as a detailed apologia of his conduct in Galilee'.[23] Without wanting to anticipate the following discussions, it may be more beneficial to consider why Josephus felt it necessary, relevant or appropriate to include the personal framework (*Life* 1–16, 414–29) when authors such as Cicero, Catulus or Caesar, authors who as we shall see later similarly focused their

---

[22] Rajak, *Josephus*, 166. She also remarks that the disproportionate structure turns *Life* into a 'curiosity'. See also Siegert, Schreckenberg and Vogel, *Aus Meinem Leben*, 4; Thackeray, *Josephus*, 5, who mentions 'brief sketches'; McLaren, *Turbulent Times*, 70–7; Feldman, *Josephus*, 381. For Barish, 'The Autobiography of Josephus', 64, the imbalance, with a focus on the 'war period', suggests that *Life* should be considered both an 'account of the war and an autobiography'. For additional explanations, see Shutt, *Studies in Josephus*, 14; Cohen, *Josephus*, 121; Rajak, *Josephus*, 154; Rappaport, 'Where Was Josephus Lying?', 288. Dormeyer, 'Biographie', 23, also argues that Josephus omitted the Jotapata episode because a military leader should die with his troops. His survival was 'schändlich'; Mason, 'Essay', 73, cf. 62.

[23] Shutt, *Studies in Josephus*, 14.

writings on a brief period within their military or political careers, did not. An approach based on generic parameters may thus explain more comprehensively why Josephus decided on the allocation of space he did.

Returning now to the more detailed breakdown, the fact that the two parallel accounts of Josephus' early and late career (A and E) are exactly the same length (sixteen verses, 3.72 per cent), cannot be a coincidence. The disputed digression against Justus of Tiberias (C2, *Life* 336–67), although prominent in content and as the basis for long discussions, is decidedly un-prominent in terms of space, constituting only 7.44 per cent, roughly the same size as three other sequences (B2, *Life* 213–44, 271–303; C1, *Life* 304–35). It must be noted that for clarity's sake, the opposition narrative (B2, *Life* 64–203) has been collapsed into one large section; it is composed of several short opposition narratives interrupted by short digressions. Thus, the large percentage should not detract from the fact that no single subsection is overwhelmingly longer than any other, and even the pivotal dream sequence or the invective against Justus of Tiberias does not claim more space than any other scene.[24] Mason suggests that Josephus uses this constant evolution to drive the narrative and to build suspense, for the benefit of the audience.[25] It is however also possible that Josephus was avoiding a narrative focused constantly on himself as author and subject, in accordance with contemporaneous literary theory conventions as discussed in Chapter 2.

Comparanda

Xenophon

Xenophon severely limits his narrative period to his time with the Persian/Greek army and his efforts to bring them back home to Greece safely (Table 2). With the exception of the odd digression looking forwards or back in time (e.g. 5.3.7–13), the space of the entire *Anabasis* is limited to the campaign, excluding any other periods in his life. Xenophon himself only appears in an official capacity in Book III; the first two books are comparatively short and offer the historical and political background to Xenophon's actions as leader.[26] For the sake of brevity and clarity, an exemplary analysis of Book IV only has been included here, which shows that Xenophon occupies large sections of the attention, either

---

24 Cf. Mason's theory of short pericopae strung together to form a whole: Mason, 'Essay', 53–4.
25 Mason, *Life*, xxiii.
26 The same conclusions apply to Caesar's *Gallic War*, in which all seven books written by Caesar are set in Gaul/Germany/Britain covering the years 58–52 BCE including only minimal references to events or themes outside the military campaigns.

Table 2 Xenophon

Passage	Content	Dates	Sentences	Percentage
Book I	Campaign origins under Cyrus/his death	401 BCE		14.3
Book II	Greek deliberations and death of their leaders	401 BCE		14.3
Books III–VII	Army under Xenophon's leadership/travelling home	401–399 BCE		71.4
Book IV			227	43.61
1.15–22	Xenophon in action			
2.9–28	Xenophon in action			
3.9–16	Dream sequence			
3.20–34	Xenophon in action			
4.12–13	Characterization			
5.7–9	Characterization			
5.16–24	Xenophon in action			
5.28–6.3	Characterization			
6.10–15	Speech			
6.17–19	Speech			
7.3–8	Xenophon in action			
8.4–6	Characterization			
8.10–14	Speech			

through speeches, military action or through characterization narratives in which he exemplifies a range of virtues through his deeds and words, such as piety or good generalship.

Libanius, Oration *1*

Table 3 exemplifies that Libanius intends to concentrate on the time he lived and worked in Antioch, with nearly the entire second half of his original narrative devoted to this period (*Oration* 1.94–155). The first part of the narrative allocates roughly the same amount of space to the periods of his life spent in various other cities, whereby his five-year residence in Nicomedia, referred to by him as one of the happiest times of his life (1.51), receives the most attention, separating his two periods of life in Constantinople. The addenda, incorporated posthumously, are almost double the length of the entire work and remain focused on his life in Antioch. All the early stages in his life lead up to his career in Antioch.

Sulla covered a wide range by narrating the majority of his life. Uncertainties remain regarding the weighting of his narrative, and whether he included the last contentious period of his life as dictator of Rome (82–79 BCE) and his final year

Table 3 Libanius

Passage	Content	Verses	Percentage (of original 155 verses)	Percentage (of whole text)[a]
1	Prologue	1	0.65	0.35
2–3	Ancestry	2	1.29	0.7
4–13	Education/childhood	10	6.45	3.51
14–29	Athens	16	10.32	5.61
30–47	Constantinople	18	11.61	6.32
48	Nicea	1	0.65	0.35
49–73	Nicomedia	25	16.13	8.77
74–93	Constantinople	20	12.9	7.02
94–155	Antioch	62	40	21.75
156–285	Addenda	156	–	45.62

[a] It is generally agreed that Libanius had originally written only verses 1–155; the additional passages (156–285) are later additions published posthumously.

in retirement (78 BCE).[27] Augustus similarly covered a larger part of his early career, including events up to the Cantabrian War. The fragments of Nicolaus' *Life*, although shorter than the texts of Sulla or Augustus, demonstrate that he covered his youth and education as well as family history (although the actual space devoted to these topics remains unknown), and continued to the end of his active career with the election of King Herod's successors. Again, we know that he allocated space for the development of his topical narrative, using himself as the example of a good philosopher's life, but it is impossible to determine the percentage of space allocated for this part of his work. Works by Catulus and Cicero covered only a limited period in their life, allocating the literary space only for specific topics and events, such as the events during, and consequences of, their respective consulships (Plutarch, *Mar.* 25, Cicero, *Fam.* 5.12.4).

We see a divide in terms of allocation of space and coverage of individual events or time periods. Authors either focus on a specific, and comparatively short, period of their life in the public eye, or cover a wider range up to an entire life account. The results do not indicate a trend changing over time. Sulla was the first of the authors discussed here to allocate space to ancestry and narrate an extensive period of time, followed by Augustus and Nicolaus, while roughly contemporary authors such as Catulus, Caesar and Cicero allocated space only to a limited time frame.

The allocation of space within Life *appears to take a middle path by framing a very limited time period to give the impression of narrating Josephus' entire life*

---

27 Smith, 'Sulla's *Memoirs*', 68.

to date, thus taking on board previous precedents and adapting them. Josephus ensures that he offers familiar territory to any audience.[28]

Summary and conclusion

We have seen that although *Life* itself does not carry an individual title in the manuscript tradition, Josephus surrounds the text with repetitive terminology as a generic catchphrase to alert the audience (*Ant.* 20.266; *Life* 413, 430). The conscious lack of a prologue can be explained by positing that whereas Josephus' other books begin with an introductory preface about himself and his aims, the epilogue/prologue in *Ant.* 20.266–68 and the opening words of *Life* (ἐμοὶ δὲ γένος) were sufficient to constitute a prologue.[29] The content analysis and allocation of space have demonstrated that while Josephus offers information on his entire lifespan to date, he balances his narrative heavily in favour of his time and deeds in Galilee. Nevertheless, no individual narrative takes the spatial limelight, regardless of the importance, or perceived importance, of the respective content.

In terms of comparing *Life* to other texts, we see some similarities as well as differences. The given titles are all interconnected in their terminology; only Xenophon's *Anabasis* stands out. The calculation of verb subjects has demonstrated a further uniformity as far as all authors take the lead in heading sentences in the nominative case, and are unwilling to allow any individual character to overshadow them; there was merely a variance regarding the margin and the prominence of the respective supporting cast; Xenophon's *Hellenes* for example statistically overshadow him. The existence and necessity of a preface have been discussed, and with the exception of Caesar's *Gallic War* and Xenophon's *Anabasis*, the texts include a brief preface or notable catchphrases. An analysis of the allocation of space each author accords the various periods of his life has

---

28 A division between these groups of works has been noted, but it is beneficial to discuss this division and its implications within the framework of a larger analysis that considers other generic features simultaneously. See the following for the generic implications of this division. *Contra* Jonathan Price, 'Josephus', in *The Oxford History of Historical Writing. Volume 1: Beginnings to 600 AD*, ed. by Andrew Feldherr and Grant Harding (Oxford, New York: Oxford University Press, 2011), 223. Price briefly judges *Life*, suggesting that by focusing on a six-month period only and not giving an account of Josephus' whole life, *Life* did not adhere to the requirements of ancient autobiography. However, Price leaves unclear how or where he defined these requirements.

29 The arguably seamless transition suggests that both *Antiquities* (at the very least Book 20) and *Life* were presented in the same literary session/reading. See further, Chapter 5, for the mode of representation (i.e. presentation to the audience) and book-lengths in antiquity (i.e. whether it would have been likely for *Ant.* 20 and *Life* to fit onto the same scroll).

revealed a division ranging from a narrative limited to a very short period to an account of the author's life up to the date of composition. Initial results reveal a general agreement on title or reference, minimal introduction, focal point of the verb subjects and presence in the text. Where a division between the texts is evident (e.g. allocation of space), the texts are evenly divided. It will be interesting to note whether this distinction continues and whether the *Anabasis,* the only text already to stand out in some features, will continue to do so.

5

External features

Mode of representation

Josephus' *Life* is a continuous first-person prose narrative set in a rough chronological framework. While the social setting, that is, the audience and occasion, will be discussed in greater detail in Chapter 6, it may prove beneficial to comment briefly on the ancient custom of *recitatio,* publicly reading one's literary compositions; the ensuing analysis also discusses *Life*'s (and the comparative literature's) oral or written presentation or dissemination, which can influence an audience's perception of genre. Part of the ancient process of making works available and accessible to one's audience, *recitatio* offered authors an opportunity of presenting drafts of their compositions to their social circles (or those of their patrons).[1] The texts presented would not have been the finished product, but works-in-progress, much like scholars might present a paper at a conference looking for constructive feedback on their own research (e.g. Pliny, *Epist.* 5.3; Cicero, *Off.* 1.147). Subsequent steps, as exemplified by Pliny (e.g. *Epist.* 5.3) include corrections and circulating a written version.[2]

Josephus, fully integrated into the contemporaneous literary world, himself adhered to the process of presenting and circulating his works within ever-growing social circles.[3] Siegert notes a consistent prose rhythm within *Life,*

---

1 It would be anachronistic to speak blithely of 'publication', even though I myself have used the term with little reflection to refer to the process of making a text accessible to an audience. For a detailed overview of the ancient publication process, especially the importance of appreciating its immediate local impact, see Mason, 'Reading Josephus'.
2 For the custom of *recitatio* in Roman culture, see further and in greater detail, Robert Ogilvie, *Roman Literature and Society* (Brighton: Harvester Press, 1980), esp. 12–16; *Ancient Literacies,* ed. by William A. Johnson and Holt N. Parker (Oxford: Oxford University Press, 2009); William A. Johnson, *Readers and Reading Culture in the High Roman Empire. A Study of Elite Communities* (Oxford: Oxford University Press, 2010).
3 Mason's pithy remark in one of his earlier publications, that 'we do not know whether Josephus first published his books by recitation' seems counter-intuitive considering the emphasis Mason places on Josephus participating in the contemporaneous literary customs. See here Mason, 'Introduction to the *Judean Antiquities*', in *Flavius Josephus, Translation and Commentary Books 1–4 / Translation and Commentary by Louis H. Feldman,* ed. by Steve Mason (Leiden, Boston: Brill, 2000), xviii.

which reaffirms our understanding of the text being read out loud.⁴ Josephus directly addresses his audience and later patron, Ephaphoditus, and he admits that his accent when speaking Greek needed help (*Ant.* 20.263). Without wanting to anticipate the discussion concerning Josephus' style (as follows), *Life* demonstrates some extreme formulaic composition, highlighted by Mason in his translation; it is likely that rhythm and repetitive constellations greatly facilitated oral presentation and aural retention of the text.⁵

Comparanda

The *Anabasis* was composed in a continuous third-person prose narrative.⁶ The narrative flows smoothly and is structured chronologically. Caesar also wrote a smooth continuous narrative in the third person, praised by Cicero (*Brut.* 261–2), strictly separating author and actor, using the first-person voice only in editorial comments (e.g. *B Gall.* 2.29: *de quibus supra scripsimus* – 'of which I have written above'). Cicero's *commentarius* was by his own admission a perfectly finished prose narrative (*Att.* 2.1) which he intended for written circulation. This is evident as he specifically sent versions to Atticus in Athens, to the historian Lucceius, and to Pomponius (*Att.* 21.2) to distribute it for him. On the other hand, Plutarch states that Cicero frequently advocated for himself and praised his own actions (Plutarch, *Cic.* 24.1, cf. Cicero, *Att.* 21.2). Given Cicero's profession and resources, it is also likely that he included a variety of speeches and documents in the account to prove his own abilities as well as to provide evidence for his actions. Similarly, Smith suggests that Sulla wrote in Latin and included various speeches that he himself had delivered.⁷ Suetonius' anecdotes

---

Mason repeatedly emphasises the importance of understanding Josephus and his works within the framework of ancient publication practices: ibid., xviii-xiv; idem., 'Should Any Wish to Enquire Further (*Ant.* 1.25): The Aim and Audience of Josephus' *Judean Antiquities/Life*', in *Understanding Josephus: Seven Perspectives*, ed. by Steve Mason (Sheffield: Sheffield Academic Press, 1998); idem., 'Reading Josephus'. For Josephus' social setting, audience and social standing, see Chapter 6.

4   Siegert, Schreckenberg, and Vogel, *Aus Meinem Leben*, 10. Siegert refers to *Life* 1, 2, 61, 263, passages ending in the *versus cretici*. Siegert does not, unfortunately, visually demonstrate the existence of such a metre. Prose rhythm was a conscious feature of ancient literature. Cicero praises those orators who were skilled at imbuing their works with a natural prose rhythm, esp. Isocrates: *Brut.* 32–34; *De or.* 3.173–181.

5   Mason, *Life*, lii. For the importance of memory in literature, see also Mason, *Life*, 13n.58 and Rajak, *Josephus*, 27–8. However, Alessandro Vatri, 'Ancient Greek Writing for Memory: Textual Features as Mnemonic Facilitators', *Mnemosyne* 68, no. 5 (2015): 750–73, suggests that mnemonic devices were used mainly for the benefit of the audience's memory. Larry W. Hurtado, 'Oral Fixation and New Testament Studies? "Orality", "Performance" and Reading Texts in Early Christianity', *New Testament Studies* 60, no. 3 (2014): 329, insightfully distinguishes between familiarisation of the text and memorisation.

6   Exceptions are editorial cross-references such as *Anab.* 1.2.5, 2.3.1.

7   Smith, 'Sulla's *Memoirs*'.

about Augustus having good enunciation, working with an elocution teacher and usually reading his own works out aloud (*Aug.* 84.2, 85.1) support the theory of a first-person narrative. Libanius' oration is similarly a polished prose narrative, although scholars continue to debate its mode of representation. Norman, who has contributed one of the seminal translations and commentaries on the work, suggests that Libanius declaimed his oration before a live audience.[8] This is supported by the pauses in the narrative, which are the result of long, drawn-out vowel sounds at the end of the paragraphs (e.g. *Oration* 1.10,13,116,147). Paul Petit, on the other hand, suggests that Libanius never intended to present his oration and that it was instead distributed by his heirs posthumously.[9] However, I suggest that considering both the mode of representation for the comparative texts as well as the content of the oration, it is unlikely that Libanius did not present his work at all, or at the very least the first, clearly more polished half (verses 1–155, see Chapter 3).

Overall, we see that the various authors endeavoured to produce polished prose narratives. *Josephus' first-person narrative falls within the boundaries of representation.*[10] All the texts offer the audience a narrative of events that they can follow easily and whose main events and general thrust they could effortlessly remember.

Length

The importance of length as a generic feature has been discussed in Chapter 2. Ancient critics frequently mentioned length as a characteristic feature of literature, and Fowler emphasizes the importance of size as a 'critical factor from a generic point of view'.[11] Josephus himself bears testament to the importance of knowing the number of lines and length of his books, as he proudly states that his *Antiquities* number exactly 60,000 lines (*Ant.* 20.267; cf. *War* 1.30). At pertinent stages in his other books, he also makes references to the length of his works:

---

8   Norman, *Libanius' Autobiography,* xvii–xvii.
9   Paul Petit, 'Untersuchungen über die Veröffentlichung und Verbreitung der Reden des Libanios (1956)', in *Libanios,* ed. by Georgios Fatouros and Tilman Krischer (Darmstadt: Wissenschaftliche Buchgesellschaft, 1983), 98–9.
10 F1 suggests that Augustus wrote in the first person, but it remains uncertain: Smith and Powell, *Lost Memoirs,* 2. Extant fragments indicate that both Scaurus (*HRR* vol. 1, 195, F6: *veni*) and Rufus (*HRR* vol.1, 189–90, F9: *veniebam;* F14: *me invitum*) wrote in the first-person singular.
11 Fowler, *Kinds of Literature,* 62.

ἀλλ' ἐπειδὴ σύμμετρον ἤδη τὸ βιβλίον εἴληφε μέγεθος, ἑτέραν ποιησάμενος ἀρχὴν τὰ λοιπὰ τῶν εἰς τὸ προκείμενον πειράσομαι προσαποδοῦναι.

But as this book already reached a suitable length, by starting another book I shall endeavour to complete the remaining parts of the matter at hand. (*Ag.Ap.* 1.320)

Referring to *Life*, Josephus states (*Ant.* 20.267) that he intends to narrate his life βραχέα – briefly. In Josephus' words, this translates to roughly 15,900 words, placing the book squarely into Burridge's medium-length category, which could be read within the timeframe of one session.[12]

Comparanda

The comparative texts differ considerably in terms of length.[13] Nevertheless, Joseph Geiger assigns the works of Catulus, Rufus, Scaurus and Sulla to the 'historical genre of monographies' on account of their length despite being aware of the disparate lengths of the respective works.[14] Cicero refers to a *liber* by Catulus, indicating a medium-length account similar to *Life*. Cicero speaks of his own *commentarius* in the singular (*Att.* 2.1), as opposed to other *commentarii* such as Caesar's, for which he uses the plural (*Brut.* 262), and suggests that Lucceius should be able to compose a work of moderate length based on Cicero's

---

12 Since *Ant.* 20 and *Life* are clearly closely linked and transition one into the other, we must consider that both books were read in the same sitting. Since Ant. 20 amounts to roughly 9370 words, the combined total of Life and Ant. (roughly 25270 words) could still be read within one (longer) setting.
13 Brief autobiographical introductions in which authors justify their choice of topic and confirm their truthfulness by claiming the benefits of *autopsy* are excluded from this analysis. Authors including Thucydides (v.26.5), Cicero (*Brut.* 88.301-97.333), Sallust (B Cat. 3-4), Diodorus Siculus (1.4.1-5), Pompeius Trogus (F165 = Justin 43.5.11-12; the reference appears to reflect a genealogical statement, in keeping with the ancient mindset that distinguished ancestors implied an author's character and social status) have included short passages, usually less than a handful of verses as part of the works' respective prefaces, to critique their literary colleagues and predecessors, to introduce themselves, and to offer up their various credentials (education, travels, languages, sources, autopsy) to justify their literary efforts and to set them apart from other authors. These short passages have little to no bearing on the main text and as Lisa Irene Hau points out, serve mainly to create a persona for the narrator of the subsequent narrative: L. I. Hau, 'Narrator and Narratorial Persona in Diodoros', *Bibliotheke* (and their Implications for the Tradition of Greek Historiography)' (2018): 277–302. See also Paul Roche, 'Latin Prose Literature: Author and Authority in the Prefaces of Pliny and Quintilian', in *A Companion to the Flavian Age of Imperial Rome*, ed. by Andrew Zissos (Chichester: John Wiley & Sons, 2016), or Marincola, *Authority*, 175, who explains that the author wishes to portray himself as the best '*narrator rerum*'. *Contra* Mason, *Life*, xii, xlii, who refers to Cicero (*Brut.* 88.301-97.333), Sallust (B Cat. 3-4), and Ovid (*Tr.* 1.10) when arguing that Josephus had followed the fashion of attaching an autobiography (thereby equating these much shorter passages with *Life* without noting the considerable discrepancy regarding length) to a longer historiographical work. See, however, Chapter 7 for a possible influence.
14 Geiger, *Cornelius Nepos*, 80n.63.

Vorlage, implying a length between 10,000 and 25,000 words to fit onto one scroll.¹⁵ Libanius' oration, consisting of 21,575 words, also remains within the confines of one medium-sized book. Augustus is quoted to have written thirteen books (Suetonius, *Aug.* 85.1), Sulla twenty-two books¹⁶ and Caesar's *Gallic War* comprises eight books, the last of which was written by Caesar's legate Aulus Hirtius, one book per year of Caesar's campaign (58–51/50 BCE); the individual books, however, are short, Book Seven (the longest) consists of only ninety verses in the Loeb edition. Divided into seven books, Xenophon's *Anabasis* reaches an extensive 58,285 words. While this appears long in comparison, other historiographical works Burridge mentions are considerably longer (Herodotus at 189,489 words; Thucydides at 153,260 words; Pausanius at 224,602 words); the *Anabasis* once again hovers in the generic boundary region.¹⁷

Taking into consideration the earlier conclusions regarding mode of representation, *we see a tentative correlation between the longer texts comprising several 'books' (regardless of the actual length of the individual books) and intentional written circulation and declamation by a third person on the one hand, and shorter, single 'books' which the author initially presented himself, on the other.*¹⁸ The comparative length of Life *indicates its affiliation with the latter group.*

Structure

The structure of *Life* follows a largely chronological framework, within which Mason has detected a concentric pattern that mirrors the larger pattern of the *Antiquities*.¹⁹ The circular pattern has the dream sequence (*Life* 204–12) at its centre, during which Josephus describes the divinely inspired dream or vision he received that convinced him to remain in Galilee despite the manifold dangers. Mason's structural depiction of *Life* helps his readers to visualize the concentric pattern.

If we approach the structure from a different angle, it becomes evident that once Josephus returns from his first diplomatic mission to Rome and effectively

---

15 Cicero, *Fam.* 5.12.4: *modicum.* Cf. Quintus Cicero, who speaks in the singular, *commentariolum* (*Comment. pet.* 58); Livy speaks of *commentarii* in the plural (e.g. 1.31.8, 1.32.22), referring to several texts or archives. For scroll sizes, see earlier.
16 *HRR* vol. 1, 203, F20.
17 Burridge is not aware of any implications when he discusses the *Anabasis* as historiography despite noting a discrepancy in the length of the *Anabasis* in relation to other historiographical works: Burridge, *Gospels,* 114.
18 The exception is Augustus' lost work; Suetonius, *Aug.* 85.1, mentions that Augustus read aloud from his thirteen-book-long *De vita sua.* However, one could argue that individual excerpts read aloud, as reported by Suetonius, should not discredit the ultimate mode of representation.
19 Mason, *Life,* xxi–xxvii. Cf. Mason, 'Essay', 56.

ends the narrative of his early career (*Life* 16), he employs various structural units to alternate accounts concerning himself and his own actions in Galilee with regular digressions. According to Mason's observations, Josephus leaves various stories initially unfinished in order to drive the narrative forwards and to create suspense.[20] I would add that Josephus alternates the accounts with a systematic regularity within his structure. Especially within the opposition narrative (*Life* 17–303, see Table 1. Josephus), Josephus jumps between his own interactions with his various opponents (John of Gischala, Justus of Tiberias, the delegation from Jerusalem) and topical digressions narrating the situation of Judeans outside of Judaea (*Life* 25–7), the situation in Galilee (*Life* 30b–61), Phillip ben Jacimus (*Life* 179–84), or situations in which he himself features, but which do not carry any tension within the narrative itself, such as the noblemen from Trachonitis (*Life* 112–13, 149–55), or the confrontation with Roman forces (*Life* 213–15). I would suggest that Josephus employed this method of structuring his narrative with the purpose of deflecting the audience's odium that manifests itself when one spends too much time talking about oneself, as advised by Plutarch (*De laude* 543B).

Comparanda

The structures of both the *Anabasis* and *Gallic War* are fairly similar, in that they follow a largely chronological as well as geographical framework with cross-references, interspersed with structural units such as speeches and various digressions. The most 'convenient' structure for Xenophon's *Anabasis*, according to the classicist Leonard Wencis, divides the narrative into three chronological sections, namely the actual 'anabasis' (*Anab.* 1.1–1.7) until the Battle of Cunaxa (401 BCE), the 'katabasis', from Cunaxa to the Pontus (*Anab.* 1.8–4.7), and the 'parabasis', the journey home (*Anab.* 4.8–8.8).[21] Xenophon takes control of the structure and directs the reader by pointing them forwards and back within their reading, and includes a variety of digressions and speeches. Caesar organized his work annually, which automatically results in a chronological sequence. The discussions about the manner of publication for the *Gallic War* have been divided, one school arguing for serial production and publication in instalments, the other side arguing for a unified narrative, with 'a tangible narrative arc and a marked beginning, complex middle and fully closural

---

20 Mason, *Life*, xxiii.
21 Leonard Wencis, '*Hypopsia* and the Structure of Xenophon's *Anabasis*', *The Classical Journal* 73, no. 1 (1977): 44–9.

end'.[22] Either way, whether reading the books individually or all together, the audience receives a chronological military account of either an individual year of campaigning or of the entire Gallic campaign. Libanius similarly structured his work chronologically; he weaves a narrative path from his childhood until the time of writing by aligning the structure with the various cities he lived and worked in. The later additions (*Oration* 1.156–285) in the second part upset this clear chronological structure, giving the work as a whole an 'air of incoherence', although the individual addenda maintain a chronological structure.[23] Within the individual episodes, there are occasional departures from the chronological structure, looking backwards or forwards, but they are conveniently highlighted for the audience, e.g. πρότερον δὲ (*Oration* 1.106).

It is more difficult to determine the structure for fragmentary texts. Misch understands the structure of Nicolaus' βίος to have been divided into a chronological narrative of his ancestry, education and life events, followed by a topical presentation of his character.[24] This follows Jacoby's alignment of the fragments of ancestry (F131), education (F132), deeds and activities (F133–36), and virtues (F137–39). From a fragment preserved in Servius Honoratus we know that already in Book Two Augustus was narrating events from the year 44 BCE, more specifically the funeral games of Julius Caesar, at which point Augustus was nineteen or twenty years old – Augustus appears to have structured his *Life* chronologically throughout, as Suetonius (*Aug.* 85.1) uses a temporal marker (the Cantabrian War) to indicate the end of the narrative. It is possible that Augustus included some topical digressions, for example on legal matters, as the following fragment suggests:

> Ulpianus libro nono de officio proconsulis: corpora eorum qui capite damnantur cognatis ipsorum neganda non sunt, et id se obseruasse etiam diuus Augustus libro decimo de uita sua scribit.
>
> Ulpian in the ninth book on the duties of a proconsul: The bodies of those who had been condemned to death should not be denied to their relatives; and the Divine Augustus too wrote in the tenth book on his own life that he observed this. (*Digest* 48.24.1)[25]

---

22 Kraus, 'Bellum Gallicum', 160. See further.
23 Norman, *Libanius' Autobiography*, xii.
24 Misch, *Geschichte*, 184. Wacholder, *Nicolaus*, 39, posits instead that the sequence of the fragments collected in the *FGrH* corresponds to the order of appearance in the original text but argues for a fully chronological structure.
25 Smith and Powell, *Lost Memoirs*, 4, F3.

Christopher Pelling remains doubtful of the structure of Sulla's lost work, suggesting it might not be as linear as expected. References to Sulla's ancestors are recorded for Book Two, as well as a speech which Pelling dates to latest 91 BCE, preserved by Aulus Gellius (*NA* 20.6.3).[26] Pelling states that he would have expected Sulla's account 'to be well underway' by his second book, and suggests that a 'simple linear structure' may not apply to Sulla; perhaps he included a generous amount of 'background information' that modern readers would not expect in the more intimate setting of an autobiography.[27]

Cicero explicitly asks Lucceius to abandon his usual chronological approach when converting Cicero's *commentarius* for publication. Cicero's request appears to indicate that he divided his account, perhaps within a rough chronological framework, into various dramatic acts, i.e. topically: *habet enim varios actus multasque mutationes et consiliorum et temporum . . .* – 'for it contains various acts and many changes of both plans and circumstances . . . ' (Cicero, *Fam.* 5.12.6).

The majority of texts including Josephus' Life have been structured chronologically with intermittent topical digressions, with the exception of Cicero, who emphasizes his extravagant thematic structure, and Nicolaus of Damascus, who perhaps divided his account into a chronological and topical part respectively. This perceived structure has some consequences for our understanding of structure as a generic feature, raising the question whether Nicolaus' structure has been misunderstood given its extremely fragmentary state, and Cicero's insistence on creating something extraordinary. *Overall, we conclude that the majority of texts were structured chronologically, and other structures may have been possible due to the inherent flexibility of genre.* Reaching out to other, more distant, literature, we see that Plato's *Seventh Epistle* includes considerable philosophical discourses (albeit within the chronological structure), and Augustine's *Confessions* are divided into a chronological narrative (Books 1–9), and a philosophical and theological discourse (Books 10–13).[28]

---

26   Pelling, 'Ancient Genre', 44. Smith agrees that the dating of the fragment is complicated in terms of structuring the text (chronological, insertions etc), and suggests that the book number is corrupt: Smith, 'Sulla's *Memoirs*', 67–8.
27   Pelling, 'Ancient Genre', 44. For a more detailed discussion of the sequence of Sulla's works, see Smith, 'Sulla's *Memoirs*'.
28   Other genres can similarly divide their structure between chronological and topical; Quintillian for example distinguishes between these structures for the encomium or panegyric (*Inst.* 3.7.10–18). Biographies can demonstrate a chronological or topical structure, or a mixture of both, cf. Burridge, *Gospels*, 135–6, 165–6.

Literary units

As just mentioned, Josephus composed *Life* with a variety of shorter narratives which he alternates consistently. These literary units have been aptly described by Mason as short anecdotes or pericopae, which Josephus utilized to illustrate his character and his relationships with the other characters.[29] Josephus plays with a variety of literary units which include speeches (both direct and indirect), dreams and prayers (e.g. *Life* 204–15), and deflective units which are not vital to the flow of the narrative (e.g. *Life* 179–84). The length of the individual literary units varies, although overall those units concerned with Josephus himself tend to be longer than the units he affords to other characters.

The literary units are connected to form a continuous, unbroken narrative with few deviations or breaks. The speeches are integrated into the narrative but do not extend to dialogue, and are kept short, whereas Josephus' own indirect speeches can be considerably longer. In order to maintain the chronological framework, Josephus uses temporal markers to forge a connection between otherwise unrelated literary units (e.g. *Life* 112, 179, 216, 309, 373, 390, 407, 426).[30] Furthermore, Josephus uses short signposts and introductory and concluding remarks to unify the disparate literary units, such as δι' αἰτίαν τοιαύτην (e.g. *Life* 31, 46, 148, 155, 265, 270, 380, 389, 428). A clear advantage of these various literary units lies in their mnemonic benefits, making it easy for the speaker and the audience to remember the flow of the narrative and events.

Comparanda

Caesar employs many different literary units which he connects to a flowing narrative. Aside from narratives about his own actions, Caesar includes speeches and units in which he describes both geographical and anthropological issues of interest, such as the composition of Gaul or Britain, as well as the cultural mannerisms of the local people.[31] Noticeably absent are philosophical discourses, personal anecdotes about Caesar himself or a proactive dialogue between the characters. Xenophon demonstrates a more expanded repertoire of units which

---

29 Mason, 'Essay', 53–4.
30 Schwartz has demonstrated that Josephus frequently uses the phrase κατὰ τοῦτον τὸν καιρὸν to indicate a change of source material in both *War* and *Antiquities*. However, he does not discuss the appearance of the term in *Life*: Daniel R. Schwartz, 'Kata Toyton Ton Kairon: Josephus' Source on Agrippa II', *The Jewish Quarterly Review* 72 (1982): 241–68.
31 But note Riggsby, *Caesar*, 11, who suggests that some of the ethnographical descriptions could be later interpolations, *contra* Mayer, 'Caesar', 197–8.

he combines seamlessly, such as speeches (e.g. *Anab.* 1.24–25), biographical passages and obituaries (e.g. *Anab.* 2.6.16–20), geographical or cultural descriptions (e.g. *Anab.* 3.4.7–9), dialogue or an active discussion in direct speech between several characters (e.g. *Anab.* 7.2.23–38), personal anecdotes such as the dedicative inscriptions Xenophon commissioned at Delphi (*Anab.* 5.3.5) or his friendship with Socrates (*Anab.* 3.1.4–7). Lastly, the various literary units employed by Libanius mirror those units just discussed; the individual episodes concerned with Libanius himself are linked with occasional digressions such as a panegyric on Antioch (*Oration* 1.2,86), and summative comparisons of the good and the bad cards that Fortune had dealt Libanius (e.g. *Oration* 1.24,66).

It is more difficult to extrapolate literary units and the quality of their linkage in fragmentary texts. However, extant fragments show that Augustus included natural phenomena such as comets (F1, F2), as well as speech and dialogue (F8). Several fragments mention Cicero (F4, F5, F13), so we might assume a digression about his life, character or abilities. Similarly, F9 mentions Augustus defeating tribes in the Alps, so it is highly possible that he included some geographical or cultural digressions in his description of military campaigns. We can make a similar assumption of Catulus' *Res gestae*, which was mainly concerned with justifying his actions during the war against the Cimbri and Teutones, and of Sulla's work. Plutarch for example preserves the reference that Sulla spoke at length and with admiration of the geographical properties of the Plain of Elatea (*Sull.* 16.1). Lastly, Nicolaus' fragments focus on Herod, his actions and family, and indicate that Nicolaus employed literary units such as anecdotes about Herod's love of history and learning (F135), and biographical sketches (included in F136). The literary units presenting the characterizations of Nicolaus himself take the form of anecdotes and philosophical discourses (F137, F138). None of these individual units are of course unique to the works discussed here but can be found as literary units and blocks within other ancient genres as well, yet it is noteworthy *that the scope of literary units employed by both Josephus and the comparative texts are similar to the point of being identical,* as they all use a combination of units including speeches, (personal) anecdotes, and geographical and cultural digressions.

Scale

The scale of *Life* is largely confined to Josephus himself. Geographically, the scale is focused predominately on Galilee, with only few diversions to Jerusalem, Rome and Alexandria, depending on Josephus' whereabouts. These diversions are brief if they leave the geographical scene (e.g. *Life* 25–27) or are diverse in content but not geography. *Life* 30b–61 describes the situation in Galilee, *Life* 179–84 focuses on Philip, son of Jacimus, but is also located in Galilee. Overall, the geographical scale is narrowly limited to Josephus' presence and the area with which he identified himself.

Similarly, the temporal scale of *Life* is kept very narrow and is limited to Josephus' life, without any temporal digressions that would serve to widen the scale. The apparent temporal imbalance has frequently been discussed, in that Josephus focuses the majority of his account on his brief command of Galilee, the period of his life where he was at his most active and influential. To counteract the imbalance of *Life*, Josephus occasionally refers his audience to *War*, where he had previously given an account of the events in Galilee subsequent to the arrival of Vespasian (e.g. *Life* 412). Josephus also successfully ensures that in the rare narrative elements where he himself is not centre stage or even present, the focus nevertheless returns to him, a technique which prohibits any extension of the scale to other characters. For example, the discussions in Jerusalem and the resulting decision to send a delegation into Galilee focus fully on Josephus (*Life* 189–203).[32] Josephus has constructed *Life* on a scale centred on himself as the main subject with limited, but continuous, digressions, continuing his genre-indicating phraseology that *Life* was about τὰ πεπραγμένα **μοι** διὰ παντὸς τοῦ βίου – 'the events throughout **my** whole life' (*Life* 430).

Comparanda

The geographical scale of the *Anabasis* is fairly wide, as it covers large parts of the Persian Empire as well as local history. A large part of the first book narrates the history of Cyrus and his family and the circumstances which led to the involvement of Greek mercenary troops. Given these informative aspects of the *Anabasis*, arguments have been raised in favour of designating the text as history or the popular contemporary travel-accounts with an autobiographical mode.[33] This is supported by the fact that Xenophon himself is only properly introduced in Book 3.[34] Subsequently, however, the scale narrows considerably to focus only

---

32 The exceptions are the aforementioned topical digressions which carry little narrative weight.
33 Cf. earlier, for a discussion of the relationship between Xenophon, autobiography and historiography. Jim Roy refers to the *Anabasis* as a 'traveller's memoir' in Jim Roy, 'Xenophon's *Anabasis* as a Traveller's Memoir', in *Travel, Geography, and Culture in Ancient Greece, Egypt, and the Near East*, ed. by Colin Adams and Jim Roy (Oxford: Oxbow Books, 2007).
34 He is mentioned briefly in earlier parts, and referred to as 'Xenophon the Athenian' (e.g. *Anab.* 1.8.15) and receives a proper introduction in Book Three: ἦν δέ τις ἐν τῇ στρατιᾷ Ξενοφῶν

on the time and place featuring Xenophon himself and ends once Xenophon and the army had reached Greek territory, effectively covering only a period of a couple of years (401–399 BCE). Caesar also limits the temporal scale of the *Gallic War* to the actual period of campaigning (58–51/50 BCE), although the geographical scale is wider as the narrative covers events in Gaul, Germany and Britain, as well as geographical, historical and ethnographical descriptions of the respective countries and peoples. Caesar's famous opening words (*Gallia est omnis divisa*..., *B Gall*. 1.1) firmly set the scene. Given these features, alongside the third-person narration, the *Gallic War* hovers uncomfortably between the generic spheres of autobiography and historiography. However, the scale remains focused on Caesar himself, the timeframe coincides with the period of Caesar's campaign only. Located in the same boundary region between autobiography and historiography is Sulla's lost opus. Sulla must have been able to include a variety of information, widening the scale, including geographical and historical information which he had collected during his various campaigns abroad for example Numidia, Cappadocia and Parthia.[35] In contrast to Xenophon and Caesar, however, we know that the temporal scale was wider as Sulla did not focus on only a short period of his life. Libanius also widens his temporal scale to include his entire life to date but ensures that the overall scale remains firmly limited to Libanius himself. Although we travel to Athens, Constantinople, Nicomedia and Antioch, Libanius does not expand the scale to offer his reader any information about the respective cities, allowing them almost to flow into one due to the very limited focus. Thus, while he writes on a wide temporal scale, the geographical narrows considerably, especially as Libanius omits many events which do not impact directly on the author and his career.[36] The background to Libanius' life remains in the literary shadows.

Other texts demonstrate a much narrower scale. Catulus is known for focusing on his consulship and the actions of himself and his counterpart Marius during the Cimbrian wars (113–101 BCE) in order to receive his due honours (Cicero, *Brut*. 132). Cicero states explicitly that he had included the time period from

---

Ἀθηναῖος, ὃς οὔτε στρατηγὸς οὔτε λοχαγὸς οὔτε στρατιώτης- 'There was a man in the army named Xenophon, an Athenian, who was neither general nor captain nor private.' (*Anab*. 3.1.4.)

35 Speaking about historiographical works, Brunt discusses the existence of digressions in a lost work that are not indicated by the transmitted title, noting the difficulties of judging the scope or chronological limits of a work. We can easily transfer his concerns onto the current discussion. Peter A. Brunt, 'On Historical Fragments and Epitomes 1', *The Classical Quarterly* 30, no. 2 (1980): 477–94 (486–7).

36 For example, Libanius omits to give the religious reasons behind several riots in Antioch despite being in the city at the time. His commentator Norman, *Libanius' Autobiography*, goes to great length to explain characters and events left anonymous or vague.

the beginning of the Catilinarian conspiracy to his return from exile in 57 BCE (*Fam.* 5.12.4; but cf. *Att.* 1.19, where he limits the temporal scale to the period of his consulship only).

Lastly, the fragments of Nicolaus' βίος indicate a narrow scale concentrating on Nicolaus himself, partly dictated by the (supposed) thematic character presentation. Mark Toher, however, has recently suggested that the scale of Nicolaus' autobiography may be wider than originally assumed, by positing the theory that Nicolaus included an account of Herod's reign in his autobiography, rather than in his *Historia universalis,* as previously assumed.[37] Toher bases his argument on the fact that Nicolaus explicitly says that he completed his historiographical masterpiece during the time of Herod's reign, on Josephus' diverse presentation of Herod and consistent depiction of Nicolaus as the 'sage advisor', and also on the contemporary political situation that sees Augustus dealing with his potential successors, a parallel situation found in Herod's family history.[38] Toher's argumentation in itself is reasonable and coherent, although he does not consider the implications of his conclusions for the size and scale of Nicolaus' autobiography, which under these circumstances would widen considerably.

In sum, the texts offer several trends for the limitations they impose. Texts with a wide geographical scale such as the *Anabasis* and the *Gallic War* have occasioned discussions about their generic relationship with historiography. Conversely, these texts, as well as others (e.g. Catulus), demonstrate only a short temporal scale, focusing on a limited time period during the author's life, which corresponds to the apparent narrative imbalance of Josephus' *Life*.[39] Scholarly explanations for such an imbalance are diametrically opposed: Smith, speaking about Sulla, argues that such an unbalanced scale focuses on the development and early career of the respective author up until his biggest triumph (military or political).[40] Toher, on the other hand, argues that the author wished to present a contentious period in his life in order to clarify and justify the situation.[41] It appears either explanation is justified depending on the individual circumstances and cannot be generalized. Other texts demonstrate a narrow geographical and

---

37 Mark Toher, 'Herod, Augustus, and Nicolaus of Damascus', in *Herod and Augustus: IJS Conference, 21st–23rd June 2005,* ed. by David Jacobson and Nikos Kokkinos (Leiden: Brill, 2009), 68–9, 71. He suggests that Josephus used the autobiography as his main source for his account of Herod in *Ant.* 15–17. Geiger, 'Augustan Age', 255, 258, appears unaware of Toher's arguments, suggesting instead that Nicolaus duplicated the narratives in both his works.
38 Toher, 'Herod, Augustus, and Nicolaus', 77–80.
39 Or what Toher refers to as 'restricted' in Toher, 'Nicolaus' Historical Fragments', 73.
40 Smith, 'Sulla's *Memoirs*', 75.
41 Toher, 'Nicolaus' Historical Fragments', 73.

historical scale, focusing instead exclusively on the life of the author (Nicolaus, Libanius) or an extended period thereof (Augustus). *Overall, therefore, the texts divide into two distinct groups fairly consistently.*

Method of characterization

As we have seen within the context of discussing the generic features of autobiography in Chapter 2, modern assumptions expect a presentation of the author's (=narrator=protagonist) character and the author's realization of that self-same character by means of an inner dialogue or self-analysis. To extend such assumptions onto ancient texts is unsound given the differences between ancient and modern approaches to literature; we should not expect to see such an inner dialogue in antiquity. Instead, ancient authors had two different methods of characterization available to them: direct and indirect. Direct characterization is the explicit description of a person's character by the narrator, using adjectives, abstract nouns, epithets or brief summaries of traits attributed to the respective person. It is instantly recognizable by the audience, allows direct communication between author/narrator and audience and it avoids confusing the audience. In contrast, indirect characterization develops throughout the narrative. The audience is allowed to form their own judgement based on a person's actions, success, deeds and speeches, implying that these actions are evocative of character. The author retains a certain amount of influence in choosing what actions and deeds to report, and how clearly he wants the character to shine through his deeds.[42] In biblical literature especially, the storyline itself can reveal the character of the protagonists: if they are pious and just, they will eventually be delivered by God and succeed against any opposition, or, *mutatis mutandis*, will fail in their endeavour if they do not exhibit these characteristics.[43]

---

[42] The methods of such indirect characterization, and how Greco-Roman society deduced character based on actions, ancestry, military training, and the company one kept (friends, patrons) have been explained in detail by both Burridge and Mason, and need not be repeated here. However, it must be pointed out that both scholars focus on indirect characterization to the near exclusion of direct characterization. Mason, *Life*, xlvii–l; Mason, 'Essay'; Burridge, *Gospels*, 117, 139–40, 170–2. For biblical characterization, see Meir Sternberg, *The Poetics of Biblical Narrative* (Bloomington: Indiana University Press, 1985), 321–64; Elizabeth Struthers Malbon and Adele Berlin, *Characterization in Biblical Literature* (Atlanta: Scholars Press, 1993). See also Tamara Cohn Eskenazi, *In an Age of Prose: A Literary Approach to Ezra–Nehemiah* (Atlanta: Scholars Press, 1988), 127–35.

[43] See Wills, *Jewish Novel*, 102, 121, on Esther's prayers as a character-revealing function, or on how Judith's character becomes evident through her speeches and thoughts rather than her deeds. Figures such as Haman are characterized by their failure; cf. Josephus' enemies who also fail in their attempts to unseat Josephus.

Turning to Josephus' method of characterization, Mason has demonstrated that Josephus uses deeds to portray his own character and that of his opponents.[44] Josephus himself explicitly conforms to the notion that actions in one's public life adduce character:

> ἤθει πολλῶν γυναικῶν διαφέρουσαν ὡς ὁ μετὰ ταῦτα βίος αὐτῆς ἀπέδειξεν.
>
> in character, she [Josephus' wife] surpassed many women, as her subsequent way of life makes clear. (*Life* 427, cf. 344)

Life also contains brief passages of direct characterization (e.g. *Life* 40, 70, 134) and employs editorial stock phrases and keywords to describe, rather than demonstrate, character. Although Josephus does not go into great detail or allow the characters to develop themselves, the terminology he employs (*Life* 29, καλοὺς κἀγαθοὺς) was sufficiently recognizable to convey character.[45] Josephus also adheres to the aforementioned concept that God saves those who are pious and good:

> διὰ τοῦτ' οἶμαι καὶ τὸν θεόν, οὐ γὰρ λελήθασιν αὐτὸν οἱ τὰ δέοντα πράττοντες, καὶ ἐκ τῆς ἐκείνων ῥύσασθαί με χειρὸς καὶ μετὰ ταῦτα πολλοῖς περιπεσόντα κινδύνοις διαφυλάξαι, περὶ ὧν ὕστερον ἀπαγγελοῦμεν.
>
> Because of this I believe that God, because those who accomplish their duties do not escape his notice, delivered me from their hand and afterwards he guided me through the many dangers that fell upon me, of which I shall report later. (*Life* 83, cf. 138)

Comparanda

Xenophon employs both direct and indirect methods of characterization. An example of direct characterization is the obituary and encomium for Cyrus, which includes editorial comments describing him as 'most kingly and worthy' (βασιλικώτατός τε καὶ [. . .] ἀξιώτατος, *Anab.* 1.9.1), or the 'character sketch' of Clearchus (*Anab.* 2.6.1-15).[46] Xenophon uses indirect characterization to portray himself as the ideal general in contrast to his competition and opponents in the Greek army (e.g. *Anab.* 4.6.1-3). Caesar proves rather reluctant to provide his audience with direct characterization, preferring a

---

44 Mason, 'Essay', 62–6, provides a comprehensive list of deeds that Josephus presents to demonstrate his character.
45 Cf. also *Life* 134 (cf. *Ant.* 17.325 for the same terminology); Mason, *Life*, 82n.640.
46 Thomas Braun, 'Xenophon's Dangerous Liaisons', in *The Long March: Xenophon and the Ten Thousand*, ed. by Robin Lane Fox (New Haven and London: Yale University Press, 2004), 100n.9.

more subtle, indirect approach, for example playing with the relative tenses to show himself as being constantly prepared and vigilant (e.g. *B Gall.* 7.11.8, 7.13.1).[47] In keeping with the military tone of the *War*, Caesar also highlights his own deeds and speeches encouraging morale among the troops to influence the audience to think of him as the ideal general. Characterizing others, Caesar uses a mix of both direct and indirect characterization, relying on catchwords and descriptive clusters.[48] Nicolaus, as has been discussed earlier, uses a combination of direct and indirect characterization to convey his own character to his audience (F137-9):

Πρὸς γε μὴν τὸ δίκαιον ἀκλινὴς οὕτω καὶ ἀθώπευτος, ὥστε καὶ ἀπειλὰς ἐνεγκεῖν τινων ἡγεμόνων ποτὲ δικάζων ὑπὲρ τοῦ μὴ τοῦτο παραβῆναι. πολλοὶ γὰρ αὐτὸν ᾑροῦντο καὶ δικαστὴν καὶ διαιτητὴν φανερᾶς εἰς πάντας αὐτοῦ τῆς δικαιοσύνης γενομένης

He was so unswerving towards the law and against flattery that he even bore the threats of certain generals when he was judging instead of overstepping the law. For many chose him both as judge and as arbitrator because his righteousness was clear to all. (F137)

Libanius, writing several centuries later, uses the same mixture of characterization, relying on direct characterization (e.g. *Oration* 1.12,90,223), epithets (e.g. *Oration* 1.31), and indirect characterization throughout. Libanius makes this characterization explicit when he argues that since Emperor Valens did not execute his friends, he was in fact a good person (*Oration* 1.171). Libanius also omits, or refuses to, name his opponents; leaving them anonymous (e.g. *Oration* 1.50, 98) is a characterization in itself.

Overall, we see that the method of characterization is highly similar, spanning languages and decades. Authors generally appear to prefer indirect characterization, although clusters of direct characterizations are a common habit (e.g. obituaries). *Josephus' method of characterization therefore fits well into the guidelines suggested by the comparative texts,* such as characterizing himself as an ideal general (e.g. *Life* 163,172, cf. Xenophon and Caesar) or insinuating an impious character by having his opponents fail (e.g. *Life* 372).

---

47 L. V. Pitcher, 'Characterization in Ancient Historiography', in *A Companion to Greek and Roman Historiography Vol. 1*, ed. by John Marincola (Malden: Wiley-Blackwell, 2011), 106, 114.
48 For Caesar's characterization of Ariovistus as a typical tyrant by means of both direct and indirect methods, see Ann Vasaly, 'Characterization and Complexity: Caesar, Sallust, and Livy', in *The Cambridge Companion to the Roman Historians,* ed. by Andrew Feldherr (Cambridge: Cambridge University Press, 2009).

Sources

The use of sources in a personal account about the actions and events of the author's life may seem redundant. Considering, however, that sometimes memory can fail and that a good number of years can lie between the events themselves and the author putting them to paper, it is worthwhile to search for any sources, personal or other, which the authors relied on in their accounts.

Richard Laqueur originally published the notion that Josephus had used a ὑπόμνημα - 'Rechenschaftsbericht' - written during his time in Galilee as the basis of both *Life* and the respective parallel sections of the *War*.[49] Josephus, so Laqueur, reacted to allegations raised by Justus of Tiberias by recycling a report he had written at a time when Josephus had been accused by a compatriot in Galilee, 67 CE.[50] It was this 'Rechenschaftsbericht' that Josephus, now settled in Rome, reused in reaction to Justus and that Laqueur felt confident could be reconstructed. The following episodes of *Life* were identified by Laqueur as pertaining to Justus, and thus interpolated into the 'Rechenschaftsbericht' some thirty years after its original composition: *Life* 34-42, 65, 88, 175-8, 186, 336-67, 390-93, 407-10.[51] He formulates as follows: 'Hinter der Selbstschilderung, welche Josephus als Antwort auf die Angriffe des Justus verfasste, steht eine ältere Schrift, die der Verfasser nachträglich zu der uns erhaltenen Selbstdarstellung ausgestaltete und erweiterte.'[52]

Although Laqueur's theory was initially well accepted, recent arguments have been raised against this two-tier layering of *Life*.[53] Rajak rejected the 'unprobable notion', and comparing the body of *Life* with the *Antiquities*, Mason presents a well thought-out structure and coherent rhetorical devices which imply that *Life* had been composed in one layer.[54] He identified a concentric pattern centred on the divine revelation Josephus experiences in Galilee (*Life* 208-9) and compares

---

49 Laqueur, *Josephus*.
50 Ibid., 122.
51 Ibid., 37-55.
52 Ibid., 53.
53 The following scholars have accepted and/or modified Laqueur's theory: Weber, *Untersuchungen*; Thackeray, *Josephus*; Gelzer, *Kleine Schriften*; Rajak, 'Justus of Tiberias'. Although Cohen, *Josephus*, 81-3, agrees with Laqueur's theory in principle, he argues that due to Josephus' treatment of source material, it is impossible to reconstruct said 'kernel'.
54 Rajak, *Josephus*, 147; Mason, *Life*, xxi-xxvii. Abraham Schalit, 'Josephus and Justus', *Klio* 26 (1933): 67-8, had already raised concerns about Laqueur's hypothesis, branding it 'eigenartig' and 'unbeweisbar'. He suggested instead that Josephus wrote *Life* as an organic whole in response to Justus of Tiberias' accusations. By demonstrating how well *Life* and *Antiquities* fit together structurally, Mason does not consider that he contradicts his earlier statement of *Life* having been written in a hurry (ibid., xiii) – it is unlikely that the fine structure discovered by Mason could have been devised 'in haste', but rather appears to have been planned well in advance.

the pattern with similar structural evidence taken from *Antiquities*, concluding that all passages in *Life* were composed together with great deliberation.⁵⁵

While we cannot fully reject the notions of rewriting and editing, looking for too many different layers – as Laqueur does – deconstructs *Life* to the level of the text being unworkable. Josephus does not refer to any such source, and the audience receives the impression that Josephus decided to narrate his life briefly, off the cuff (βραχέα, *Ant*. 20.266), relying solely on his outstanding memory and education (*Life* 8). Josephus does mention that he himself had kept notes of events in the Roman camp outside Jerusalem which he subsequently used as source material for *War* (*Ag.Ap*. 1.49–50) and also refers to the imperial Flavian *commentarii* (*Life* 342) that he had used to write the history of the war, but he does not imply that either source was relevant for the composition of *Life*. The letters by King Agrippa, some of which Josephus quotes verbatim (*Life* 365–66) provide little support to the narrative.⁵⁶ The letters, however, that Josephus received from, and sent to, the delegation from Jerusalem (*Life* 217–19, 226–27, 229, 235) qualify as an integral source, although we cannot say whether Josephus had kept copies of his correspondence throughout the years (as evidence?) or whether he recreated the letters from memory.

Mason recently proposed that Josephus had used Justus of Tiberias' history as a source for the sections in *Life* which he could not have known for himself, such as the account of Philip son of Jacimus (*Life* 46–61, 179–84, 407–9).⁵⁷ Mason does not elaborate on his theory, but the framing introductions and conclusions to the respective sections are consistent with other instances where Josephus tries to smooth the transition between sources by using temporal markers or summative formulations such as κατὰ τοῦτον δὲ τὸν καιρόν.⁵⁸ A brief comparison of *Life* with Nicolaus' biography of Augustus, *Bios Kaisarios* (*BK*), of which we have several long fragments (*FGrH* 90 FF125–130), shows some parallels in terms of topoi and motifs, but no linguistic parallels. Both Josephus and Augustus liberate high-ranking prisoners (*Life* 13–16, *BK* VII 16), practice abstinence at a time when not to practice it would have been excused in young men (*Life* 80, *BK* XV 36), and describe scenes of themselves being accosted by soldiers in the safety of their home and fleeing upstairs to the first floor (*Life* 146–7, *BK* XXIX

---

55 Ibid., xxvi.
56 Ibid., 150n.1501, comments on the presence of typical Josephan language within the letters, doubting their authenticity.
57 Ibid., xlix.
58 See also Schwartz, 'Many Sources', for Josephus' transitions between source materials.

117–8).⁵⁹ Given the lack of linguistic parallels and a full Greek version of the *BK*, it must remain unclear for now whether Josephus simply remembered some intimate details of the biography, whether he had perhaps read the (original) imperial Latin autobiography or had it translated, or whether the parallels are coincidental.⁶⁰

Comparanda

Letters, or despatches, have also been suggested to form the basis of Caesar's *Gallic War*, much in the way that Laqueur had originally suggested Josephus re-used his 'Rechenschaftsbericht'.⁶¹ Caesar himself mentions the regular despatches he sent to Rome throughout his campaigns (e.g. *B Gall.* 2.35) and Suetonius confirms that Caesar's letters to the Senate survived in Rome to his day (*Iul.* 56). Recently, however, Riggsby rejected these despatches as the immediate source for the *Gallic War* and suggests instead that Caesar wrote a 'running record' of his activities which in turn formed the basis of the narrative and the despatches.⁶² Either way, Caesar did not rely wholly on his memory but incorporated his own earlier writings. In addition, as Caesar at times reports events at which he himself was not present or topical digressions of an anthropological nature, it is reasonable that here he had recourse to reports he received throughout the campaigns.⁶³ We also know that Sulla had previously already written about his past deeds with the aim of justifying his actions before the Roman people and/or the Senate, including letters, speeches and reports, all of which may have been incorporated into his larger work. He gave a speech before the crowd offering to justify his actions upon his resignation in 79 BCE (Appian, *B Civ.* 1.104), wrote a letter to Valerius Flaccus advocating the advantages of a dictatorship (Appian, *B Civ.* 1.98) and had sent a report to the Senate justifying his past actions which ultimately led to civil war (Appian, *B Civ.* 1.77).⁶⁴ Similarly, Cicero and Augustus would

---

59 The scenarios for these parallel motifs differ to varying levels, but intimate details such as both fleeing to the first floor may well indicate *Life*'s reliance on the imperial biography.
60 Cf. Cohen, *Josephus*, 108, who notes that both Josephus and Augustus use their wives' immoral behaviour as cause for divorce (*Life*, 426; Suetonius, *Aug.* 62.2) and deliberates whether the similarity can put attributed to Josephus' familiarity with the imperial text.
61 H. J. Edwards, *Caesar, the Gallic War, with an English Translation by H. J. Edwards* (Cambridge, MA: Harvard University Press, 2004), xvi.
62 Riggsby, *Caesar*, 148–9.
63 Cf. Suetonius, *Iul.* 56, quoting Asinius Pollio: *cum Caesar pleraque et quae per alios erant gesta temere crediderit . . .* – 'and Caesar for the most part heedlessly trusted the accounts which came from the others . . .' cf. also Caesar, *B Gall.* 1.29 and Lucian, *Hist. conscr.* 20, where he mentions despatches sent by the general's officers for his information.
64 Cf. Behr, *Selbstdarstellung Sullas*, 13, who suggests that Sulla must have used his past speeches and letters as source material.

have had access to their numerous publications, mentioned earlier in Chapter 3, even if they are not quoted explicitly. Xenophon evidently uses his own memory when projecting himself as an actor (e.g. *Anab.* 1.8.15–17), and Robin Lane Fox has mentioned his reliance on his own personal notes for topographical details.[65] In addition, Xenophon mentions other sources. Some remain anonymous, e.g. ὡς παρὰ πάντων ὁμολογεῖται τῶν Κύρου δοκούντων ἐν πείρᾳ γενέσθαι. – 'as all agree who are reputed to have known Cyrus intimately' (*Anab.* 1.9.1), or only ἐλέγετο – 'it is reported' (*Anab.* 1.8.9), and some he mentions by name, such as the physician Ctesias (*Anab.* 1.8.26), who wrote a history of Persia, or his colleague Clearchus, from whom it appears Xenophon received verbal reports about Cyrus' war councils (*Anab.* 1.6.5–10, 1.8.12, cf. 1.9.28).[66]

The use of previous personal writings as well as other literature is evident in extant texts, and can reasonably be suggested for fragmentary or missing texts based on their author and his circumstances. *We see that personal and official reports to authoritative bodies, letters and alternative sources for digressions and background information are all acceptable sources which help to supplement the author's own memory, and this is mirrored by Josephus' use of his source material.*

Summary and conclusion

The external features of Josephus' *Life* can be summarized as follows: *Life* is presented as a continuous prose narrative of medium length in the first-person singular, fitting the confines of one book. The chronological structure alternates

---

65 Robin Lane Fox, *The Long March: Xenophon and the Ten Thousand* (New Haven, London: Yale University Press, 2004), 30. Cf. also P. J. Stylianou, 'One *Anabasis* or Two?', in *The Long March: Xenophon and the Ten Thousand*, ed. by Robin Lane Fox (New Haven, London: Yale University Press, 2004). Also Jim Roy, 'Xenophon's Evidence for the *Anabasis*', *Athenaeum* 46 (1968): 37–46, who argues that Xenophon based the *Anabasis* largely on his own notes as they reflect the changes in his strategic position throughout the campaign. But see George Cawkwell, 'When, How and Why Did Xenophon Write the *Anabasis*?', in *The Long March: Xenophon and the Ten Thousand*, ed. by Robin Lane Fox (New Haven, London: Yale University Press, 2004), 54–6, who argues that Xenophon cannot have kept a diary on the march due to the adverse physical conditions while on campaign and the fact that he finds little evidence for the habit of keeping diaries at all in the fifth century. Instead, Cawkwell argues for Xenophon's reliance on a Persian itinerary detailing the distances between cities and rivers.

66 Ctesias was a Greek doctor at the court of Persian king Artaxerxes II (fifth century BCE). Fragments of his *Persika* are collected in *FGrH* 688. Bradley, 'Irony', 536–9, thinks that Xenophon's references to other (historiographical) sources such as Ctesias indicate that Xenophon treated the *Anabasis* as history, or rather, wants to suggest to the reader that they are reading a work of history. This is not necessarily so, although it adds to the (confusing) perception of the *Anabasis* as a boundary text. Bradley has overlooked that, as is evident, other authors had also included a variety of sources into their narratives; Bradley must be more careful if he insists on a historiographical genre just because Xenophon includes historiographical sources.

between accounts of Josephus himself and roughly contemporary digressions excluding the main character, creating a flow of episodes and suspense. Within this framework, Josephus uses a variety of literary units such as speeches, prayers and geographical digressions, although the scale remains focused on Josephus. As an author, Josephus prefers the method of indirect characterization, and relies on previous personal writings first, and external, third-party sources second.

The comparative texts were composed as continuous prose narratives, either in the first- or third-person voice. They vary in length, ranging from Catulus' *liber* to Sulla's massive and exceptional feat of twenty-two books. The structure is generally chronological, with the possible exception of Cicero and Nicolaus, for whom topical arrangements have been suggested (or a division). The texts all share the same selection of literary units (speeches, geographical descriptions, anecdotes). The geographical and temporal scale is generally focused on the author and his movements only. Characters are preferably introduced to the audience in an indirect fashion as opposed to direct characterization. Lastly, while all texts by their nature rely on the author's memory, the reference to personal writings and external sources is consistently evident. These external sources, such as the Flavian imperial *commentarii* or the Caesarian despatches, have official character or had been published previously, for example, Cicero's works, and thus help to uphold the alleged truthfulness of the author.

A consistent family resemblance is evident. There are few explicit deviations such as Sulla's length or the topical structure demanded by Cicero. It is noteworthy that the *Anabasis,* which had stood out in the opening features and subject matter, does not stand out in its external features. Within these parameters, Josephus' *Life* does not stand out either but aligns itself with its literary precedents and successors. The most distinctive common external features these texts demonstrate are the insistent focus on the author (scale) and the ostensible reliance on memory and personal source material. On the one hand, this reinforces literary critics' assertion that no one feature or characteristic is indicative of genre, but that a genre demands a family resemblance made up of various features from a pool of possibilities. On the other hand, given the limited literary variations in ancient literature, it may be necessary to pinpoint certain features as highly indicative. However, the internal features of the texts will be discussed before pulling all the threads together.

6

Internal features

The previous two chapters have analysed *Life* alongside other roughly contemporary texts in the search for genre-parameters. Prior to reaching overarching conclusions regarding ancient autobiography, this chapter encompasses the final set of features to be analysed, including setting, topoi, style, atmosphere, quality of characterization, social setting, time of composition and purpose.

Setting

The geographical and dramatic setting, or the backdrop, of a text represents an important literary element that can offer the reader a clear indicator of the author's chosen genre. The setting and its various aspects facilitate the audience's access to the narrative by providing background information. The main geographical settings of *Life* include Jerusalem, Rome and Galilee, all of which represent important and formative stages in Josephus' life. The narrative follows these settings depending on Josephus' whereabouts; alternatively, Josephus is implied as the off-stage focus of attention. For example, when Josephus decides to send his own delegation to Jerusalem to plead his case, he (and the storyline) accompanies them up to the border of Galilee and Samaria; when Josephus parts with the delegation, so does the narrative (*Life* 270). Josephus sets the scene by placing himself in a Galilean city (e.g. *Life* 68, 77, 86, 115) or in a very public space such as a market or forum (e.g. *Life* 92, 107, 138). His mere presence in a city or a public space, visible to everyone, portrays him as a governor travelling through his territory and asserting his power – the setting has a very immediate impact on the narrative.

Similarly, it is exceedingly rare for Josephus not to be part of the dramatic setting, either in person or as the object of discussion; the exceptions are various digressions such as an overview of the situation in Galilee prior to his appointment (33–61), a digression on Philip, son of Jacimus (179–84), or Vespasian's early movements in Galilee (407–10).[1] We see that the geographical and dramatic settings were integral to the narrative and that Josephus ensured that, where reasonably possible, he was the focus of *Life*'s settings

Comparanda

The geographical settings of the *Anabasis* are all focused on the exotic regions of the Persian Empire. Xenophon himself usually appears in a military setting, such as in battle, army camps or war councils (e.g. *Anab.* 1.2.9–13, 4.1.6, 4.1.19, 4.5.21, 4.5.34, 6.6.6–21). Similarly, Caesar's geographical settings depend on the location of his military campaigns all through Gaul, Germany and Britain, and are representative of Caesar's position as general of an army. An occasional shift in location back to Rome usually at the end of a book (e.g. *B Gall.* 2.35, 4.38, 6.44) serves to ground the narrative and remind the audience for whose benefit Caesar was campaigning. The fragments of Nicolaus' *Life* indicate that the setting followed Nicolaus on his travels, including Rhodes and Ilium (F134), Jerusalem (F135), perhaps Arabia (F136) and Rome (F136), and socially we always find Nicolaus in the company of kings or other high officials. Libanius' geographical settings are highly representative of a successful orator. When Libanius takes an active part in the narrative, he is most frequently found in a setting such as the city hall (τό βουλευτήριον, *Oration* 1.87,112), or wherever a large group of people could assemble and listen to him, priding himself on filling public baths (1.55), or in the company of his illustrious supporting cast.

In terms of the dramatic settings, the *Anabasis* stands out in that the entire first book is devoted to the Persian royal family without any mention of Xenophon himself. However, once the Greeks take control of their army and Xenophon is elected leader, the dramatic setting focuses entirely on the author himself as an individual or as part of the larger group of Greeks trying to fight their way home. Similarly, except for the opening verses (*B Gall.* 1.1–6), which describe the local situation in Gaul as background information, Caesar's focus is on Caesar. The only other exception is found in one notable digression during 56 BCE (*B Gall.* 3.17–27), which focuses on the achievements of other Roman

---

[1] Coincidentally, but without remarking on the relevance for the dramatic setting, it is exactly these passages which Mason, *Life*, xlix, suggests Josephus had taken from Justus of Tiberias' history.

generals in his army.² We see a parallel in Libanius' narrative order; except for a brief panegyric on Antioch (*Oration* 1.2–3), Libanius remains the constant focus of the dramatic setting, delegating even his imperial cast into the background. Nicolaus' fragments demonstrate that although a variety of high-class actors appear regularly (Herod, Agrippa, Augustus), Nicolaus is the focus of the dramatic settings as the voice of reason and the trusted messenger.

The geographical settings are always highly representative of the ideal persona and position the author wishes to reflect and the author as subject is the focus of both the geographical and dramatic settings. Digressions that carry the focus away from the author's geographical or dramatic setting are highly unusual. Notably, all the fully extant texts feature a digression at the beginning of their narratives which temporarily refocuses the settings away from the subject onto the respective background information that will form the setting of their later actions: the wars in Gaul necessitate Caesar to campaign, the tumultuous situation in Galilee was the focal point of Josephus' actions, Libanius saw himself as the guardian of Antioch and the Persian royal family constituted the ultimate cause for Xenophon's predicament.

Topoi

Mason stresses that Josephus consciously included several typical topoi which his audience would instantly recognize, to demonstrate his belonging to the aristocracy and his ideal character, and to offer himself up as an ideal example of the success of Judean culture.³ In support of his theory, Mason has compiled a comprehensive list of topoi within *Life*, many of which we find repeated in the comparative literature.⁴

(a) Ancestry

Josephus opens *Life* with a reference to his ancestry, his paternal family connections with the highest of priestly classes and his maternal connection

---

2   Except for one campaign against the Veneti, which Caesar narrates in *B Gall.* 3.7–16, he did not campaign that season, but was preoccupied with political matters in Rome and the conference at Luca in the spring of 56 BCE with Pompey and Crassus to reconfirm the First Triumvirate.
3   Mason, 'Essay'.
4   Ibid., 57–66. Mason compares the topoi with a variety of Greco-Roman literature, not autobiography alone. As Burridge, *Gospels*, 118, has stated, it is unlikely that topoi can be considered a firm generic feature if they transcend generic boundaries consistently.

to the Hasmonean family (*Life* 2).⁵ This opening section is overrun with praise and mention of his ancestors' highest qualifications and honours, and Josephus moves through a genealogy reminiscent of biblical lists until he concludes the section with his father Matthias' reputation, which implicitly reflects directly onto Josephus and his brother.

Neither Caesar nor Xenophon mention their ancestors, and based on Cicero's status as *novus homo*, it is unlikely that he mentioned any distinguished ancestors. Extant fragments show that both Nicolaus (F131) and Sulla mention their ancestry. While Nicolaus praised only his parents, Aulus Gellius (*NA* 1.12.16) preserves a fragment mentioning Sulla's ancestor Publius Cornelius, causing Christopher Smith to assert that the beginning of Sulla's work was 'heavily bound up ... with ancestry.'⁶ Suetonius states that Augustus intentionally limited his remarks about ancestry, which is not surprising as Caesar was merely his adoptive father:

> ipse Augustus nihil amplius quam equestri familia ortum se scribit vetere ac locuplete, et in qua primus senator pater suus fuerit . . . Nec quicquam ultra de paternis Augusti maioribus repperi.
>
> Augustus himself merely writes that he came of an old and wealthy family in which his own father was the first to become a senator . . . That is all I have been able to learn about the paternal ancestors. (Suetonius, *Aug.* 2.3)

Libanius, however, includes an overview of his successful and prominent Antiochene ancestry, emphasizing their long-standing local history (*Oration* 1.2-3). We know from other genres that ancestry was a popular motive in ancient literature, used frequently to characterize or introduce a character, both positively and negatively; as Libanius wryly notes, many good people had been reduced to silence on account of the bad reputation of their ancestors (*Oration* 1.7).⁷

(b) Birth, childhood, education

Josephus makes no mention of his birth. He claims to have been a precocious child, educated in the traditional Judean system, which, according to Mason, Josephus presents as parallel to the typical Roman education for elite young

---

5 For details on Josephus' pedigree, see Mason, 'Essay', 57-61.
6 Smith, 'Sulla's *Memoirs*', 67.
7 The reference to Hadrian's ancestry (*SHA Hadr.* 1) is traced back to his *De vita sua*.

men, including rhetoric, memory and understanding (*Life* 8-9).[8] Josephus stresses his religious education by stating that he actively partook in the various Judean movements in order to understand them individually before choosing the one he deemed most fitting (*Life* 12).[9] Josephus gives the overall impression of a peaceful, studious, boyhood.

Other authors who mention their childhood and education are Nicolaus and Libanius.[10] Nicolaus' father ensured a good education for his children, and Nicolaus himself stresses his proficiency in various fields of scholarship (F131, F132). Libanius includes an account of his childhood and early education (*Oration* 1.4-13). Scholars have also suggested that Sulla possibly included references to his early upbringing, hand in hand with a report of his ancestry, but we have no firm evidence.[11]

(c) Great deeds

Josephus boasts of military deeds (e.g. *Life* 114-21, 165-68), political achievements such as his diplomatic mission to Rome (*Life* 13) his appointment as general of Galilee, and literary achievements (*Life* 361-7, 412-13). Interestingly, Josephus does not narrate his greatest metaphysical achievement, his interpretation of the ancient prophecy nominating Vespasian as the next emperor of Rome (*War* 3.399-403). Other authors are similarly eager to portray their respective skills and achievements. Many passages of *Anabasis* and *Gallic War* are concerned

---

8   Mason, 'Essay', 57-61. See also Siegert, Schreckenberg and Vogel, *Aus Meinem Leben*, 27n.20 and Rajak, *Josephus*, 35-7.
9   The mathematics in this passage do not add up, supporting the rhetorical nature of Josephus' statement. He claims that between the ages of 16-19, he studied the various Judean philosophical schools and spent three years in the desert with Bannus. Shutt, *Studies in Josephus*, 2n.3, suggests replacing παρ' αὐτῷ with παρ' αὐτοῖς, but see Mason, *Life*, 20n.86. For a longer discussion, see Steve Mason, *Flavius Josephus on the Pharisees: A Composition-Critical Study* (Leiden, New York: E.J. Brill 1990), 342-5.
10 Augustine's *Confessions*, especially Book One, contain considerable reflections about the author's childhood and education, even though he understands that he cannot remember aspects of his childhood, even if there were recounted to him (e.g. *Confessions* 1.6). Although the present analysis has, for reasons of limitations, excluded Augustine's *Confessions*, nevertheless it is pertinent to raise the point, especially as Augustine himself was a contemporary of Libanius.
11 See Tatum, 'Late Republic', 165; Behr, *Selbstdarstellung Sullas*, 14, 24. Suetonius, *Aug.* 89, remarks on Augustus' education during his youth and his old teacher, Apollodorus of Pergamon. Perhaps this titbit of information was common knowledge; it is not included in the list of possible fragments for Augustus' lost work. Dormeyer, 'Biographie', 19, argues that praise of one's own childhood (as found in *Life*, 8-9) and abilities were unusual in antiquity. According to Dormeyer, authors avoided praising a child's abilities. M. Aurelius was modest with his childhood, Augustus' *RG* narrate the emperor's achievements from the age of 19, biographies (tacitly) agree that wonderous abilities were set on only in public life. Josephus, so Dormeyer, deviates embarrassingly from this pattern ('peinlich abweicht'). However, I consider it unlikely that Josephus would stray from accepted conventions.

with highlighting their respective author's military and diplomatic achievements and capabilities. From Plutarch's comments about Catulus, we know that he wanted to emphasize his successful involvement and achievements during the war against the Cimbri and Teutones (e.g. *Mar.* 23.6), and Cicero himself asked Lucceius to write about his actions and deeds from the time of Clodius' conspiracy to his return from exile (*Fam.* 5.12.4). Appian claims that Augustus consciously wrote not about other people's achievements (πράξεις), but his own (*Ill.* 15.43). Libanius highlights his oratorical success and that of his school and students and prides himself on his literary achievements that had caught the imperial eye (*Oration* 1.129). The fragments of Nicolaus' autobiography include a short story about how he actively petitioned Marcus Agrippa to negate the punishments he had intended for the Ilians for failing to help his wife, Caesar's daughter Julia, during a dangerous river crossing (F134). The other fragments focus on his skills as a philosopher and mediator (e.g. F137), highly regarded by leading royal and imperial figures.

(d) Virtues

Josephus does not include a topical discussion of his own virtues, or those of the other characters, but relies on his deeds to demonstrate his outstanding character (cf. *Life* 82).[12] The virtues thus emerge indirectly, but consistently. Similarly, the other authors are content with allowing their virtues to emerge through their deeds and actions. The only author who provides direct analysis of his virtues is Nicolaus, who offers up himself as the ideal example for leading a philosopher's life (FF 137–39).

(e) Divine intervention

Another topos that Josephus includes is that of divine intervention. Josephus centres *Life* on the dream he had convincing him to remain in Galilee (*Life* 208–11), and occasionally intersperses his account with instances of divine intervention and protection (*Life* 14–14, 80–83, 299–303).[13]

Xenophon mentions two instances where his decision was swayed by divine intervention (*Anab.* 3.1.11–12, 6.2.15), and both Sulla and Augustus have had fragments preserved which indicate frequent reference to the supernatural and

---

12 Cf. Mason, 'Essay', 62–6, for an overview of 'deeds proving character' in *Life*.
13 Ibid., 64. On the pivotal position of the dream sequence, see Mason, *Life*, xxvi.

divine intervention.[14] Libanius refers most frequently and consistently to divine intervention. He presents his work as a summation of the good and the bad cards dealt him by the hand of Fortune, insisting that Fortune was responsible for his continuous success. He also includes a divine dream sequence (*Oration* 1.67) and the conviction that he was healed by the god Asclepius (*Oration* 1.143). The *Gallic War* stands out by not showing any interest in divine intervention.[15]

(f) End of career/retirement

Although it does not constitute the end of *Life,* Josephus' fall from his horse in a skirmish (*Life* 403) metaphorically marks the end of his career in Galilee within the narrative sequence of *Life*; the next scene already introduces Vespasian and sees Josephus wrapping up his narrative. Upon his arrival in Rome, Josephus offers little information about his daily life apart from the imperial honours he received (*Life* 422, 425, 428–9), some domestic information (*Life* 426–8), and how he was subject to slander (*Life* 424). We see that once Josephus had recorded the events in Galilee, he was unwilling or unable to present anything else relevant to his presentation of himself.

None of the other texts except for Nicolaus' fragments make any reference to their retirement or end of career. In F136, Nicolaus mentions that although he had planned to retire, having reached the age of sixty, Herod's son Archelaus convinced him to travel to Rome to support Archelaus' claim to his father's throne. It is possible that Sulla referred to his decisions to withdraw from active political life in Rome, but, as Smith mentions, it remains unclear whether Sulla included the last active years in his work.[16] Neither Josephus nor Nicolaus held any active political or military positions in Rome, both socially considered foreigners, at the time of composition (see the following) and could legitimately admit to having retired.

Of all the topics discussed, the only element all texts share is the emphasis on a certain set of deeds and achievements, which by default omits larger tales

---

14 See Wiseman, 'Augustus, Sulla and the Supernatural', for a close discussion of the supernatural elements in Augustus and Sulla. The *RGDA*, in contrast, have only minimal reference to the divine, for example Chapter 9: pr]iva[ti]m etiam et municipatim universi [cives unanimite]r con[tinente]r apud omnia pulvinaria pro vale[tu]din[e mea s]upp[licaverunt]. – 'Moreover all citizens in private and as a municipality have, with one accord, repeatedly offered prayers for my good health at all public feasts.' Text and trans. Alison E. Cooley, *Res Gestae Divi Augusti: Text, Translation and Commentary* (Cambridge: Cambridge University Press, 2009), 68.
15 The narrative does refer to religious matters, but mainly on an explanatory level, for example, when describing the religious convictions of the Gauls, *B Gall.* 6.16–18.
16 Smith, 'Sulla's *Memoirs*', 68, and above. See also further, 'time of publication'.

of setbacks, and how they reflect on their author's respective virtues. Overall, given the fragmentary state of many texts it is difficult to conclude a range of topics, although some topics feature more heavily (such as deeds and divine intervention) and some are usually avoided (such as the end of one's career). It is also not possible to conclude a definite cultural divide or evolution over the years.

Style

In *War* 7.455, at the end of his narrative, Josephus asks his audience to judge *War* on its style, which in contrast to the truthfulness of the history might be found wanting. Josephus later admits that learning Greek had been a difficult process and eventually compliments himself on succeeding on a level rarely reached before among his compatriots (*Ant.* 20.26–4).[17] The fact that he admits to the help of several secretaries (*Ag.Ap.* 1.50) has resulted in discussions about whether and to what extent Josephus was himself the author of the majority of his corpus; such theories have now largely been rejected in favour of Josephus as the sole author.[18] In fact, several recent publications have positively discussed various aspects of Josephus' rhetorical abilities.[19] As Mason notes, throughout

---

17 Rajak, *Josephus*, 46–64, suggests that apologizing for the lack of Greek linguistic skills constituted a rhetorical feature in ancient literature, and looks closely at the presence of Greek language and culture in Josephus' Jerusalem. Several scholars suggest that Josephus did not grow up with Greek, incl. Rajak, *Translation*, 230–2; Eric Koskenniemi, *Greek Writers and Philosophers in Philo and Josephus* (Leiden, Boston: Brill, 2019), esp. 279. On the other hand, it can be argued that since Josephus had been elected to travel to Rome to free two priests, he must have had at least basic Greek (Latin is extremely unlikely) in order to negotiate their release.

18 Thackeray adhered to the theory that Josephus had received considerable help in writing *Antiquities*, and that only *Ant.* 20 and *Life* were written by Josephus himself. Richards, 'Composition', opposes this view, citing consistent literary evidence which assumes that Josephus wrote the entire draft of *Antiquities* himself, some of which was revised by Greek helpers for a second edition. Rajak, *Josephus*, 233–6, offers a comprehensive overview of arguments and counter-arguments; she points out a series of methodological flaws in Thackeray's arguments, not least the fact that Josephus does not mention any help in writing *Antiquities*, and that the various styles that Thackeray believes to have found must be attributed to Josephus' personal reading material at the time of writing. See also Shutt, *Studies in Josephus*, 29–35, who concludes based on his own linguistic analysis of *War* and *Antiquities* that common terms and constructions between the two works imply a single authorship. He sees the assistants' presence only in polishing and improving Josephus' Greek in *War*. Geiger, 'Jewish Biography', 70, stands out when he suggests that *Life* was written in a rough style precisely because Josephus (for whatever reason) wrote without the help of the assistants who had supported him in the composition of *Antiquities*.

19 For example, Tamar Landau, *Out-Heroding Herod: Josephus, Rhetoric, and the Herod-Narratives* (Leiden, Boston: Brill, 2006); Mark Andrew Brighton, *The Sicarii in Josephus' Judean War: Rhetorical Analysis and Historical Observations* (Atlanta: Society of Biblical Literature, 2009); John M. G. Barclay, 'The Empire Writes Back: Josephan Rhetoric in Flavian Rome', in *Flavius Josephus and Flavian Rome*, ed. by Jonathan Edmondson, Steve Mason and James Rives (Oxford: Oxford University Press, 2005); Hansen, 'Anmerkungen'; Honora Howell Chapman, 'Spectacle in Josephus'

Josephus' corpus, his works are 'imbued with the rhetorical spirit' and Josephus himself knew how important style was for the audience (*Ant.* 14.1); he prides himself on his linguistic abilities (*Ant.* 20.263–4).[20]

It is noteworthy, therefore, that of all of Josephus' books, *Life* is generally considered to be bad in style and language, and devoid of rhetorical ability. Thackeray refers to a 'crudity of style' and Cohen emphasizes the repetitive formulations (e.g. *Life* 166, 328; 26, 100, 171, 377; 102, 306, 375, 384), suggesting that these repetitions were the remnants of the unpolished ὑπόμνημα which lay at the basis of *Life*.[21] Mason offers the overall impression 'of extreme repetitiveness and formulaic construction', representing Josephus' 'unassisted personal style'.[22]

However, considering the care and attention to detail that went into the composition of all his works, and the level to which they conform to the contemporaneous literary conventions, it seems reasonable to argue that Josephus worked hard on his Greek and literary knowledge base. Considering further that Josephus clearly had put much thought into *Life*'s construction, aims and characterization, we cannot dismiss the literary style of *Life* as simply unrevised or as Josephus' 'own style', composed quickly, in a rush.[23] Josephus was pushing a highly personal and important agenda, speaking about himself – why should he now neglect literary conventions? I would like to consider the possibility that Josephus purposefully and deliberatively composed *Life* in the way he did, adhering to literary conventions as he had done in his other compositions, including stock phrases and repetitive terminology which result

---

Jewish War', in *Flavius Josephus and Flavian Rome*, ed. by Jonathan Edmondson, Steve Mason and James Rives (Oxford: Oxford University Press, 2005). See also Martin Friis, *Image and Imitation: Josephus' Antiquities 1-11 and Greco-Roman Historiography* (Tübingen: Mohr Siebeck, 2018), for Josephus' knowledge of conventional genre-features, esp. 10, 55, 147, 193.

20 Mason, *Life*, xxxviii. See also idem., 'The Importance of the Latter Half of Josephus's Judaean Antiquities for His Roman Audience', in *Pentateuchal Traditions in the Late Second Temple Period* (Leiden: Brill, 2012), 129–53 (151).

21 Thackeray, *Josephus*, 18–19; Cohen, *Josephus*, 124–5, also 110; Stern, 'Josephus and Justus', 393; Schwartz, *Josephus*, 23. Siegert, Schreckenberg and Vogel, *Aus Meinem Leben*, do not comment on *Life*'s style.

22 Mason, 'Essay', 35; Mason, *Life*, liii, cf. xv: 'careless and unimaginative'. Cf. Thackeray, *Josephus,* 115, who suggests that in *Ant.* 20 and *Life*, we come as close as we could imagine to the 'ipsissima verba' of Josephus. Speaking of Josephus' 'unassisted' style, it appears that Mason despite, alongside the majority of contemporary scholars, rejecting Thackeray's *amanuensis*-theory, tacitly assumes that Josephus did have a measure of help. Koskenniemi, *Greek Writers,* 285–7, also devalues the level of Josephus' (written) Greek in later life while composing *War*/*Ant.*/*Life*. He asks if Josephus had in fact learnt Greek continuously during his life in Rome, why *Ant.* 20 and *Life* were written in such 'basic Greek', especially when compared to *Ag.Ap.* Koskenniemi suggests that Josephus struggled with Greek all his life and that he did not feel comfortable with the level of his Greek in Roman society.

23 See, for example, Steve Mason, 'Figured Speech and Irony in T. Flavius Josephus', in *Flavius Josephus and Flavian Rome*, edited by Jonathan Edmondson, Steve Mason and James Rives (Oxford: Oxford University Press, 2005), 243–88; idem, *Life*, xv.

in the perceived appearance of bad, low style, to convey an air of truthfulness and spontaneity, not having to hide behind the text, and to facilitate the oral presentation of *Life*, although we must distinguish between reading aloud from a text, and reciting from memory.²⁴ Considering that Josephus was narrating his own life, it might have been more convincing, more urgent, if he used the scroll only occasionally. He was not necessarily reciting *Life* from memory – he was no trained orator – but instead reciting a text with which he was intimately familiar. This thought is further strengthened by Josephus' introduction of *Life* in *Antiquities* as a spontaneous narrative which could be delivered ad hoc. As Barish has noted, the formulation κατὰ περιδρομὴν (*Ant.* 20.267) can be translated 'cursorily', or 'a cursory account';²⁵ this is paralleled by Josephus' use of βραχέα, and his suggestion that he quickly recount the events of his life while witnesses to his testimony were still alive (*Ant.* 20.266).²⁶ Josephus in his other works relies on prefaces and prologues to introduce his works and themes, and the brevity with which *Life* is introduced further enhances the impression of spontaneity.

Here we reach an opportune moment to re-address the connection between *Ant.* 20 and *Life*. In their style analyses, scholars have also noted the same, lower, level of style for the final book of *Antiquities*.²⁷ For both Thackeray and Mason, this same inferior style of Greek and various shared expressions found nowhere else in the Josephan corpus are a sign for the contemporaneous composition of both books by Josephus himself, without revision or assistance, and especially for Mason, highlight the importance of reading *Antiquities* together with *Life*.²⁸

---

24 For *War* specifically, see Steve Mason, 'Of Audience and Meaning: Reading Josephus' Bellum Judaicum in the Context of a Flavian Audience', in *Josephus and Jewish History in Flavian Rome and Beyond*, ed. Josephus Sievers and Gaia Lembi (Leiden: Brill), 71–100. Studies have demonstrated that the repeated use of word patterns and prose rhythm indicate an author's reliance on his memory, enabling him to recite with minimal recourse to notes or the scroll, for example Walter J. Ong, *Orality and Literacy, the Technologizing of the Word* (London, New York: Methuen, 1982).
25 Barish, 'The Autobiography of Josephus', 67. Josephus was evidently trying to strike a balance between brevity and maintaining interest, as can be seen by his use of διεξελθεῖν/διεξέρχομαι, translated by Liddell/Scott as recounting with an emphasis on a full, detailed account.
26 On the desire to give the impression of speaking ex tempore, see Rosalind Thomas, *Literacy and Orality in Ancient Greece* (Cambridge, New York: Cambridge University Press, 1992), 92. Thomas suggests that Greek orators, her field of focus, wanted to give the impression of spontaneity and improvisation despite having a text prepared and memorized, and she extends the concept to historians as well (125–6).
27 Thackeray, *Josephus*, 18–19, 100–24; Mason, *Life*, xv; idem, 'Josephus's Autobiography', 60, mentions 'a continuum of style and diction'. Again, Mason suggests that the similar style, in contrast to the previous books of *Ant.*, reflect Josephus' 'natural voice'. Zeitlin, 'A Survey of Jewish Historiography', 66, argues that the perceived similarities of style and expression shared by *Ant.* 20 and *Life* need not imply that they were composed as a unit, but that Josephus simply reused Greek terms and phrases he was familiar with and had used previously.
28 Mason, *Life*, xiv–xv.

If we accept this explanation, we might ask why Josephus felt it necessary to hide his natural voice in the other books, or alternatively why he suddenly felt comfortable enough to write in his natural style. In *Ant.* 20, Josephus had included a range of shorter, seemingly gossipy and unrelated stories, replete with inconsistencies or questionable statements.[29] These include the Adiabene narrative (*Ant.* 20.17-96) or notices of political appointments or marriages (e.g. 20.142, 145-7, 148, 158) and Agrippa's building projects (20.211-12). Josephus includes two episodes in which the actions of a single Roman soldier resulted in dramatic consequences; baring his genitals ultimately resulted in the death of 20,000 people (20.108-112). The other soldier was beheaded for tearing apart a holy book to avoid a similar uproar (20.115-17). Attentive readers might also ask why Poppaea Sabina detained the high priest and the treasurer as hostages after their successful and peaceful demands of Nero to preserve the newly built wall in the temple (20.195), or why Agrippa subsequently simply appointed a new high priest (20.196).

Throughout *Antiquities* 20, Josephus jumps around introducing a multitude of characters, places and events which seem somehow connected although the transitions and connections are not always clear.[30] While Josephus generally was more careful ensuring that his audience would not get too lost in his narrative, *Ant.* 20 and *Life* more resemble a literary labyrinth. Merely arguing that this is Josephus' natural voice does not do justice to Josephus' efforts. *Antiquities* 20, just like *Life*, was an important book. Carefully structured, roughly halfway through *Antiquities* 20, Josephus refocuses his narrative to Rome and the rumours surrounding the death of Claudius and Nero's accession, followed by an intense personal statement criticizing other historians for either pandering to Nero or reviling him to the point of lying (20.154-155). In contrast, Josephus himself does not wish to add further lies to the topic but instead emphasizes his aim of offering an account of his people's history and their misfortunes (20,156-157).[31] *Ant.* 20 also narrates the rise of the restive local atmosphere which ultimately led to the revolt and destruction of Jerusalem's temple, and Josephus frequently

---

[29] See Gelzer, *Kleine Schriften*, 229, who had previously commented on the 'gossipy' sections of *Ant.* 20 in connection to the Herodian descendants, suggesting that Agrippa cannot have been alive at the time of composition. Harold W. Attridge, 'Josephus and His Works', in *Jewish Writings of the Second Temple Period. Apocrypha, Pseudepigrapha, Qumran Sectarian Writings, Philo, Josephus*, ed. by Michael Stone (Philadelphia: Fortress Press, 1984), 188, 210-11, also refers to the passages portraying Agrippa in a rather negative light but concludes that *Life* was published contemporaneously with *Ant.* 20.

[30] The Brill translation and commentary on *Antiquities* 20 had not been published at the time of submission, although it is hoped that it will shed some more light on the discussion.

[31] See Mason, *Life*, xxi-xxvii, esp. xxiii-xxiv, on the importance of Josephus' concentric literary structures.

mentions that these specific events would lead to the city's downfall (20.157, 160, 166, 181, 184, 210, 214, 218, 252, 256).³² As part of the impending disaster, he also emphasizes envy and competition between the priests and Levites (20.179-181) and among the numerous high priests themselves (20.205-207, 213–14). It strikes me as unlikely that Josephus would neglect considerations of style.

If we expand our view and take into consideration insights arising from the present discussion, we might surmise that Josephus knowingly adapted his style – in contrast simply to an unrevised style.³³ The episodes and stories narrated in *Ant.* 20 and *Life* should all have been very familiar to Josephus. At the same time, this more simple, seemingly less polished style would allow the audience to take in and memorize events and the sequence of events without thinking too much about detail – on which Josephus was occasionally fudgy. Both *Ant.* 20 and *Life* contain several inconsistencies or unclear sequences, noted earlier, which easily went unnoticed or not considered important given the superficial style Josephus had chosen, a fact which has already been noted by scholars approaching *Life* from different angles. It was evidently less important for Josephus that his audience remember detailed particulars of the stories, but rather that they could walk away with a more general understanding of the main thrust of the events or stories narrated, resulting in an emotional response.

Comparanda

The *Anabasis* is generally the first unrevised Greek text students encounter, chosen for its simple and clear style, a feature already appreciated by Quintilian (*Inst.* 10.1.82–83). Similarly, Caesar's *Gallic War* is also regularly used as an entry-level text for students of the Latin language, given its simple and

---

32 For a detailed discussion of the war's timeline and causes, see best Steve Mason, *A History of the Jewish War A.D. 66-74* (Cambridge: Cambridge University Press, 2016).

33 In support of this theory, Thackeray, *Josephus*, 105, points out that this manner of stylistic decline towards the end of a long work was not unique to *Antiquities*; he notes a similar change in the style of *War* 7 and the final book of Thucydides' history, Thackeray suggests, has also escaped revision. See also Donald A. Russell, *Quintilian: The Orator's Education, Books 11-12* (Cambridge, MA: Harvard University Press, 2001), 187, who considers the final book of Quintilian's *Institutio Oratoria* to be 'puzzling and scrappy'. It has further been suggested, although not without controversy, that *War* 7 was a later addition under Domitian, based on the more pronounced role the third Flavian emperor plays in the last book and an inferior style compared to *War* 1–6: Cohen, *Josephus*, 87; Thackeray, *Josephus*, 31–5; Barnes, 'Sack of the Temple', 139–40; Seth Schwartz, 'The Composition and Publication of Josephus' Bellum Iudaicum Book 7', *HTR* 79 (1986): 373–86. See, summative, Mason, *Life*, 148n.1493. Christopher P. Jones, 'Towards a Chronology of Josephus', *Scripta classica Israelica* 21 (2002): 113–22 (13–14); Daniel R. Schwartz, 'Josephus, Catullus, Divine Providence, and the Date of the *Judean War*', in *Flavius Josephus; Interpretation and History*, ed. by Jack Pastor, Pnina Stern and Menahem Mor (Leiden, Boston: Brill, 2011).

straightforward, yet highly polished, style.³⁴ Caesar's literary style is praised by contemporary and later critics including Cicero (*Brut.* 261–2), Quintilian (*Inst.* 10.2.114) and Tacitus (*Dial.* 21), as well as by his subordinate Aulus Hirtius (*B Gall.* 8 preface 5). Cicero praises his own work just as enthusiastically, suggesting that both his own and Caesar's literary results were something remarkable and extraordinary; Cicero went beyond what might be expected to ensure (in vain) the success of his *commentarius* on his consulship (e.g. *Att.* 1.19, 2.1; *Fam.* 5.12). Tongue-in-cheek, perhaps he overemphasized his style knowing full well that Atticus would understand the irony when he refers to using Isocrates' perfume box or Aristotle's rouge (*totum Isocrati Myrothecium . . . ac non nihil etiam Airstotelia pigmenta*, *Att.* 21.2.1). Interestingly, Riggsby notes that the 'aggressively plain style' employed by Caesar did not come naturally to him but was employed consciously.³⁵ This insight, the author's conscious use of a determinedly simple style, stands in contrast to rather harsh scholarly reactions to the sharp decline noticed in Josephus' penmanship which Wacholder has also witnessed in Nicolaus' βίος. Wacholder deems the text 'as a piece of literature . . . an utter failure' compared to Nicolaus' other works, using terms such as 'incoherence', 'repetitive' and 'cumbersome', contrasting the style to Nicolaus' 'skilful pen' in his other writings.³⁶ The only explanation Wacholder can offer is the lack of a Greek autobiographical literary tradition and consequently a lack of examples and precedents, not noticing that he contradicts himself, as he had previously stated that Nicolaus' title was in direct and conscious opposition to the 'usual Greek memoirs' and his βίος a synthesis of Greek and Hebrew/Eastern traditions.³⁷ It remains unclear to me why a lack of precedents should cause a skilled author suddenly to employ a less thought-out style. Similar evaluations have been submitted for Libanius' style. Although Libanius' style in the revised first half of the *Oration* is still the most rhetorical of all the texts in this analysis, it is interesting to note that when compared just within his own corpus, this work constitutes one of his less rhetorical and less-polished texts. Petit refers to a largely unknown German dissertation by Carolus Rother, who compiled a statistical review of the density of rhetorical features in Libanius' individual

---

34 Michael von Albrecht, *A History of Roman Literature: From Livius Andronicus to Boethius with Special Regard to Its Influence on World Literature*, trans. by Frances Newman and Kevin Newman, 2 vols (Leiden, New York, Köln: E.J. Brill, 1997), 416–18. See also for example Hall, 'Ratio and Romanitas'. Hall notes that Caesar's controlled style is meant to emphasize his own control over himself, his Romanness and rationality. Cf. Dilke, 'Literary Output', 85, who mentions a 'simplicity of style'.
35 Riggsby, 'Memoir and Autobiography', 273.
36 Wacholder, *Nicolaus*, 39.
37 Ibid., 37, 43.

speeches; based on the purely numeric findings of Rother, Petit concludes that Libanius' *Oration* 1, in comparison to Libanius' whole corpus, contains little rhetorical embellishment – it is one of the 'an rhetorischem Schmuck ärmsten Reden'.[38] Libanius' style must have been intentional; as mentioned previously, *Oration 1*'s second part is a largely unedited list of events added at various stages during Libanius' later years, perhaps awaiting editing. We can easily read the differences in style and composition, a clear indicator that the style Libanius adopted for the first, published part must have been carefully chosen.

It is impossible to assess the style of lost or very fragmentary texts, and we are dependent on contemporary critics. Cicero notes Catulus' general erudition (*Brut.* 259) and praises him for writing in the style of Xenophon (*Brut.* 132), implying a simple style compared to Cicero's own.[39] Augustus' style of speaking and erudition in general are praised by Suetonius (*Aug.* 86-9), but he does not refer to Augustus' lost work specifically. However, Suetonius' report that Augustus declaimed his work (*Aug.* 85.1) suggests a sufficiently polished narrative.[40] Plutarch's reference that Sulla dedicated his books to Lucullus and wanted him to polish his works (*Luc.* 1.1) should not be taken literally, nor should one subsequently assume a bad style, especially considering his appraisal by Sallust as *litteris Graecis atque Latinis iuxta atque doctissime eruditus* (*Iug.* 95.3). Instead, Plutarch uses the reason for the dedication to highlight Lucullus' linguistic abilities and erudition which set him apart from his contemporaries:

> ἦν γὰρ οὐκ ἐπὶ τὴν χρείαν μόνην ἐμμελὴς αὐτοῦ καὶ πρόχειρος ὁ λόγος, καθάπερ ὀτῶν ἄλλων τὴν μὲν ἀγορὰν . . . ἀλλὰ καὶ τὴν ἐμμελῆ ταύτην καὶ λεγομένην ἐλευθέριον ἐπὶ τῷ καλῷ προσεποιεῖτο παιδείαν ἔτι καὶ μειράκιον ὤν.

> For the style of Lucullus was not only business-like and ready; the same was true of many another man's in the Forum. . . . But Lucullus, from his youth up, was

---

38 Petit, 'Untersuchungen', 102. See Carolus Rother, 'De Libanii Arte Rhetoria Quaestiones Selectae' (Breslau, Phil. Diss., 1915). Based on the comparatively low style, Petit concludes that Libanius did not intend to publish his speech widely, if at all.

39 Candau, 'Republican Rome', 150, praises the literary style in two epigrams attributed to Catulus, who was also known for his successful poetry. Catulus was no stranger to composition and what Candau calls a 'refined' style. Overall, Candau also recognizes the 'low literary quality' of autobiographies from Republican Rome, Ibid., 155. Candau's contribution comes as part of an edited collection of essays, which has been discussed in Chapter 1. While he does voice his suspicions concerning the style of autobiography in general, he is unable to draw any firm conclusions for the genre without a more comprehensive analysis or overview such as attempted in this study.

40 Malitz, 'Autobiographien', 233-4, praises the 'high literary style' of Augustus' *de vita sua*. But see Anton Powell, 'Augustus' Age of Apology: An Analysis of the Memoirs – and an Argument for Two Further Fragments', in *The Lost Memoirs of Augustus and the Development of Roman Autobiography*, ed. by Christopher Smith and Anton Powell (Swansea: The Classical Press of Wales, 2009), 174, who suggests that Augustus was not match to Caesar's skills.

devoted to the genial, and so-called 'liberal' culture then in vogue, wherein the Beautiful was sought. (*Luc.* 1.3–4)

Augustus similarly dedicated his work to Agrippa and Maecenas (Plutarch, *Comp. Dem. Cic.* 3.1); however, because he is also known for mocking Maecenas' literary style (Suetonius, *Aug.* 86), it is likely that these dedications were understood as honorific gestures. Lastly, as Smith points out, several fragments have survived because later authors were interested in Sulla's choice of language.[41] On the other hand, looking at the bigger picture, Eleanor Huzar suggests that Claudius' works were lost, or rather not transmitted, due to the hostility of his successors and, importantly, a lack of style.[42]

Cicero's emphasis on the amount of work he invested into his *commentarius* is usually taken to imply an unusual feature. However, this discussion has shown that, contrary to the expectations raised by Xenophon's and Caesar's boundary status, other comparative texts demonstrate a polished, if (consciously) simple style.[43] Quintilian stresses that at times, a simple style can be more insistent and convincing than elaborate rhetorical masterpieces. Sometimes, according to Quintilian, the simpler the expression, the more natural the text can appear, and the content becomes much more accessible to an audience (*Inst.* 8 *praef.* 18–22). This should be not understood as a general statement preferring a simple style to rhetorical flourishes, but rather as a concession that speakers sometimes wished to convey natural spontaneity and authenticity, perhaps especially so when writing about their own lives.

In their current format, this suggestion must exclude Xenophon and Caesar, whose works were circulated from abroad and who used a third-person voice to distance themselves slightly from the text. Nevertheless, while their simple, but by no means basic, style, cannot be compared to the simple style of Josephus or Nicolaus on a like-for-like level, it can still be considered a generic characteristic in the sense that simplicity and purity of style may convey honesty, truthfulness and furthermore is easy for an audience to listen to and take on board.[44] Any overly rhetorical passages, consequently, would be even more memorable.

We must consider that *authors consciously adapted their style in favour of a simpler, repetitive style* and that such a simple style prevented any odium on the

---

41 Smith, 'Sulla's *Memoirs*', 67.
42 Eleanor Huzar, 'Claudius – the Erudite Emperor', *ANRW* II.32, no. 1 (1984): 611–50 (613).
43 This realization stands in contrast with the generally less-than-polished style of non-autobiographical *commentarii* that were discussed earlier, for example by Frontinus or Quintus Cicero.
44 Cf. Riggsby, 'Autobiography and Memoir', 273, who argues that the plain style employed by Caesar suggests that in his private notes, Caesar had no reason to lie to himself.

part of the audience by presenting an authentic, serious, sober, straightforward account which implied an author imbued with the same characteristics. The less rhetorical embellishments the author includes, the more spontaneous and authentic the account can appear to be delivered, and gives the audience the impression that the author cannot – and need not – hide behind such embellishments.[45] Simultaneously, the audience does not need to pay constant attention, given the simplicity of the narrative, but instead can take in and remember the general gist of the stories and arguments more easily.

Atmosphere

The tone of *Life* is rather serious in that there is little humour or light-hearted narrative. Josephus is narrating something very important to him and will brook no interference nor allow his audience any relaxation. At times, the tone ranges between being overly defensive, especially when Josephus narrates his own actions, and very aggressive and driven when he speaks about his opponents. The mood consequently varies depending on Josephus himself and the situation he finds himself in. The audience receives the impression of a constant battle which is evoked by the mood alternating between aggression and defence, struggle and jubilation, anger and rare moments of calm deliberation, depending on the action of the scene and Josephus himself. The pace is always active, even panicky at times, until it reaches its climax with the success-narratives (*Life* 304 onwards, excluding the aggressive digression against Justus of Tiberias). During this sequence which ends with the arrival of Vespasian (*Life* 407), the mood calms down considerably as Josephus absolves himself of any authority in the narrative and becomes a shadow of his previous bravado.

The attitude towards the other characters can indicate reverence and respect towards pious figures such as Bannus and the imprisoned priests (*Life* 11–12, 14), or towards figures of authority such as King Agrippa II. The text's attitude towards Josephus' opponents is variable, often expressing frustration, as well as pleasure or glee at their defeat. As Mason has pointed out, the masses are treated as rabble, malleable background noise which can be swayed into any direction.[46] The values advocated are those of piety and virtue, courage, the balance between

---

45 Quintilian notes that some people in fact prefer a more simple, raw, and impulsive delivery, and admits that he agrees to the extent that natural ability and delivery are the basis for any artistic enhancements (*Inst.* 11.3.10–12).
46 Mason, *Life*, 38n.188.

a merciful and strict ruler, as well as the knowledge that the just (in this case Josephus) will ultimately prosper. The audience receives the overall impression of a serious, volatile atmosphere, giving respect where it is due, and a strong defensive undercurrent mixed with pride at the author's achievements.

Comparanda

Throughout the *Anabasis*, Xenophon creates moments where the mood turns darkly suspicious or the audience experiences dramatic tension between the characters, interspersed with joyful release ('the sea!!'); this mood-interchange has been aptly described as cycles of 'optimism and pessimism', and Xenophon succeeds in retaining his audience's attention through his cyclical creation of different moods.[47] Frequent direct speeches add pathos and urgency to the atmosphere, creating a sense of immediacy which further draws the audience into the text rather than adding light-hearted or relaxing tones. The attitude the text extends towards Xenophon is modest at first (he does not appear as the main actor until the third book), before celebrating him for possessing the values which the *Anabasis* advocates, virtue, loyalty, courage, piety and leadership. The occasional reflections pointing forwards and backwards in time explaining Xenophon's decisions add a defensive tone. Overall, the audience encounters a serious atmosphere intermixed with a sense of both pride and defensiveness.

The tone of the *Gallic War* is also serious, omitting any jokes or light-hearted moments, and Caesar as the author does not waste a word. The frequent battle scenes create an aggressive mood and the manner of their narration, in short, staccato-like sentences exemplified by the narrative of the siege of Alesia (*B Gall.* 7.63–90), create an urgency that is relieved through the long indirect speeches which allow the audience to distance itself from the events, again creating a cycle of tension and release dependant on the actions of the main character. Caesar pulls the audience into the narrative by employing the first-person plural pronoun frequently (e.g. 'our army', 'our soldiers' etc.).[48] The values advocated are identical to the virtues advocated by Xenophon: courage, loyalty, leadership skills and *Romanitas*.[49] The overall atmosphere, therefore, is serious because the audience comes to understand the volatile situation Caesar is in; simultaneously,

---

47 Bradley, 'Irony', 541; Wencis, '*Hypopsia*', 44–5.
48 Hall, 'Ratio and Romanitas', 12.
49 For *Romanitas*, ibid.; for *virtus*, see Riggsby, *Caesar*, 83–105. Compare *Romanitas* with the notion of Panhellenism suggested by Rood, 'Panhellenism', who argues that Xenophon was advancing Panhellenism through his *Anabasis*.

the audience perceives pride at the achievements of Caesar and his army on behalf of Rome.

The mood that Libanius projects depends strongly on the events he is describing – the audience feels sadness when Libanius narrates the death of family members (e.g. *Oration* 1.117–18) and ecstatic joy at Emperor Julian's accession (*Oration* 1.119). The mood turns considerably darker in the later additions, during which Libanius frequently talks about death and loss, giving way to his 'natural morbidity'.[50] The rhythmic interchange between accusations, defence and vindication of Libanius against his numerous accusers results in cycles of suspicion, aggression and relief – Libanius goes as far as to evoke a picture of war – πόλεμος – in his evocative vocabulary (*Oration* 1.91). The values that Libanius advocates are primarily those of friendship (*Oration* 1.28, 56–7, 173), piety through the consistent references to Fortune, and local patriotism towards the city of Antioch (*Oration* 1.2, 86).

The extant texts tend to have similar features: a serious atmosphere, cycles of urgency interspersed with periods of calmness, an aggressive attitude towards opponents, the evocation of an almost patriotic sentiment, and lastly, the audience feels either pride or self-defence underneath the surface.[51] Speeches in the third-person singular narratives (*Anabasis, Gallic War*) add pathos and intensity, perhaps to compensate for the more neutral narrative voice. *In comparison, Josephus' Life aligns itself fully with the comparative texts, and no text falls out of line.*

Quality of characterization

David Daube's study of typology in Josephus had demonstrated that Josephus characterized himself as adhering to biblical models and, more frequently, vice versa, rewrote biblical narratives to reflect Josephus' own actions, and Daube offers a few subtle parallels in *Life*.[52] For example, Daube shows how Josephus rewrote the Book of Jeremiah to have the prophet ask for Baruch's release in *Ant.* 10.156–58 (compared to Jer. 40:1), a scene which is subsequently reflected by Josephus asking Titus for the release of his brother and friends (*Life* 419–21).[53]

---

50 Norman, *Libanius' Autobiography*, 180.
51 Toher, 'Herod, Augustus, and Nicolaus', 76, describes the surviving fragments of Nicolaus as tragic and pathetic.
52 David Daube, 'Typology in Josephus', *JJS* 31 (1980): 18–36.
53 Ibid., 27.

Elsewhere, Josephus added the extra-biblical detail that Joseph's wife was a virgin (*Ant.* 2.91 vs. Gen. 41:45), comparable to the prisoner Josephus himself married on Vespasian's orders (*Life* 414). Daube's findings are insightful and show how prominent biblical characters were during Josephus' composition process, and how he rewrote the narratives subtly to align more closely with Josephus' own experiences and character.[54] However, Daube himself notes, without elaborating, that only a 'meticulous' reader would have noted the implied characterizations and hints;[55] I would add that the parallel characterizations were subtle and spaced far apart – the biblical narrative covers the first half of *Antiquities* and the suggested parallels in *Life* would hardly have been presented in the same sitting.[56]

Mason meanwhile has demonstrated comprehensively that Josephus characterizes himself as the ideal Judaean historian, statesman and general, following established Greco-Roman literary conventions.[57] By attributing to himself a variety of positive, worldly qualities such as piety, leadership skills, diplomacy and erudition, Josephus presents himself as a Judaean aristocrat on par with the Roman elite.[58] On the surface, Josephus' characterization of himself takes on many stereotypical facets, and by default, so must the characterization of his opponents; these, according to Mason, are portrayed as the typical counter-image to the ideal statesman, exhibiting the negative values to Josephus' positive ones, such as greed, corruption and constant rabble-rousing.[59]

However, the quality of characterization within *Life* is not straightforward. Josephus introduces a level of complexity by portraying himself as both naive and devious at the same time; he insists that he was unaware of any hidden agenda planned by John of Gischala on his alleged trip to the hot baths of Tiberias (*Life*

---

54 Ibid., 27–8. Despite going into great detail, Daube overlooks several parallels with Nehemiah which Josephus has integrated into *Life*. See Davina Grojnowski, 'Nehemiah, Josephus, and Self-Presentation: An Analysis of Parallels', *Journal for the Study of Judaism* 46, no. 3 (2015): 345–65, for a more detailed discussion of these parallel scenes.
55 Daube, 'Typology', 26.
56 Without wanting to detract from Daube's insights, his argument exhibits a flaw of a temporal nature. Josephus wrote the early books of *Antiquities* (which include the adapted characterizations) prior to *Life*. We must wonder whether he inserted the extra-biblical details in the Jeremiah or Joseph narratives knowing that in *Life*, many books and stories later, he would include subtle parallels to enhance his characterization as prophet, or whether he adapted his self-portrayal in *Life* to reflect the biblical portrayals, as suggested in a different context by Finn Damgaard, *Recasting Moses* (Frankfurt: Peter Lang GmbH, 2013).
57 Mason, 'Essay'.
58 Scholars have frequently remarked that according to the ancient mindset the character of a person did not develop, but remained static. Therefore, it would be anachronistic to expect to see the inner development of a character throughout a text, and one should not apply modern expectations to the quality of ancient characterization. Cf. Pitcher, 'Characterization in Ancient Historiography', 102–3, or *B Gall.* 1.40, where Caesar points out that his *innocentia* was visible throughout his life.
59 Mason, 'Essay', 63–70.

86), but shortly afterwards congratulates himself on feigning ignorance of a plot (*Life* 107).⁶⁰ Contrary to the attempted stereotypical portrayal of Josephus' opponents, the reality at times emerges through the narrative. His enemies are capable men with high-flying connections (e.g. *Life* 87, 124, 177, 190); rather than brutes one needs to conquer forcefully, his enemies are ambitious men similar to Josephus against whom he must struggle to succeed, and Josephus himself admits that at various times he fell into great danger because of his enemies' actions (e.g. *Life* 125, 272).⁶¹ Josephus further admits his occasional fears or other weaknesses (*Life* 20, 175, 206, 304), and as Rajak has pointed out, is capable of omitting or altering information in his characterization of those he wanted to protect or defend.⁶²

We see the discrepancy most clearly in Josephus' construction of John of Gischala's character. While the two men shared many characteristics in terms of background, ambition, education and their social environment and connections, Josephus cleverly characterizes John as his arch-enemy.⁶³ In the following passage, Josephus the narrator inserts himself into the narrative by editorializing, creating a rather negative image of John:

> *Vita* 74: **For he claimed that the Judeans living in Philip's Caesarea**, who had been confined at the order of the king [. . .] since they had no pure olive oil that they could use, **had sent to him [Ioannes] requesting that he make provision** [. . .] so that they would not violate the legal standards by having to use the Greek kind [of oil]. (75) **Yet Ioannes was not saying these things in the service of piety, but on account of the most blatant, disgusting greed**. Knowing that among those in Caesarea one would sell two pitchers for one drachma, whereas in Gischala it was eighty pitchers for four drachmas, he sent for as much oil as was there! He had ostensible received authority from me. (76) **It was not willingly that I agreed, but through fear of the mob – so as not to be stoned to**

---

60 See also Mason, 'Figured Speech and Irony T. Flavius Josephus', 243–88. Wills, *Jewish Novel*, 61, 152–4, states that irony was not wholly the remit of Greco-Roman literature, but also evident in Jewish novels.
61 For more details on the historical relationship between Josephus and his opponents, see Martin Goodman, *The Ruling Class of Judaea: The Origins of the Jewish Revolt against Rome A.D. 66–70* (Cambridge: Cambridge University Press, 1987), 183–5. For Justus especially, see Rajak, 'Justus of Tiberias'.
62 Mason, *Life*, 109n.982, suggests it is 'surprising' that Josephus would so openly admit his fears, but it is also possible to understand these expressions in the tradition of deflecting a negative audience reaction, in line with the aforementioned rhetorical methods. For disparities in characterization of friends, see Rajak, *Josephus*, 165–6.
63 Mason, *Life*, 48n.259; Uriel Rappaport, *John of Gischala: From the Mountains of Galilee to the Walls of Jerusalem. The Author's Electronically Circulated Translation by R. Toueg, of His Yohanan mi-Gush Halav: me–Hare ha–Galil el Homot Yerushalayim* (Haifa: University of Haifa Press, 2006) [Hebrew], 81: 'at a certain stage, there were no great differences in outlook between John of Gischala, Justus of Tiberias, and Josephus.'

death by them if I refused. So with my consent, Ioannes realized considerable wealth from this sordid business. (transl. Brill, emphasis my own)

If we can look beyond Josephus' harsh editorializing, what we have left is a rather garbled account of a group of Judaeans confined in some manner for unknown reasons by King Agrippa. These poor people had reached out to John, who is allegedly, if we follow Josephus' lead, the evil character in this scenario; the confined Judaeans view him as their saviour.[64] These Judeans, in effect prisoners in their own city, relied on John as much as the imprisoned priests had relied on Josephus in Rome. The presence of the elusive mob in this scene, the excuse Josephus uses to explain his involvement in the scene, remains inexplicable.

Similarly, Josephus' editorializing in the following scene forcibly casts John in the character of a villain. In *Life* 301–4, Josephus narrates how he was being accused by Jonathan (a member of the delegation sent from Jerusalem) for being a power-hungry tyrant. Jonathan's men try to grab Josephus and dispose of him. Into this scene, Josephus inserts that he was rescued from John by divine providence (301). John, however, was not even in the scene: in *Life* 301, Josephus tells us that John was merely approaching the scene with armed soldiers. John does not feature as a threat again until v. 304, where Josephus simply avoids him en route. We see a degree of tension between Josephus' character stereotypes and reality in his characters.

Comparanda

Xenophon successfully characterized himself as the ideal general who saved the Greek army from destruction and led them back home. The success of his characterization is evident in the praise he has evoked up until modern times as one of the prime examples of generalship and leadership. He is always accessible for his subordinates and works alongside them (e.g. *Anab.* 4.3.10, 4.4.12) – all these deeds are part of the recipe for high morale among troops.[65] However, it is uncertain how far Xenophon actually lived up to the ideal general, and in how far he is portraying himself as a stereotypical character; as Tim Rood

---

64 For kosher olive oil in antiquity, see Mason, *Life*, n.406; Martin Goodman, 'Kosher Olive Oil in Antiquity', in *A Tribute to Geza Vermes: Essays on Jewish and Christian Literature and History*, ed. by Philip R. Davies and Richard T. White (Sheffield: Sheffield Academic Press, 1990); Siegert, *Aus meinem Leben*, 167.
65 Cf. Cawkwell, 'When, How and Why?', and Michael Whitby, 'Xenophon's Ten Thousand as a Fighting Force', in *The Long March: Xenophon and the Ten Thousand*, ed. by Robin Lane Fox (New Haven, London: Yale University Press, 2004), on Xenophon as the upkeeper of troop morale.

states, the characterization is 'too good to be true'.[66] In fact, many of the actions Xenophon describes are common motives frequently attributed to successful generals and have become part of the ancient repertoire.[67] Simultaneously, scholars have detected a discrepancy between the characterization of other actors in the *Anabasis* and reality, notably the characterization of Cyrus. In his discussion of the contrast, Thomas Braun concludes that Xenophon consciously misrepresents his friends in the *Anabasis* if necessary.[68] Caesar also characterizes himself as the perfect general, by sending away his horse before a battle (*B Gall.* 2.25, 7.87; cf. Tacitus, *Agr.* 35.7; Plutarch, *Crass.* 11.6; Xenophon, *Anab.* 7.3.45), singling out individual troops for motivational purposes (e.g. his preferred tenth legion, *B Gall.* 1.40; cf. Alexander's Companion in the Cavalry, Arrian, *Anab.* 1.16.4), or informing his subordinates to ensure a calm atmosphere (*B Gall.* 4.23, 8.8, in contrast to unsuccessful commanders who lose their nerves and control, *B Gall.* 3.3–6, 5.53).[69] However, the stereotype of the ever-present, ever-calm commander breaks down occasionally; there are instances when he is not able to coordinate or control his troops, nor is he able to supply for his army (e.g. *B Gall.* 2.20–27; 7.17). Comparably, as much as Caesar portrays himself as the stereotypical Roman general, the quality of his opponents' characterization remains one-dimensional and has collectively been accused of being 'schematic', a 'literary construct'[70] and sparse, as Caesar hardly defines his actors.[71] Lastly, Libanius characterizes himself as the highly successful orator who was always the victim of professional jealousy. However, as Raffaela Cribiore has pointed out, the clashes between Libanius and his competitive accusers are highly stylized and follow the same basic pattern – in addition, the fact that Libanius leaves

---

66 Rood, 'Panhellenism', 322.
67 See, for example, the military manuals compiled by Frontinus (*Strategemata*), Onasander (στατηγικός) and Vegetius (*Epitoma rei militaris*). Powell, 'Augustus' Age of Apology', would like to include two additional fragments into the list of extant fragments for Augustus' lost work. In these fragments, Augustus also portrays himself as the ideal general who always looks out for his troops regardless of his situation, although elsewhere he was frequently accused of not having any military talent – hence also the defensive note regarding his (lack of) military actions in the extant fragments.
68 Braun, 'Dangerous Liasons', esp. 116–17.
69 Cf. also Adrian Goldsworthy, '"Instinctive Genius": The Depiction of Caesar the General', in *Julius Caesar as Artful Reporter: The War Commentaries as Political Instruments*, ed. by Kathryn Welch and Anton Powell (London: Duckworth with The Classical Press of Wales 1998), and Riggsby, *Caesar*, 213, who points out that Caesar's self-representation is 'entirely conventional'.
70 Riggsby, *Caesar*, 68.
71 Pitcher, 'Characterization in Ancient Historiography', 106. Also Vasaly, 'Characterization and Complexity'. Jonathan Barlow, 'Noble Gauls and Their Other in Caesar's Propaganda', in *Julius Caesar as Artful Reporter: The War Commentaries as Political Instruments*, ed. by Kathryn Welch and Anton Powell (London: Duckworth with The Classical Press of Wales, 1998), 157, discusses Caesar's characterization of the Gallic leaders, concluding that the *Gallic War* places 'a slant on existing realities'.

some opponents anonymous demonstrates their interchangeability and hints at a stylized, unrealistic account.[72]

In sum, we have seen that the main character/narrator continuously presents himself as a stereotypical example of his chosen profession (e.g. Xenophon or Caesar the ideal general; Nicolaus the ideal philosopher). The respective opponents and secondary characters are either characterized as stereotypes reflecting the negative traits to the main character's (the author's) positive self-representation or are reduced to generic figures serving as a passive object to the main character's (the author's) actions. As a result, considerable tension is evident between the quality of characterization and the historical situation as far as we can trace it.[73] *Taking the findings concerning* Life *into consideration, the quality of characterization is highly similar among all the texts discussed here.*

Social setting and occasion

This category was included because a text's social setting (audience, occasion) can reflect its genre participation. What audience did the author envision, what audiences would be able to interpret the genre and the text correctly, what would be a suitable occasion to present the text? Some genres were more suited to certain occasions than others, and some audiences would be more likely to decode the text along the author's expectations.

Scholarly arguments have been advanced for various constellations of *Life*'s audiences: Roman, Greek, Judean, mixed. As Mason has demonstrated, Josephus' consistent portrayal of himself as a Judean aristocrat and his denigration of the 'crowd' – ὁ ὄχλος – indicates an elite, educated audience.[74] As Josephus addresses his patron Epaphroditus in his end credits (*Life* 430), it is reasonable to suggest

---

72 Raffaella Cribiore, *The School of Libanius in Late Antique Antioch* (Princeton: Princeton University Press, 2007), 92, who brands Libanius' characterization as 'highly unlikely'. Cf. Wintjes, *Leben Des Libanius*, 84–7.
73 The quality of characterization by Nicolaus has consciously not been discussed here. There are too few remaining fragments to receive a rounded impression, although Toher, 'Herod, Augustus, and Nicolaus', 76–80, based on his theory that Josephus in his *Antiquities* relied on Nicolaus' βίος rather than on the *Historia universalis*, has recourse to a much larger selection of excerpts from which he deduces the quality of Nicolaus' characterization of both himself and Herod. However, the fact that Josephus filtered the original text, as well as Toher's lapidary comment (ibid., 77) that Josephus might have read either the original or perhaps a secondary edition embedded into Nicolaus' *Historia* must result in a more cautionary reading.
74 Mason, *Life*, 38n.188. Cf. Mason, 'Reading Josephus', 100, who mentions a 'sophisticated Roman audience' for *War*. The link between *Antiquities* and *Life* suggests the same audience constellation, and in fact Mason, 'Introduction', xviii, argues for a continuity of audience between all of Josephus' works.

a literary circle arranged by his patron, and Josephus' reference to imperial and royal support indicates some distribution of the material to a high-profile audience in written form as well (e.g. *Life* 365–7).[75] However, Mason, Hannah Cotton and Werner Eck have all thrown some doubt on Josephus' status within Roman society. Mason understands Josephus' dedication of his later works to Epaphroditus as evidence that Josephus had lost his earlier imperial patronage, despite his emphasis on continued favour under Domitian and his wife Domitia (*Life* 429).[76] Josephus lists the imperial privileges he received (land in Judea, accommodation in Rome, citizenship, a stipend, protection against accusations, *Life* 422–6), but Mason does not consider these privileges as being either very impressive or extraordinary when compared with contemporary Roman policy and patron–client relationships. On the contrary, he compares Josephus with truly successful Judaeans in Rome, such as the Herodian dynasty and the family of Philo's brother, Alexander the Alabarch, who all had demonstrably close relationships with the imperial family.[77] Lastly, for Mason, the fact that roughly contemporary Roman authors such as Suetonius or Dio see Josephus only as a 'curiosity' and mention him in passing (Suetonius, *Vesp.* 5.6.4; Dio 65.1.4 but cf. Eusebius, *Hist. eccl.* 3.9.1–2) cements the impression of Josephus' lack of prominence in imperial circles which impacts on his potential audience.[78]

On the other hand, direct parallels with the Book of Nehemiah might indicate a devout or knowledgeable Judean audience, and support Goodman's hypothesis of Josephus' influential position in the local Judean community.[79] Josephus uses motifs which are highly reminiscent of Nehemiah's actions: he insists that he

---

75 The identity of Epaphroditus remains unclear and is not strictly relevant in this discussion of genre. See Hannah M. Cotton and Werner Eck, 'Josephus' Roman Audience: Josephus and the Roman Elites', in *Flavius Josephus and Flavian Rome,* ed. by Jonathan Edmondson, James Rives and Steve Mason (Oxford: Oxford University Press, 2005) for a discussion. See also Steve Mason, *Orientation to the History of Roman Judaea* (Eugene: Cascade Books, 2016), 91–2, on the term 'patron'.
76 Mason, 'Should Any Wish to Enquire Further (*Ant.* 1.25)', 66. Cotton and Eck, 'Josephus' Roman Audience', go as far as to suggest that Josephus was both isolated and lonely in Rome. See also Ross Shepard Kraemer, *Unreliable Witnesses [Electronic Book]: Religion, Gender and History in the Greco-Roman Mediterranean* (New York: Oxford University Press, 2011), 229. She suggests that Josephus refers to his female imperial patronage because they were his only access to imperial power.
77 Mason, 'Should Any Wish to Enquire Further', 75–6. Also Rajak, *Josephus,* 185–222.
78 Ibid., 77. For a detailed discussion of the benefits Josephus received in comparison to how he presented them to his audience, see William den Hollander, *Josephus, the Emperors, and the City of Rome. From Hostage to Historian* (Leiden, Boston: Brill, 2014).
79 Martin Goodman, 'Josephus as Roman Citizen', in *Josephus and the History of the Greco-Roman Period: Essays in Memory of Morton Smith,* ed. by Fausto Parente and Joseph Sievers (Leiden, New York: E.J. Brill, 1994). Goodman suggests that Josephus was made welcome in the Roman Judean community as influential spokesperson, and maintained his social environment in Rome. He cites the large Judean communities in Rome, the fact that Josephus, thanks to his access to the imperial court and to the Herodian descendants, made a desirable patron, and that Josephus proudly emphasized his heritage, including giving his sons traditional names such as Hyrcanus, Justus, and Agrippa (*Life*, 5). Cf. also *War* 6.107.

did not accept the tithes due to them as priest or governor (*Life* 80; cf. Neh. 5:14–18), and employs a communication motif – both Josephus and Nehemiah offer letters as justification that they had attempted to communicate with their opponents. Their respective opponents demand a meeting, whereupon Josephus/ Nehemiah pretend they are too busy and ask for the meeting to be relocated to a location more convenient for them (*Life* 216–231; Neh. 6:1–9).[80] The educated Judeans in Rome, which include the Herodian descendants and those of Philo's family, received a classical education presumably supplemented by knowledge of scripture (e.g. *Ant.* 18.143, 19.360), which raises the possibility that Josephus envisaged them – or others like them, members of their circle – as part of his intended audience, and presumably they were able to pick up on similarities and references that others (including ourselves) might have overlooked.

Despite the lack of an academic consensus regarding the religious or ethnic identities of Josephus' intended audience, especially since the range of definitions can fluctuate, we can for the moment conclude a social setting of a multi-faceted, educated audience, which Josephus trusts to pick up on various subtleties within the text, be they genre-related, political or religious.[81] The dedication to Epaphroditus suggests a social occasion of a literary circle, in which Josephus could also interact with other authors. This is implied by the final sentences in both *War* and *Life,* in which he directly addresses his audience asking them to judge him either on style (*War* 7.455) or his character (*Life* 430), expecting them to be able to do so.[82] The final chapter will be able to offer further deliberations on Josephus' audience after all aspects of the literary analysis have been interpreted.

Comparanda

The social setting of the *Gallic War* has long been assumed to rest among the senatorial elite in Rome; the emphasis on *Romanitas* as well as the frequent despatches sent to the Senate have caused scholars to suggest a setting among the higher Roman classes. This is supported by our knowledge of Cato's speech against Caesar in the Senate, rather than in a public place (Plutarch, *Cato Min.* 51) as well as internal evidence such as the constant praise for prominent Roman colleagues. However, some arguments have been raised to suggest a more popular

---

80 For further parallels between Josephus and Nehemiah, enhancing the argument for a Judean target audience, see Grojnowski, 'Nehemiah, Josephus, and Self-Presentation', 345–65.
81 Cf. Mason, 'Figured Speech and Irony T. Flavius Josephus', 282, 285. See also Mason, 'Reading Josephus', on the importance of understanding a local audience in a first instance.
82 Cf. the rhetorical questions he asks in *Ag.Ap.* 2.291–296, in which he reflects on the ideas and concepts he has just presented, and addresses Epaphroditus again.

social setting that reaches the less privileged Roman citizens, scholars relying on internal evidence such as Caesar's respectful treatment of his ordinary soldiers, or the clusters of notes, explanations or geographical digressions which bring the distant Gaul to life for a rather uneducated audience.[83] Considering the support for Caesar among the popular masses of Rome (Cicero, *Cat.* 4.9; *Att.* 16.16), as well as the fact that political decisions were made in the Senate, Caesar aimed at a mixed audience well-informed about Caesar himself; he did not need to educate his audience about himself. The internal evidence supports this, Caesar omits any reference to his personal history.[84] The social occasions during which the *Gallic War* was read correspond with the social setting; either they were read in the Senate or private gatherings of influential men, or as Wiseman suggests, before a large public audience.[85]

Just as Caesar was largely writing for his hometown, Sulla's audience was undoubtedly Roman; his biggest dispute lay with the city of Rome and its constitution. The fragmentary nature of Sulla's works allows for educated assumptions at best. The length (twenty-two books) would have required several sessions of reading (see mode of representation, earlier). Xenophon leaves internal clues in the *Anabasis* that suggest an Athenian audience, more specifically those men whom he thought would be interested in (and informed about) his fate as opposed to that of the army, and his references to Socrates and philosophic discourses imply an educated audience. However, it is interesting that some very recent volumes do not discuss Xenophon's audience further than admitting the difficulties of locating Xenophon's intended audience, or remarking on the very generic 'contemporary Greek audience' or 'fellow Athenian as well as Greeks from other cities'.[86] As noted previously, given Xenophon's exile and use of a pseudonym, we do not know how much influence he had over the occasion of the *Anabasis*' presentation to the public. Libanius' frequent praise of Antioch

---

83 T. P. Wiseman, 'The Publication of *De Bello Gallico*', in *Julius Caesar as Artful Reporter*, ed. by Kathryn Welch and Anton Powell (London: Duckworth with The Classical Press of Wales, 1998). Cf. also Hall, 'Ratio and Romanitas', 29, who suggests a Roman middle-class audience which could not speak or read Latin fluently, hence the simplified Latin style, above.

84 Mellor, *Roman Historians*, 170-6, has proposed an additional aspect to the social setting, which remains largely unremarked upon, namely an elite Gallic audience whom Caesar wanted to convince to accept Roman domination. We see here a continuation of the trend which expects an educated social setting knowledgeable about Caesar.

85 Wiseman, 'The Publication of *De Bello Gallico*', 5. But see Riggsby, *Caesar*, 13, who points out the flaws in Wiseman's theory regarding public lectures; he points out that we do not have any evidence for a large public audience listening to 'full-scale . . . narrative'.

86 Rood, 'Panhellenism', 323, 327; Michael A. Flower, *Xenophon's Anabasis, or the Expedition of Cyrus* (New York: Oxford University Press Inc., 2012), 44. External clues such as praise and the copying of Xenophon's manuscripts indicate that educated Greeks and Romans including Cicero continued to read and appreciate Xenophon's literature.

and the focus on his time there hint at a local audience. His habit of leaving characters anonymous suggests that he expected his audience to be able to fill in the gaps easily, and his oblique references to historical events and literary figures (e.g. *Oration* 1.12, 15, 152) indicate that he was writing for an educated audience aware of his personal and professional circumstances. However, as mentioned previously, scholarship remains undecided on whether Libanius ever actually published his oration; the later additions were certainly not intended for publication, given their abrupt and haphazard style. Regarding the original first part of the oration, Petit claims that because of the controversial content (i.e. Libanius himself), Libanius never published his speech, a theory which Norman modifies by suggesting a very small, select audience consisting of his closest friends. Both Petit and Norman approach the issue under the impression that writing about oneself was unpopular and best avoided, although neither attempts to explain this attitude considering that Augustine published his *Confessions* within the same generation.[87] Libanius himself directly addresses his audience several times, suggesting an intimate social setting (*Oration 1*. 12, 37). We can see the benefits of the literary analysis and a comparative approach, which show that none of the other authors discussed here attempted to hide their work. It allows the conclusion that it remains unlikely that Libanius should carefully construct an account of his life and subsequently suppress its publication.

In the extant fragments, Nicolaus emphasizes his education, his courage, his royal connections, as well as the advantages of a philosophical life; given the fact that we know he stayed in Rome following Herod's death, Toher suggests that Nicolaus wrote for an educated Roman audience. Toher advances the theory that Nicolaus wrote with Augustus in mind, given that Augustus was facing problems with his potential successors, parallel to the domestic issues confronting Herod.[88] His audience must have been familiar with philosophy and general history.

Again, we must rely on external evidence rather than internal clues when determining the social setting of the fragmentary texts. Cicero for example, by asking Lucceius to publish on his behalf, expected a social setting among Lucceius' accustomed audience; the references he makes in his 'Letter to Lucceius' (*Fam.* 5.12) regarding his audience and previous literature, historical events and philosophical matters (e.g. *Fam.* 5.12.4–5) imply Cicero's expectations of an educated audience. From his previous publications concerning the events that had transpired during his consulship, we know that Cicero expected people

---

87 Cf. also Pausch, 'Formen', 311, stating that autobiography had a considerable 'Rezeptionsproblem'.
88 Toher, 'Herod, Augustus, and Nicolaus'.

to know about his achievements and tribulations, and envisioned his works to be read in social settings as varied as the military surroundings of Pompey (Plutarch, *Caes.* 8.3) or the more studious Athenian audience (*Att.* 2.1.1), or he again attempted to encroach on the social settings reached by other authors such as Archias (*Att.* 1.16.15), and, given this expansive distribution, we must assume a wide variety of social occasions. We know from Suetonius' comment (*Aug.* 85.1) that Augustus read aloud from his works at small social gatherings of friends, and we might expand this circle to include the circles surrounding Agrippa and Maecenas as the official dedicatees.

While these conclusions are admittedly fragmentary, the trend towards an educated audience in the author's native social surroundings is evident, which is supported by the preferred method of indirect characterization which in itself requires an educated and attentive audience able to catch the implied character traits.[89] The occasions at which the works could have been presented vary, and it is noticeable that Life *does not stand out among these texts*.

Time of composition/publication

The question of dating *Life* has long been of interest in Josephan scholarship. Since *Life* is usually appended to *Antiquities* 20, it would follow that it was published simultaneously.[90] The final book of Josephus' *Antiquities* was published in 93/94 CE during the reign of Emperor Domitian, as *Ant.* 20.267 clearly states: τῆς νῦν ἐνεστώσης ἡμέρας, ἥτις ἐστὶν τρισκαιδεκάτου μὲν ἔτους τῆς Δομετιανοῦ Καίσαρος ἀρχῆς – 'this present day which is the 13th year of Caesar Domitian's reign'.

The problem, however, lies in two contrasting statements concerning the time of death of King Agrippa II. *Life* 359 assumes the death of Agrippa II: βασιλέως Ἀγρίππα περιόντος ἔτι καὶ τῶν ἐκ γένους αὐτοῦ πάντων – 'while King Agrippa and all of his family were still among us'. Consequently, Agrippa II's death must have occurred prior to the publication of *Ant.* 20 and *Life* in 93/94 CE. The tenth-century historian Photius, however, dates the death of Agrippa II to 100 CE.[91] Scholars were faced with either discounting the evidence of Photius, or the

---

89 Cf. Cohn Eskenazi, *Age of Prose*, 128, who claims that indirect characterization requires readers/audiences to be attentive to nuanced details.
90 Manuscript tradition has *Antiquities* and *Life* linked almost consistently; for a comprehensive discussion of the manuscript tradition, see Schreckenberg, *Die Flavius-Josephus-Tradition*.
91 Photius, *Bibliotheca* 33=*FGrH* 734 T2.

option, comprehensively formulated at the beginning of the twentieth century by Laqueur, that *Life* was appended to the last book of the *Antiquities* in a second edition.[92]

Disparate evidence has forced scholars to come up with complex theories in an attempt to harmonize the evidence.[93] Nevertheless, the majority of recent scholarship, including the present author, agrees with an earlier (93/94 CE) rather than later (100 CE) date, a dating which does look more persuasive considering the strong links between *Life* and *Antiquities*.[94] In addition to these comprehensive discussions, relevant comparative material might also be considered, as well as their method of publication. Which other ancient authors appended an autobiography to their larger corpus? At what stage in their life did they publish, that is, were they already well-known, respected, citizens or mid-career? Approaching the text based on its genre may well offer further aspects that can contribute to the discussion of dating *Life*. It remains necessary to point out that Josephus had reached the end of his active military career, and had already published several books; he had spent at least twenty years in Rome at the earliest possible time of publication, 93/94 CE.

Comparanda

Xenophon does not mention when he wrote his *Anabasis,* but most scholars agree on a date roughly thirty years after the events themselves (401–399 BCE). Based on the internal evidence Xenophon supplies regarding the age of his sons and a digression pointing forwards to his life in exile (*Anab.* 5.3.7), Cawkwell summarizes the view that Xenophon wrote and published the *Anabasis* in the early 360s BCE, roughly contemporary with the writing of *Cyropaedia*.[95]

---

92 Laqueur, *Josephus*, 1–6.
93 Bilde, *Josephus*, 106. He disagrees with those scholars who, by inference, reject Josephus' own words on the dating of *Life*. Emil Schürer admits that the evidence is inconclusive in: *The History of the Jewish People in the Age of Jesus Christ (175 B.C.–A.D. 135), Revised and Edited by Geza Vermes & Fergus Millar* (Edinburgh: Clark, 1973), Vol. 1.54. Jones, 'Chronology', gathers the various arguments together but also fails to offer a conclusive answer. For a comprehensive review of previous theories attempting to date *Life*, see primarily Mason, *Life*. It would require a whole chapter to review and discuss the various theories that have been advanced. This study fully accepts the *communis opinio* that *Life* was published alongside *Ant.* 20. Geiger, 'Biography', 69, tries to sit on all chairs, suggesting that Josephus wrote *Life* in Domitian's thirteenth year (93–4 CE), but didn't publish until after Agrippa's death in 100 CE (following Photius' dating).
94 Cf. Rajak, 'Justus of Tiberias', 361. For a full discussion of dating *Life*, see most comprehensively with further references, Mason, *Life*, and idem., 'Josephus' *Autobiography*'.
95 Cawkwell, 'When, How and Why?', 47–51. But see Roy, 'Xenophon's Evidence', 45n.29, for a selection of older views on a publication between 390 and 377 BCE. Cawkwell, 'When, How and Why?', 60–2, argues that Xenophon waited 30 years prior to publishing because he reacted to a rivalling account by Sophaenetus of Stymphalus, who was also part of the campaign and who

Consequently, Xenophon must have written the *Anabasis* late in life, in a period of literary accomplishments, having retired from any active military or political life, and effectively living in exile from his original home in Athens.⁹⁶ Several generations later, Sulla had placed himself in a voluntary exile outside of Rome, having retired from active political life in 79 BCE at the age of 59/60, and took to writing (Plutarch, *Sull.* 37). From the internal evidence in Nicolaus' fragments (F138), we know that Nicolaus spent a considerable amount of time in Rome after the death of Herod (4 BCE) before writing his now lost work, a time he had originally planned to spend in retirement, indicating an advanced age.

The format of Caesar's *Gallic War* has caused some debate regarding its time of publication, and scholars have recently argued for an annual publication, overturning the previous scholarly assumption of a single publication after the events in 51 BCE, based on internal evidence such as Hirtius' comment about the speed with which Caesar was able to compose his books (*B Gall.* 8 praef. 6) and conjunctions linking the different books together (e.g. *B Gall.* 2.1: *ita uti supra demonstravimus*).⁹⁷ Either way, scholars are arguing over a very narrow time period between 58 and 51 BCE, at a time when Caesar was in his 40s; ultimately, Caesar wrote during his active political and military career. Cicero's letter to Lucceius is dated to 56 BCE, shortly after his consulship and a year after his return from exile (57 BCE); by that date, he had already written a poem about his consulship (*Att.* 1.191.3), sent several reports to Atticus for publication (*Att.* 2.1.1), and had expected other historians to write about him

---

allegedly had written an account entitled *Anabasis* (*FGrH* 109). Cawkwell suggests that Xenophon had not fared well in this second account and composed his own *Anabasis* to set the record straight, making it his own 'personal apologia', ibid., 67. But see Stylianou, 'One *Anabasis*', contra Cawkwell, who based on internal linguistic evidence argues that the second *Anabasis* by Sophaenetus never existed, but that all extant accounts ultimately derive from Xenophon.

96 We also know that when Rutilius Rufus wrote his *De vita sua* in exile around 90 BCE, he had already reached the end of his career with little hope of a return to Rome. Rufus' work is not discussed in this study as the evidence is too fragmentary to be of substantial help in a literary analysis. Scholars discussing Rufus have largely focused on summarizing his career and the extent fragments, for example Candau, 'Republican Rome', 139–47; Lewis, 'Imperial Autobiography', 662–5; Hans Beck and Uwe Walter, *Die frühen Römischen Historiker. Band II von Coelius Antipater bis Pomponius Atticus* (Darmstadt: Wissenschaftliche Buchgesellschaft, 2004), 100–8.

97 Annual publication: Kathryn Welch, 'Caesar and His Officers in the Gallic War Commentaries', in *Julius Caesar as Artful Reporter: The War Commentaries as Political Instruments*, ed. by Kathryn Welch and Anton Powell (London: Duckworth with The Classical Press of Wales, 1998), collects the arguments given for annual publication, arguing that Caesar suffered from his prolonged absence from Rome and wanted to stay on Rome's political radar. Wiseman, 'The Publication of *De Bello Gallico*', uses internal evidence to argue that Caesar in the early books did not know of events in later books; for example, Caesar's conviction in *B Gall.* 2.28.1 (57 BCE) that he had summarily defeated the Nervii stands in contrast to his comment that the Nervii were besieging Quintus Cicero (*B Gall.* 5.49.1). Cf. Riggsby, *Caesar*, 9–11. In contrast, Matthias Gelzer, *Caesar, Der Politiker Und Staatsmann* (Wiesbaden: F.Steiner Verlag, 1960), 119n.16, argues for a single publication in 51 BCE.

(*Att.* 1.16.15). Cicero, similarly to Caesar and Augustus, did not write at the end of his career, but rather wanted to restart his political life by making an account of his achievements widely known. Scholars generally agree that Augustus wrote and published his autobiography in the mid-20s BCE, at a pivotal point of his career, at the end of the Cantabrian War (cf. Suetonius, *Aug.* 85.1) and shortly after the inauguration of the principate.[98] Libanius remarks that at the time of writing, he was approaching his sixtieth birthday (*Oration* 1.51). Since he also claimed to be fifty at the time of the first Olympic Games hosted in Antioch (364 CE) after the death of the emperor Julian (363 CE), it follows that he was born in 314 CE and writing in 374 CE.[99] Given his age and the political circumstances in Antioch, Libanius was writing at a time he thought to be the end of his career, having lost both the political influence he had enjoyed during the reign of Julian and his professional success.[100]

Cicero makes an illuminating comment regarding the difficulty of pinpointing a date of publication for ancient literature and the general problem of compositional layers. By saying that he had already seen parts of the historical work Lucceius was still writing, he demonstrates how ancient authors had the habit of sending out parts of their compositions to friends prior to the completion of the entire work (*Fam.* 5.12.2); it is difficult to determine a single date of composition or publication. Diodorus Siculus (first century BCE) tells us that while he had completed his masterpiece, the books had not yet been handed out (I.4.6); his emphasis on this circumstance marks his approach as unusual. As Mason argues in detail, we must not underestimate the issue of compositional layers and the problems of ancient publication, lack of copyright, and second and third editions: reprinting an original was not a simple process – scripts had to be copied by hand, and it is possible that the author wrote something, put it down, picked it up, changed it etc.[101] Mason also notes that authors published, got feedback and added/amended parts of the narrative based on that feedback. However, we can still see two trends emerging concerning the time of publication of the works under discussion in the present analysis: those

---

98 See further Dobesch, 'Nikolaos von Damaskus', 124, and Smith and Powell, *Lost Memoirs*.
99 Cf. Wintjes, *Leben Des Libanius*, 40.
100 For a detailed overview of Libanius' dark period and the historical background, see ibid., 163–76. For a discussion of the composition dates for the various later additions, see ibid., 17n.3, and Norman, *Libanius' Autobiography*, xiii–xiv. Both agree that although the individual sections (from *Oration* 1.156–285) were written at different stages, they were only woven together into a coherent narrative and attached to the original work after Libanius' death.
101 Mason, 'Reading Josephus'. For the publication and dissemination process, see also Larry Hurtado and Chris Keith, 'Writing and Book Production in the Hellenistic and Roman Periods', in *New Cambridge History of the Bible Vol. 1: From the Beginnings to 600*, ed. by James Carleton and Joachim Schaper (Cambridge: Cambridge University Press), 63–80.

works which cover only a narrow temporal scale tended to be published closer to the events themselves, as opposed to those works which ostensibly cover a wider temporal scale and were published later in the author's life.[102] Xenophon here proves an exception; his *Anabasis* treats only two to three years, but was published roughly thirty years after the events. *Josephus, therefore, who purports to narrate over a wide temporal scale, fits in with some of the comparative texts, whereas others share the feature of contemporaneous publication.*

Authorial intention and purpose

Various intentions have been attributed to Josephus in writing *Life*; this diversity demonstrates the different ways in which an audience reacts to and interprets a text and that no one reason can necessarily be attributed to the author; it could also be argued that, given the temporal distance between Josephus himself and modern scholarship, his programmatic statements had been misunderstood.

(a) Encomiastic

Neyrey has suggested that Josephus wrote *Life* as an ideal example of the Greco-Roman literary encomium to praise himself.[103] Neyrey's theory is not without faults (see Chapter 1), but he was certainly correct in pointing out that Josephus was intent on presenting his best features. While Josephus demonstrates his

---

102 Such a conclusion allows for the theory that Catulus also published very soon after his military campaign; as Plutarch attests (*Mar.* 25), Catulus demanded recognition for his achievements, and it is likely that Catulus published soon after the events during the struggle for prizes, rewards, and an illustrious career following a successful campaign. However, Mellor, *Roman Historians*, 167, suggests that Scaurus, Catulus and Rufus all wrote during their retirement (as opposed to during their active career when they could have benefitted from a different perspective of themselves in the public eye). This theory might also help understand the composition and publication of Augustus' lost work; while we know that Augustus ended his account with the Cantabrian War, we have little to no information 'as to the date of composition or publication', Rich, 'Cantabrian Closure', 158. While there is general agreement on a composition date in the 20s BCE, the reason behind the composition remains disputed: Rich rejects previous views that Augustus was moved to its composition by the severe illness which struck him in 23 BCE (cf. Cassius Dio 53.30–31). For a more detailed review, see ibid., 158n.52 and also Pausch, 'Formen', 312–14. Rich suggests instead that Augustus ended his account with the Cantabrian War because it was his last active military campaign. Cf. Zvi Yavetz, 'The *Res Gestae* and Augustus' Public Image', in *Caesar Augustus: Seven Aspects*, ed. by Fergus Millar and Erich Segal (Oxford: Clarendon Press, 1984), 4, who also suggests that following the Cantabrian War, Augustus did not return to his autobiography. However, Rich would have done better to clarify expressively that this mindset on the part of Augustus must have been a conscious decision (i.e., not to take part in any military campaigns), as otherwise Augustus could not have known at the time that the Cantabrian War would constitute his last campaign.
103 Neyrey, 'Josephus' *Vita*'.

greatest talents and achievements, he does not explicitly present himself as a continuous shining star but admits faults and the occasional setbacks. Such a strategy has been advised by various orators and literary critics such as Quintilian and Plutarch to remove the odium of praising oneself constantly. Moving forward, according to Mason's almost universally accepted theory, Josephus wrote *Life* to demonstrate his excellent character.[104] Josephus evidently intended to portray himself in the best possible light, while simultaneously ensuring that his audience did not react negatively to self-praise.

(b) Exemplary

As a secondary purpose of the encomium is 'to provide a model for the audience to follow', one might suggest that Josephus intended his self-portrayal to encourage his audience to act likewise.[105] However, considering that in the end Josephus lost his cause and found himself unable to bring his narrative to a successful conclusion, we can reject this notion. Outside the military and political sphere, Josephus does set himself up as an exemplary historian by demonstrating that he, contrary to others who had also written about the war, notably Justus of Tiberias, had undergone scientific research by reading the imperial *commentarii* and by proving that he had imperial and royal backing (e.g. by including Agrippa's endorsing letters, *Life* 365–66). This can be understood as Josephus offering up his credentials for writing the *Antiquities,* to which he had appended *Life.*[106]

(c) Informative

Josephus himself states that he wrote *Life* to inform his audience about the events of his life (*Ant.* 20.266–267, *Life* 430, cf. 82). Although McLaren does not consider these indications a comprehensive mission statement, given the observations of this analysis so far, there is little reason to doubt that Josephus wished to inform his audience about himself and certain events and experiences.[107] While it is

---

104 Mason, 'Essay'. See also Chapter 1.
105 Burridge, *Gospels*, 208.
106 Mason, 'Essay', 48, cf. 53, emphasizes the connection between *Antiquities* and *Life,* suggesting that Josephus wrote *Life* 'in support of his claim as author'. Bilde, *Josephus,* 110–13, had argued along the same lines.
107 McLaren, *Turbulent Times*, 69. As has been discussed, however, Josephus was not always overly concerned with providing historical facts as we would understand them. Cf. Wacholder, *Nicolaus,* 17, who wryly notes that in antiquity, publication of literature was less concerned with the presentation of facts but an expression of ideals. Rajak, *Josephus,* 146–55, understands *Life* as Josephus' effort as a survivor of the war to explain to a Judean aristocracy why he had failed as a commander in the war and why he had been rejected by the authorities in Jerusalem.

unlikely that Josephus at the point of writing *Life* was an unknown quantity in Rome, having lived and worked there for twenty years, there are several passages within *Life* in which Josephus demonstrably wishes to remind his audience of a given situation such as the conditions in Galilee (*Life* 30–61).

(d) To preserve memory/raise awareness

Josephus had been living in Rome for roughly twenty years prior to the publication of *Life*. Considering Mason's theory that his standing in Rome was less than prominent, one might suggest that Josephus wrote to regain some of the attention he had enjoyed immediately after the war. Alternatively, Cohen had advanced the theory that Josephus wanted to re-emphasize his Pharisaic leanings to garner the support of the rising Rabbinic faction in Yavneh following the destruction of the temple and the restructuring of Judaism.[108] Seth Schwartz argues that Josephus wrote *War* and *Antiquities* 'to memorialise the characters and events described in them.'[109] Schwartz considers the importance of memory in the Greco-Roman culture in terms of building works, epigraphy and literature, and discusses how Josephus reflects that awareness in a Judean socio-cultural context. We must consider the issue of memorialization in relation to the contemporaneous composition of autobiographies in the Greco-Roman literary context.[110]

(e) Didactic

A didactic purpose for *Life* is unlikely as Josephus did not follow a philosophy or religion he wanted to teach his audience. This stands in contrast especially to *Antiquities*, which Mason understands as a 'handbook for Gentiles', highlighting the benefits of a Judean constitution.[111]

---

108 For Mason's theory, see earlier, 'social setting', alongside the more extreme Cotton and Eck, 'Josephus' Roman Audience'. Cohen, *Josephus*, 145–7.
109 Seth Schwartz, 'Memory in Josephus and the Culture of the Jews in the First Century', in *Common Judaism: Explorations in Second-Temple Judaism*, ed. by Wayne O. McCready and Adele Reinhartz (Minnesota: Fortress Press, 2011), 187.
110 Schwartz does not discuss the issue in relation to memorialization of oneself and autobiography, yet a promising avenue of research would benefit from future investigation.
111 For example, Mason, 'Should Any Wish to Enquire Further', 79. Cf. Daube, 'Typology', 19.

(f) Apologetic and polemic

The notion that Josephus intended *Life* as an apologia against the accusations of Justus of Tiberias has long received a positive reception in Josephus' scholarship. Previous generations of scholars had argued that Justus, and other anonymous Judeans, had accused Josephus of various crimes against which Josephus intended to defend himself in *Life*. Clearly, Josephus directs a distinctly polemical section at Justus, in which he attacks his compatriot for being the real reason behind the revolt of Tiberias and for spreading lies about Josephus (*Life* 336-67).[112] Although recent trends have moved away from attributing a dual apologetic and polemic purpose to *Life*, it is worthwhile reiterating, if only to respect previous audience's reception of the text.

Several intentions may lie behind Josephus' decision to write his *Life* and one should not reject all for the benefit of only one.[113] Any work of literature can operate on several different levels, and it remains possible that the author intended for a variety of reactions, and perhaps received several reactions he had not anticipated.

Comparanda

The previously mentioned omission of prefaces and programmatic statements in the texts discussed here complicates a discussion of authorial intentions, and we rely on internal evidence as well as comments by third parties.

(a) Encomiastic

Rood has noted that later audiences attributed a celebratory aspect to the *Anabasis*, suggesting that the *Anabasis* has transcended into a myth of liberation.[114] Cicero insists in his letter to Lucceius that he was pressuring the historian so that his name could be celebrated (*celebretur*, *Fam.* 5.12.1) and to enjoy fame both during his lifetime and for posterity. Similarly, Marc Mayer attributes to Caesar the ultimate purpose of self-glorification in his *Gallic War*.[115]

---

112 See in more detail Cohen, *Josephus*, 132-7, and also Rajak, *Josephus*, 14. Hadas-Lebel, 'Le récit autobiographique', argues strongly that we should understand *Life* as a polemic history.
113 Cf. also Burridge's findings when discussing the intentions behind biographies: several purposes can easily be attributed simultaneously to the same text: Burridge, *Gospels*, 148.
114 Rood, 'Panhellenism', 328.
115 Mayer, 'Caesar', 196.

(b) Exemplary

Nicolaus' purpose shines through the extant fragments, as he presents himself as the ideal example of how to lead a virtuous philosopher's life. He portrays himself as a role model for other philosophers, setting up an exemplary blueprint on how best to maintain a philosophical lifestyle, suggesting that education ideally should lead to philosophy as opposed to wealth (F132), simultaneously acknowledging that persons preoccupied with material wealth on account of their position were easily distracted from this ultimate life goal (F135).[116]

(c) Informative

The numerous anthropological and geographical digressions in the *Gallic War* indicate Caesar's wish to inform his audience in Rome of the situation he and his army were facing in Gaul and Germany. Simultaneously, scholars have consistently advocated a propagandistic purpose for the *Gallic War*, suggesting that Caesar wanted to 'spin' the situation for his benefit, by re-educating and informing Rome about his view of the wars.[117] In his letter to Lucceius, Cicero makes several references to his potential audience and claims that his audience would be highly interested in an account of Cicero's achievements and the events of his past few years (*Fam.* 5.12.4–5). Libanius insists that he wrote in order to correct (πειρατέον ἐπανοτρθῶσαι, *Oration* 1.1) the misunderstandings in circulation about himself and to correct people's assumptions about himself – he wanted to ensure that his audience knew of his past and present circumstances (ὡς εἰδεῖεν ἅπαντες, *Oration* 1.1)

(d) To preserve memory/raise awareness

Cicero, alongside his wish for a contemporary audience, in his letters makes several references that he wanted to preserve a good memory of himself as he feared the judgement of later generations (*Fam.* 5.12.1; *Att.* 2.5.1).[118] Welch has suggested that Caesar insisted on an annual publication of the individual books of the *Gallic War* because he wanted to ensure that Rome would remember him

---

116 Wacholder, *Nicolaus*, 39; Misch, *Geschichte*, 184; Sizoo, 'Autobiographie'.
117 The definition of propaganda according to the Oxford Dictionary: 'information, especially of a biased or misleading nature, used to promote a political cause or point of view'. This fits with the serial publication of the *Gallic War* favoured by Welch, 'Caesar and His Officers', and Wiseman, 'The Publication of *De Bello Gallico*', who suggest that Caesar endeavoured to keep Rome informed of his progress and to maintain his popularity.
118 Cf. Kurczyk, *Cicero*, 62, who posits that Cicero pressured Lucceius in order to influence actively what posterity would think of him.

during his prolonged absence.[119] Lewis meanwhile has suggested the interesting issue of legitimate inheritance of power and succession as a leading purpose for imperial authors and their potential heirs in their literary pursuits.[120]

(e) Didactic

Rood has detected a didactic Xenophon in a variety of his speeches, in some of which he actively uses teaching terminology (e.g. διδάξων, *Anab.* 7.7.20) to instruct his characters on the art of leadership.[121]

(f) Apologetic and polemic

The earliest autobiographies had claimed defensive purposes, e.g. Plato's *Seventh Letter* 352A, or Demosthenes, *De cor.* 3-4. Scholarship has subsequently fairly consistently attributed apologetic purposes to later authors. Toher has claimed that the main characteristics of Hellenistic and Roman autobiography are self-defence and self-justification – evidenced by the proliferation of apologetic intentions attributed to the various texts.[122] Although Xenophon does not claim any purpose, given his omission of any programmatic statements, scholars have continuously attributed an apologetic purpose to the *Anabasis*, responding to a variety of accusations levelled against him, most prominently the participation in Cyrus' campaign for which ancient sources confirm he was sent into exile from his hometown of Athens (Pausanius 5.6.5; Dio Chrysostom, *Virt.* (*Or.* 8) 1).[123] Xenophon mentions several attacks against his decisions, actions and reputation in the *Anabasis*, and has his character defend himself simultaneously within the text as well as to his reading/listening audience; furthermore, Cawkwell suggests that Xenophon also had to deal with attacks against his person and behaviour years after the events.[124] Sulla's defensive aim is evident as he stresses the divine favour and directions he received, his reliance on dreams for difficult decisions, and his emphasis on his *felicitas* (e.g. Plutarch, *Sull.* 9.4).[125] From a comment

---

119 Welch, 'Caesar and His Officers', 85.
120 Lewis, 'Imperial Autobiography', esp. 703-4.
121 Rood, 'Panhellenism', 324.
122 Toher, 'Herod, Augustus, and Nicolaus', 73-4, where Toher suggests an apologetic purpose evident in Nicolaus' fragments, to answer any criticism about his lifestyle.
123 Hartmut Erbse, 'Xenophon's *Anabasis* (an Inaugural Address, Largely Unrevised, Delivered in Tübingen 14 Dezember 1965)', in *Xenophon,* ed. by Vivienne J. Gray (Oxford: Oxford University Press, 2010). Lane Fox, *Long March*, 21-2, states that the apology in the *katabasis* is most clearly evident in the direct speeches. See also Bernhard Zimmermann, 'Exil und Autobiographie', *Antike und Abendland* 48 (2002): 187-95 (190-2, 194).
124 See Rood, 'Panhellenism', 323-4, for a selection of such speeches; cf. also Cawkwell, 'When, How and Why', 67.
125 See further Tatum, 'Late Republic', 170-1; Thein, 'Felicitas'.

by Suetonius, it is clear that Augustus also had to deal with attacks against his person, more specifically his ancestry (*Aug.* 2.3), and Powell makes it very clear that the majority of extant fragments transmit a defensive note.[126] Powell uses the same method that Yavetz had applied to the extant fragments over twenty years earlier, although it does not appear that he was aware of Yavetz's approach, by picking up Augustus' positive statements and re-creating the negative attack to reconstruct the accusations against which Augustus had to defend himself.[127] Plutarch attests both a defensive purpose for Catulus, fighting for approval, as well as a polemic intention of accusing Marius:

ὅμοια δὲ καὶ τὸν Κάτλον αὐτὸν ἀπολογεῖσθαι περὶ τούτων ἱστοροῦσι,

πολλὴν κατηγοροῦντα τοῦ Μαρίου κακοήθειαν πρὸς αὐτόν.

And we are told that Catulus himself also made a similar statement in defence of his conduct in the battle, and accused Marius of great malice in his treatment of him. (Plutarch, *Mar.* 25.6)

Libanius, on the other hand, in his preface and throughout the narrative does mention numerous opponents and accusers but does not transmit an overly apologetic purpose. His preface notes that he would like to clear up rumours about himself and to correct people's opinion, but the narrative itself reads more celebratory than apologetic, strongly reminiscent of Josephus' laudatory undertones; I am unable to detect a 'Rechtfertigungszwang', as Wintjes formulates.[128] On the other hand, what appears to be an impromptu outcry suggests an underlying polemic purpose. Libanius narrates how he was consistently accused and attacked by various opponents, and the polemic is visible to the extent that, although most of them remain anonymous, he does relish the fact that many of them come to unfavourable ends. He makes his (adversary, polemic) emotions explicit, exclaiming that ideally, a third party should have reported these events because they would not have 'an axe to grind' (*Oration* 1.37, transl. Loeb).

---

126 Powell, 'Augustus' Age of Apology', esp. 174: 'it is authoritatively agreed'. Mellor, *Roman Historians*, 178 also notes that fragments suggest a polemical/defensive tone in response to accusations raised by Augustus' political opponents during the civil war 44–31 BCE, such as a low family status, no talents, accusations of cruelty and treachery. The emperor's autobiography, so Mellor, was part of a campaign to transform his image. Note Suetonius, *Aug.* 27, for an emphasis on loyalty and clemency as imperial characteristics. Dobesch, 'Nikolaos von Damaskus', 125, also interprets the imperial autobiography apologetically, as a justification of the new political landscape.

127 Yavetz, 'The Res Gestae', 3, 6. He finds 'apologetic, defensive, occasionally polemic undercurrents', reacting to 'slander', 6. A popular approach, used similarly by Rajak, 'Justus of Tiberias', in an attempt to reconstruct the allegations raised by Justus of Tiberias.

128 Wintjes, *Leben Des Libanius*, 176.

We see that a variety of purposes can be attributed to the same text and that an *apologetic purpose has been attributed to almost every text here discussed, including* Life.

Summary and conclusion

The setting of *Life* is representative of its author and confined to his movements. The repetitive, simple style does not compare well to Josephus' other works, and *Life* evokes a rather serious atmosphere, perhaps reflecting the author's wish to be taken seriously. The tension between the quality of characterization of both Josephus and his opponents as opposed to the historical situation, as far as we can trace it, is discernible, although perhaps not at first glance. Nevertheless, Josephus directed *Life* at an educated audience able to pick up various subtleties within the text. Due to the vagaries of ancient publishing, it remains difficult to confirm an exact publication date, although a rough timeframe places the publication late into Josephus' life. A variety of purposes have been attributed to *Life*, implying that the purpose behind a text is dependent both on the author and audience, and can change – or be perceived differently – depending on the parameters.

The comparative texts exhibit similar internal features. The author/subject remains the focus of the settings, and a variety of *topoi* are used. The style of most texts is simple, especially when compared within the respective author's own corpus, but still polished, except for Cicero who praises his own style extensively. The atmosphere in all texts is serious with an underlying current of either pride or self-defence, and the quality of characterization results in a dynamic tension between the characters portrayed and their historical situation. An educated audience can be assumed for all texts, although there remains a difference between whether the audience was local and aware of the author's situation and experiences, or whether the text was directed at an audience in a social setting foreign to the author. An even divide has become evident with authors either publishing their texts immediately after the events in question, in which case the temporal scale is generally more limited or towards the end of their careers, with a more generous temporal scale. Xenophon here proves an exception – the date of publication for the *Anabasis* is generally held to be thirty years after the events. An apologetic authorial intention can be attributed to all texts.

It is evident that in terms of the internal features, no text falls out of line consistently except for the *Anabasis*' time of composition. There are also common points of reference between all texts, expressively including *Life*. It is noteworthy that the differences that do occur can be divided evenly into two categories and do not cover a wide span of possibilities, thus preserving a streamlined harmony between the various texts.

7

Conclusions of the analysis

This study of Josephus' *Life* has drawn on several fields of expertise to discuss the existence of the genre of autobiography in antiquity, and to situate *Life* in its relationship to, and position within, the genre. Classical literature and history, literary theory and knowledge of Josephus himself have all added valuable information to our understanding of the genre, its constituents and how far Josephus as author reacted to his literary milieu. Individual summaries have been included at every stage, leading to the final conclusions that ancient autobiography indeed existed as a recognizable genre, that *Life* belongs to the genre, and that Josephus wrote in reaction to, and in relation to, the parameters of that genre.

Review of the previous chapters

The first chapter provided a survey of the various genre proposals put forward for *Life*. The earliest scholarly assessments had rejected *Life* as autobiography based on modern expectations of insight and an expressive self-consciousness. Scholars have since understood that ancient literature must be evaluated on its own terms and feel able to use the appellation autobiography much more freely and confidently. Nevertheless, several scholars have recently suggested other genres, such as the encomium, or have instead moved away from *Life* and focused on Josephus' autobiographical narrative in *War*.[1] Opinions within the scholarly discourse range from rejecting the existence of the genre based on modern expectations to an acknowledgement that some ancient texts offered important precursors to the modern genre of autobiography to accepting the existence of ancient autobiography. This lack of consensus has of course fuelled recent discussions, and the field has seen a rise in publications on the genre of autobiography in antiquity. However, while the concept and terminology of genre

---

1   For example, Neyrey, 'Josephus' *Vita*'; Hirschberger, 'Historiograph'; Villalba Varneda, 'Early Empire'.

and autobiography have been freely applied in the academic discourse, we have seen few approaches with genre theory as a methodological basis. Consequently, Chapter 2 outlined the basic concepts of ancient and modern genre theory. The coherence on genre allows for the application of an approach based on modern genre theory, as previous studies in other genres within classical and biblical literature have successfully demonstrated by employing a variety of established opening, external and internal features to formulate a generic framework.

To that end, Chapter 3 considered a range of Greek and Latin works which had at some point in their wider reception history been associated with autobiography because of their potential direct and indirect influence on Josephus and because of their influence on the literary and social milieu that Josephus was dialoguing with. The list of features used in the literary analysis in Chapters 4–6 was comprehensive, encompassing an analysis of title, preface, an analysis of verb subjects, allocation of space, mode of representation, size/length, structure, scale, literary units, sources, method of characterization, settings, topoi, style, atmosphere, quality of characterization, social setting, time of composition, and authorial intention and purpose.

The present chapter will now discuss the practical results of the analysis, beginning with the question of how far a framework for the genre of ancient autobiography can be established, keeping in mind that such a potential framework must not be equated with strict guidelines. In the next chapter, the implications of the analysis and understanding *Life* as an autobiography will be discussed in the form of a brief re-reading of *Life* and suggestions of further avenues along which *Life* might be interpreted differently *qua* autobiography. Building on previous scholarship and existing interpretations of *Life* and Josephus as its author, we gain new insights into how Josephus uses genre to encourage his audience to identify with himself and how he subsequently leads his audience(s) on a merry journey of veiled criticism, irony and encouragement. The present study offers a further reading model for *Life* and the following evaluation of the analysis and re-reading of the book suggests the value of asking different questions of a text and approaching it from different angles and different theories.

Conclusions of the literary analysis

Pattern

From this study several important conclusions and contributions were drawn for the genre of ancient autobiography and *Life*. Foremost in terms of general classical scholarship, the existence of a genre based on family resemblance emerged. The literary analysis has demonstrated an overall pattern regarding many of the features examined. The following features have shown consistent and continuous results: title words (except for Xenophon's *Anabasis*), the calculation of verb subjects, allocation of space, mode of representation, structure (except for Cicero's *commentarius*), literary units, method of characterization, sources, geographical and dramatic setting, topoi, style, atmosphere, quality of characterization, social setting and intention. The conclusions allow us to understand and visualize the existence of a recognized genre, enabling us to move away from modal perceptions of autobiographic or autobiographical and instead to conceptualize ancient autobiography. The present analysis has highlighted several features which the texts share with only a minimal degree of variation. Among the features discussed, the reception history/title attributed, verb statistics, allocation of space and purpose all display a high level of agreement among each other. For example, the titles and title phrases are all inter-related across the Latin/Greek language barrier using a combination of terms including *res gestae*, βίος/*vita*, *commentarius* and ὑπόμνημα; the authors as subjects dominate the number of sentences and passages in which they feature either actively or passively; the allocation of space divides consistently between authors who either focus on a specific, and usually comparatively short, period of their life in the public eye, or cover a wider range up to an entire life account. It is notable that these features are easily recognizable to a listening audience and thus allow a quick, intuitive recognition and subsequent interpretation of the text as part of a generic discourse. Notably, Josephus' *Life* shares all these features, and more, to a high degree of assimilation.

Within this established pattern, we cannot expect the texts to be 100 per cent identical in their use and application of the respective features. Genres are dynamic, and genre theory is not an exact science; nevertheless, the texts all found themselves in the same region of a given spectrum, demonstrating a high degree of Wittgenstein's family resemblance. The individual usage of features allows us to see which texts move close to the centre of the genre and which texts move towards the blurred boundary regions and share features borrowed from their *genera proxima*, notably the *Anabasis*. The inherent fluidity of genre, which allows for such movements, also prohibits us from prescribing a pattern of set, mandatory features which may be misunderstood as being 'standard'.[2]

---

2   Cf. Lewis, 'Imperial Autobiography', 658: 'Republican grandees had in the late second and early first centuries B.C. developed prototypes which allowed some degree of variation to suit individual requirements but were in essentials standardised.' Lewis correctly points to individual variation,

This extends to the concept of a hierarchy, as a text closer to the centre of a genre, presenting a large number of visible features, is not 'better' at its genre than a text at the fringes of the genre.

The literary analysis has simultaneously demonstrated some variations in a few features. In these cases, it was evident that the works separated into two groups in their application of the respective features.[3] Within these divisions, we tend to find on the one hand the works of Augustus, Nicolaus and Libanius, and the works of Catulus, Cicero and Caesar on the other. The division into two distinct groups shows us the existence of two sub-genres based on content, specifically allocation of space. They either narrate the author's entire life up to the date of composition (e.g. Nicolaus, Augustus, Libanius), or focus the content on only a brief, but intense, period of their lives (e.g. Catulus, Cicero, Caesar). Scholars have of course previously noted the existence of a division, but have failed to account for the relationship between what Lewis calls 'commentarii' and 'comprehensive autobiography' or Pausch's Augustan and Caesarian modes.[4] Lewis points out the difficulty of deciding between 'autobiography in the strictest sense' and those accounts that cover only a small portion of a life.[5] The concept of genre and sub-genres effectively solves this problem.

Following on from determining the existence of a genre based on family resemblance, a name is necessary. Given the organic nature of genre and constant mutations, we must not be surprised that we have not been able to define a definitive name for this genre. Modern contributions to the topic have used a variety of terms such as autobiography, autobiographic, autobiographical or memoir, at times seemingly without coherence or distinction between the

---

but in his discussion places too much emphasis on the 'standard' form or features found in ancient autobiographies, for example, 663, 665, 669, 688, 694, 695, 700. The variations found within the family resemblance highlighted in this study should preclude us from expecting such standard autobiographies, although of course those examples which move towards the centre of the genre, thus displaying the highest degree of family resemblance, may appear to be standard.

3   The features in which a division was evident: the use of a prologue, a discrepancy regarding the respective length of the various works, topoi, the scale, mode of presentation, as well as the time and circumstances of composition. It must be said, however, that our lack of knowledge, resulting from the fragmentary state of several works, does impact on these conclusions.
4   Lewis, 'Imperial Autobiography', 629; Pausch, 'Formen', 319. cf. also Tatum, 'Late Republic', 162–3.
5   Lewis, 'Imperial Autobiography', 630. Cf. also Villalba Varneda, 'Early Empire', who in his discussion of early imperial autobiographies and memoirs distinguishes between 'personal memoirs', 'memoirs/reports' and 'Josephus'. For a review of Varneda's contribution to the discussion of *Life*, see Chapter 1. The concept of sub-genres within ancient autobiography may also help towards countering Pelling's negative argumentation. Pelling, 'Ancient Genre', 44, treats the works of Sulla, Cicero, Caesar, Augustus, and the *RGDA* together despite sharper differences, and from them derives a 'looseness of generic expectations', doubting the existence of the genre as a whole. See Chapter 1 for a review of Pelling's position.

concept of genre or mode. Ancient authors and critics knew corresponding works under different and overlapping titles such as ὑπόμνημα, *commentarius*, *de vita sua*, βίος.[6] This mixing indicates the existence of a relationship between all of them and an ancient genre awareness of that relationship, and simultaneously a process to determine a comprehensive appellation.[7] Applying the term 'autobiography' therefore is justified if the term is used free of any modern value judgement.[8]

It has been pointed out that literary theory recognizes shifts in the development and life of a genre; we know that 'not only do generic labels change with time, but also ... the same labels come to be used in different ways'.[9] At certain points in the life-cycle of a genre, shifts and mutations occur; the designation continues to exist but comes to be understood differently, or *mutatis mutandis* the same texts come to be designated by a different, evolved, term. Therefore, applying the term 'autobiography' to ancient autobiography as the genre defined in this study is in line with such generic shifts and does not open us up to the charge of anachronism.[10] Recent suggestions rejecting the term 'autobiography' for the ancient period can therefore be put aside.[11]

We see a precedent for the lack of a definitive genre title in the genre of the ancient novel, or rather the hunt for the ancient novel, quoting Albrecht Dihle: 'more often we do not know whether the Greeks had an unequivocal

---

6   Cf. Chapter 3. It is a serious scholarly omission that to date little work has been done to explain the various titles and designations attributed to a single work by classical authors roughly contemporaneous with each other (Plutarch, Suetonius, Tertullian, Appian).
7   Ancient genre awareness is demonstrated by Cicero: *scribam ipse de me, multorum tamen exemplo et clarorum virorum. sed, quod te non fugit, haec sunt in hoc genere vitia: et verecundius ipsi de sese scribant necesse est si quid est laudandum et praetereant si quid reprehendendum est.* – 'Namely I will write about myself – and yet I shall have many illustrious precedents. But I need not point out to you that this genre has certain disadvantages. He who writes about himself must needs write modestly where praise is due and pass over anything that calls for censure.' (Cicero, *Fam.* 5.12.8, transl. adapted from Loeb). Regardless of the implications suggested by Cicero inherent in writing autobiography, there existed a genre awareness.
8   These ancient catchphrases retained their genre-defining power in later literature, as is evident in titles of autobiographies such as Gerald of Wales' *De rebus a se gestis* (c. 1146–1223) or Peter Abelard's *Historia calamitatum* (c. 1079–1142).
9   Fowler, *Kinds of Literature*, 130.
10 Here the present study differs from Burridge, *Gospels*, 60, who preferred the term 'βίος' as distinct from biography precisely because of any modern connotations and expectations. In his later works, however, Burridge has moved away from his earlier terminology and instead refers to ancient biographies.
11 For example, Irmgard Männlein-Robert, 'The Meditations as an (Philosophical) Autobiography', in *A Companion to Marcus Aurelius*, ed. by Marcel van Ackeren (Chichester, Malden: Wiley-Blackwell), 363, who quotes Momigliano ('there was no established ancient term for the phenomenon we call autobiography') and suggests based on modern autobiography theory that there was no such genre, and that we should use terms such as 'autobiographic texts'. Cf. also Villalba Varneda, 'Early Empire', who insists on placing autobiography in quotation marks, as does Rajak, *Josephus*, 107, 166, on occasion. *Contra* also Cohen, *Josephus*, 101, arguing that a 'precise place' for *Life* in the development of autobiography could not be found.

term for the type in question'.¹² Tim Whitmarsh has recently gathered together the disparate group of ancient texts generally referred to as ancient novels and asks whether it makes sense to study a range of texts in Greek and Latin, composed over a long period of time, together.¹³ Whitmarsh notes that while antiquity lacked a distinctive name for the novel, we know of varied terms such as *fabula, argumentum, fabella,* λόγος, μῦθος.¹⁴ In parallel to the present approach, Whitmarsh argues that we must use the concept of genre flexibly, as 'the non-existence of the *name* "novel" in ancient Greek does not outweigh the fact that there are so many parallels of structure, form and theme between the different texts'.¹⁵ The texts and their authors demonstrate the marks of generic organization and awareness, and we must credit authors and audiences with the ability to compose and recognize genres and generic relationships.

Writing about oneself in antiquity was frequent enough to create guidelines and genre awareness. It is significant that the text which finds itself outside the pattern, Xenophon's *Anabasis,* comes from an earlier period of experimentation. We see the evolution of a literary consciousness at work; the overall demonstration of a family resemblance, and especially the title words indicated a period of evolution and formation. While the genre is not explicitly defined to the extent of other genres such as tragedy or comedy, it is certainly part of the literary milieu and recognized as such by critics, authors and audiences.

---

12 Albrecht Dihle, 'Rev. Of *What Are the Gospels?* By Richard Burridge', *International Journal of the Classical Tradition* 1 (1995): 124.
13 Tim Whitmarsh, *The Cambridge Companion to the Greek and Roman Novel* (Cambridge: Cambridge University Press, 2008). See also the comparable exercise undertaken for the similarly debated genre 'apocalypse' by the Society of Biblical Literature genres project, in John J. Collins, *Apocalypse: The Morphology of a Genre* (Semeia 14. Missoula: Scholars Press, 1979). Collins, similarly to Whitmarsh and the present study, coherently argues that while most works referred to as apocalypse by scholars were not explicitly designated as such in antiquity, the genre is not a modern construct. See also idem., *The Apocalyptic Imagination: An Introduction to Jewish Apocalyptic Literature*, 3rd edn (Grand Rapids: Wm. B. Eerdmans Publishing Co., 2016), 3–5. Here, Collins refers to Fowler's three phases of generic development and argues that the earlier apocalypses lacked the generic self-confidence evident in the second phase of generic development, but had nevertheless already assembled themselves into a genre. According to Collins, the presence or absence of a title cannot be regarded as a definitive criterion for the identification of a genre. Instead, as I argue in the present study, one must ask whether a group of texts shares a cluster of features or traits that distinguishes them from others. See further Chapter 2; Fowler, 'Life and Death'; and the discussion as follows on the relative position of *Life* in Fowler's phases.
14 Ibid., 3. See also Gert-Jan van Dijk, *Ainoi, Logoi, Mythoi: Fables in Archaic, Classical, and Hellenistic Greek Literature; with a Study of the Theory and Terminology of the Genre* (Leiden: Brill, 1997).
15 Whitmarsh, *Novel,* 190.

Texts outside the pattern

It is important to point out that no individual texts determined as relevant fall out of line consistently except for the *Anabasis*, which varies significantly from the other texts in regard to several features (e.g. title, structure, mode of representation, time of composition).[16] Furthermore, Xenophon only introduces himself as an actor in the narrative in the third book, using instead the authorial pseudonym Themistogenes (Xenophon, *Hell.* 2.4.2, cf. Plutarch, *Glor. Ath.* 345E). This could be explained by noting that several centuries lie between the composition of the *Anabasis* (around 370 BCE) and the other texts, most of which date to the first centuries BC and BCE; we must imagine a literary and generic evolution in which the *Anabasis* represents Fowler's proto-stage. Literary genres develop naturally, and it is evident that we can trace the development process which came to fruition centuries after the composition of the *Anabasis*, but which was already in motion at the time. Authors roughly contemporary with Xenophon such as Isocrates (436–338 BCE) and Demosthenes (384–322 BCE) also attempted to write about themselves, but simultaneously felt the need to set up a fictional framework (a fictional law court) to facilitate the transmission of their works – comparable to Xenophon's pseudonym.[17] We see here authors experimenting with various genres and possibilities to express themselves within the contemporary cultural restrictions, and the result of these experiments is visible in the remainder of the texts discussed in this analysis.

Life

The place of Josephus' *Life* within ancient literature can now be more comfortably determined. Previously, scholars had instinctively noted that *Life*, as autobiography, adhered to previous literary models, emphasizing its participation

---

16 The title of the *Anabasis* remains an interesting feature that may warrant further discussion. It is attested by Diogenes Laertius, third century CE, and has been accepted without question. On the one hand, a title without any generic connotations correlates with the contemporary titles of Isocrates' *Antidosis* and Demosthenes' *De Corona*; all three works incorporate the life of the author in an artificial framework. However, Plutarch's intriguing comment about Xenophon becoming his own history by writing about his generalship refers to the *Anabasis* (*Glor. Ath.* 345E), and he clearly expects his audience to make the connection: Ξενοφῶν μὲν γὰρ αὐτὸς ἑαυτοῦ γέγονεν ἱστορία.

17 Isocrates, *Antid.* 1–13, cf. Demosthenes, *De cor.* 1–4 where he apologizes in advance for talking about himself. However, in his *Evagoras* (esp. 8–11), Isocrates is proud to attempt something new by praising a man in prose rather than verse. This hiding behind a narrative must not be taken for evidence that writing about, and praising oneself was frowned upon and not well received generally, but rather as evidence for the fact that the custom had not yet been established. These circumstances have at times been read in combination with Cicero's letter to Lucceius to suggest that only desperate or socially less secure men would reach to autobiography, overlooking the time and cultural differences between the two authors.

in the genre.[18] However, the extent to which Josephus composed his *Life* in line with the contemporaneous literary models had been underestimated. Josephus' *Life* as an independent text conforms to the parameters of the genre, presents itself as a conservative representative thereof and is simultaneously highly innovative. Overall, the study has shown a high degree of correlation between *Life* and the other comparative texts within the broad category of autobiography. Every feature which Josephus as author employs is typical and conforms well to the overall family resemblance, and, notably, he employs features found on either side of the aforementioned sub-genre division. He merges the two sub-genres identified in the course of the present literary analysis, which are distinguished by their content, specifically allocation of space. Josephus accomplishes this by framing his military period in Galilee with an abbreviated account spanning his entire life.

Consequently, we can now ascertain how far Josephus aligned *Life* with the pattern and framework provided by the other texts, and how far he contributes to the development of the genre. Considering that Josephus wrote in Rome as one of the later authors from a chronological perspective, it is unsurprising that *Life* moves comfortably within the established pattern of the generic features, employing a variety of features reminiscent of other texts. What is significant, however, is the regular consistency with which *Life* conforms to the features. While the texts compared in this study will stand out at times in terms of one feature or another, *Life* does not exhibit any unusual patterns but rather stands out by its lack of deviation.[19] Some parallels might of course be due to the contemporary literary milieu in which Josephus was writing, and its influences, as well as the constrictions imposed on ancient literature. However, the lack of any deviation at all indicates that Josephus was highly aware of his literary construct while writing and intent on writing in a conservative fashion. He presents his audience with a mix of both sub-genres, by framing a short, military-minded period of his life with details about his ancestry, youth and private life (*Life* 1–27, 412–30), and repetitive βίος terminology. Josephus consciously transcends the boundaries of the two sub-genres while still staying within the limits of the familiar generic features.[20] He adapts the different trends highlighted in regard

---

18 See Chapter 1, and most recently, Adams, *Greek Genres*, 251.
19 For example, Xenophon's title; Cicero's topical structure and elevated style; Catulus' single-minded purpose; Caesar's omission of the divine in any manner; the method of characterization by Nicolaus; Sulla's excessive length; the intermediate time span covered by Augustus, who neither wrote an account of his whole life, nor focused on a short, intense period.
20 This contradicts the assumption voiced by Price that Josephus, by focusing on a short period only and not giving an account of his whole life, did not adhere to the requirements of ancient autobiography: Price, 'Josephus', 223.

to the allocation of space, earlier, and we see the generic awareness and literary sensitivity he demonstrates by picking up on these trends and adapting them to his own needs. Josephus wanted to write conservatively, to stay within the parameters of the genre, but at the same time by structuring *Life* as he did, he offers an original contribution to the genre by actively merging the two subgenres. In this aspect, *Life* is the first fully extant example of its kind, although we must note the loss of much material. It remains possible that Josephus merely copied his structure and blend from a literary predecessor, although the results of the literary analysis have not indicated the presence of such a combination.[21]

Returning briefly to *Life*'s relationship to *Antiquities*, we had earlier noted that several authors had included brief autobiographical notices in works participating in other genres and it remains likely that Josephus, inspired by what Mason correctly refers to as a fashionable trend, by connecting *Life* to *Antiquities*, proved innovative and expanded on these brief notices which served to create a specific authorial persona.[22] If we develop that thought further, we can more confidently understand the relationship between *Life* and *Antiquities*; the inherent fluidity of genre and genres highlights their compatibility. Josephus evidently understood that by expanding on these brief accounts, by incorporating his thought-out autobiography into the final words of *Antiquities*, he benefitted from the relationship between the genres which he could successfully connect while retaining their individual independence and recognizability.[23] Josephus very successfully manipulates and responds to his audiences' expectations and transitions between genres. The gentle but clear transition also serves to highlight Josephus as standing at the end of Judean antiquities, both figuratively and literally. The inclusion of a fully worked out and thought-out *Life*, as opposed to a brief autobiographical reference, at the end of his masterful narrative presents Josephus as an equal part of contemporaneous Judean history.[24]

Fowler's developmental stages

Josephus' aforementioned process of blending and merging encourages us to consider the developmental stages of the genre. Scholars have frequently traced

---

21 The loss of Nicolaus' autobiography is unfortunate, as we know that Josephus was intimately acquainted with his literature. As Toher, 'Herod, Augustus, and Nicolaus', suggests, it is possible that Josephus took much of his Herod material from Nicolaus' autobiography rather than his *Historia universalis*.
22 Cf. Mason, *Life*, xii, xlii, and Hau, 'Narrator'.
23 See also Adams, *Greek Genres*, 254.
24 Cf. Damgaard, *Moses*, 130.

a process of development from the early attempts by Xenophon to the later, more established and confident texts.[25] The results of the literary analysis, however, demonstrate the relative stages of the process and the interdependencies, as well as Josephus' position within this process. Looking again to literary theory, the basis of this study's approach, Fowler understands the life of a genre to consist of the proto-state, the primary, secondary and tertiary levels. When we adapt these stages to ancient autobiography, we see the earliest attempts, the proto-state and origins, in Xenophon and contemporaneous authors, who struggle to express themselves in their search for a suitable vehicle. The primary stage, a recognizable group, emerges, including many texts discussed in my analysis, such as Sulla, Augustus and Catulus, who all contribute to the formation of the genre. The classical concepts of μίμησις/*imitatio* and propriety are germane to this development.[26] Josephus, then, creates the secondary stage, as he consciously reacts to and modifies the primary stage. The third state, in which an author takes the genre and creates something radically new, is evident in the Christian aspect, which begins to focus on the inner self and its journey *qua* autobiography.[27]

Within the endless cycle of the life and death of literary forms, this third stage can represent a shift within genre and simultaneously can be the first stage of a new genre. The end becomes something new. In the case of ancient autobiography, we see its third stage culminate in Augustine's *Confessions*, who takes the genre on to a new journey and who represents the third and first stage respectively, and brings us full circle to the question of who actually wrote the first autobiography.[28] We see that Augustine can in fact be considered as a first author in the history of autobiography, in so far as he represents the first

---

25 See, for example, the recent compilations by Reichel, *Antike Autobiographien*, and Marasco, *Political Autobiographies*, who offer individual chapters on various periods or individual authors. Their approach, while it offers valuable insight into these individual periods, cannot highlight to the same level any continuous threads or developments as a comprehensive literary analysis can.
26 Cf. Burridge, *Gospels*, 44.
27 Note Fowler, *Kinds of Literature*, 82, that this need not be a chronological process, but rather relative to the development of the genre.
28 Scholars frequently nominate Augustine as the author of the first autobiography, based mainly on his ability to present an inner self-awareness and self-knowledge. Gusdorf, 'Conditions'; Pascal, *Die Autobiographie*, 22–3; Weintraub, *Value of the Individual*, 1, 45. Sturrock, *Language*, begins his discussion of autobiography with Augustine. See also Smith and Watson, *Reading Autobiography*, 105. It is notable that these literary theorists do not consider what Augustine himself thought he was writing. Very recently, Paula Fredriksen, historian rather than literary theorist, has asked exactly this question, suggesting that an approach that understands the *Confessions* primarily as an autobiography comes at the cost of the coherence of the work as a whole: Paula Fredriksen, 'The *Confessions* as Autobiography', in *A Companion to Augustine*, ed. by Mark Vessey with the assistance of Shelley Reid (Chichester, West Sussex, Malden: Wiley-Blackwell, 2012), 89. We see here different interpretations of the *Confessions* other than autobiography, and the difficulty of reading and interpreting ancient texts when we do not know the genre, or rather interpret a text according to the interpretative framework offered by differing genre understandings.

stage of a new period within the life of that genre and not the first author of autobiography.²⁹ He clearly expresses his wish that his audience, with sufficient literary knowledge, read the *Confessions* as a book about himself (*a primo usque decimum de me scripti sunt*, Retract. 2.6.1, cf. *Epist.* 231.6), expecting them to acknowledge and interpret the book(s) accordingly.

---

29 For a refreshing article reading Augustine's *Confessions* as autobiography, see Michael Stuart Williams, 'Augustine's *Confessions* as Autobiography', in *The Oxford Handbook of Ancient Biography*, ed. by Koen de Temmerman (New York: Oxford University Press, 2020).

8

A new reading

Implications: Re-reading *Life* through autobiography

In this study, we understand genre as a vehicle that helps the author to communicate a message to the audience; the audience as part of the process becomes, in a sense, a co-conspirator. The value of reading a text through its genre is explained by Burridge who offers the example of Mark's depiction of the disciples lacking in faith.[1] The disciples are frequently presented as failing to understand Jesus' teachings, and previous interpretative approaches have suggested the rather slow disciples represent other early leaders whom Mark is attacking in the narrative.[2] Burridge instead suggests that when read through the genre of βίος, the passages become much clearer: the purpose of these misunderstandings and errors was not related to the disciples, but rather as a reflection of the narrative subject; biography focuses on the central figure, Jesus. The point to be made is that Jesus was difficult to understand but he will teach even those who struggle.[3]

If knowing and understanding the implications of a text's genre is important for interpretation, then the focus of interpreting *Life* must rest on Josephus and how he presents himself in relation to his narrative content and context. The question closes in on what Josephus' choice of genre tells us about himself and the text. The choice of genre constitutes a deliberate act, a continuity with the author's literary precursors. Using the theory of genre and moving forward from the results of the present analysis, discussed earlier, we can approach *Life* with an even more nuanced understanding, which must of course impact on the way we read the text. The present reading of *Life*, while brief, will hopefully open further avenues of research and deepen our understanding of its content and

---

1 Burridge, *Gospels,* 289–90.
2 Ibid.
3 Ibid., 290.

context; the immediate results are threefold, yet all related. Using the genre of autobiography, Josephus asks his audience to identify with himself, as a Judean; it enhances his statements and message concerning, and reaching out to, the Judean aristocracy, as writing *Life* suggests that Josephus was as good, if not better, at being Roman as the Romans, which in turn leads to further insights into Josephus' use of irony and criticism of the Flavian imperial family and the imperial institution.

Living *Life* through its characters

Within the genre of autobiography, the lead character the audience is asked to identify with is Josephus himself. The first-person perspective adds additional power to this process, and as has been shown in the analysis, Josephus preferably uses the personal pronoun ἐγώ in addition to the first-person verb form, further emphasizing the perspective and strengthening the perceived ties between himself as a character and the audience. He pulls the audience in by introducing himself in the prologue and offering himself and his character up for judgement. Subsequently, Josephus takes the audience along with him on a ride through his life, sharing his inside knowledge with them and thus reeling them into his side.

Mason, as part of his discussion on Josephus' use of irony, has highlighted Josephus' use of doublespeak. Mason demonstrates how Josephus includes the audience in his decision-making process, for example by explaining his decision to agree publicly with the masses intent on revolt due to the fear he and his like-minded peers experienced (*Life* 20–3), or by explaining that he only appointed seventy leading Galileans his friends in order to keep an eye on them (79).[4] Reading these passages with our renewed understanding of autobiography, we are afforded new insights and can see that not only do the passages demonstrate Josephus' literary capabilities and grasp of irony, but they serve the additional task of allowing the audience to understand the situation better from Josephus' point of view and, importantly, to side with him, that is, to identify with him and to carry the decisions alongside him.

Consequently, the audience can feel the suspense alongside Josephus and celebrate his success. As mentioned earlier in the analysis, the atmosphere especially in the main narrative of *Life* is a cycle of suspense and relief. Josephus finds himself in a dangerous situation and heroically rescues himself only for the narrative to jump to another such cycle. For example, Josephus' opponents

---

4   Mason, 'Figured Speech', 276, 279.

in Tiberias arrange for a public fast and call for the people to come unarmed, hoping thereby to catch Josephus unaware and unable to defend himself (*Life* 290–2). Josephus, however, arrives at the meeting with two guards and is forced to defend himself publicly against several accusations; during this questioning, the mood of the originally hostile crowd swings in Josephus' favour (294–300). The cycle of suspense and relief continues as a group of armed soldiers under John's leadership approaches, again endangering Josephus' life (301–2). We next read of mobs rushing to Josephus' aid, throwing stones, and of Josephus being rescued suddenly and unexpectedly from this danger (303–4).

It is this sense of success which shapes the last part of the main narrative dealing with Josephus' enemies, a euphoria which carries over into the epilogue when Josephus returns the focus back to the Romans. Josephus continues to be celebrated by Vespasian and Titus whereby the audience, having spent the previous part of *Life* identifying with him, can sympathize and feel equally special, superior and successful.

Reading the Flavians through the author

As mentioned earlier, Mason in detail presents and explains Josephus' artistic use of irony in his writings, suggesting it was employed to critique the Flavians subtly and to present a version of them that strongly differed from their preferred self-presentation.[5] Successful irony demands from the audience a certain amount of circumstantial knowledge in order to understand an implied message that transcends the explicit statement. Given the pervasive presence of irony in his writings, targeting for example Titus, Mason concludes that Josephus must have been secure in the knowledge that his audience would appreciate the irony and that Josephus himself was 'a master of oblique discourse, misdirection, and irony'.[6]

If we now remember that Josephus wrote in a genre that was recognizable in Rome and strongly associated with the imperial families, in itself an ironic choice, we can read the passages that reflect directly on Rome and the imperial position and we can see how Josephus says one thing but expects (parts of) his audience to understand something different.[7] In *Life* 1–16, Josephus presents

---

5 Ibid.
6 Ibid., 288.
7 Genre impacts on historical reliability, so it is little wonder previous scholars despaired of *Life* with its perceived inconsistencies. However, the focus of this discussion is not the historicity behind the narrative. See instead recently the relevant notes in Mason, *Life,* and den Hollander, *Josephus,* 31, who delves into the 'lived reality' behind the events narrated. Instead, this discussion focuses on the

himself as better at being Roman than the Romans, and especially in *Life* 407–30, we detect a further layer of critique aimed against the Flavians as Josephus presents himself, and by implication his audience, as superior to Vespasian and Titus.

For example, Josephus' trip to Rome (12–16), has been interpreted in a variety of ways, most recently as an opportunity for Josephus to parade his diplomatic and international success and to showcase his high-reaching contacts at the imperial court, reflecting on his character.[8] Knowing the genre of *Life* and the generic implications as outlined earlier, we can add a further layer of interpretation to this passage that compares Josephus directly with the imperial position. Josephus recounts how he was sent to Rome to secure the release of unnamed priests. Reaching Rome after an arduous and dangerous journey, Josephus narrates how through Aliturus, an actor favoured by Nero, he gained access to the emperor's wife Poppaea Sabina and was able to bring about the priests' release. There are several implicit comparisons within this narrative, between Josephus on the one hand and Roman characters on the other. For example, in *Life* 13, the procurator Felix and the emperor are paired against Josephus and the priests whom he describes as close acquaintances and καλοὺς κἀγαθοὺς.[9] Comparison between Josephus and the imperial position is heightened by the respectively associated characters: Josephus claims to be as close to the mindful priests who were undeserving of such harsh treatments, surviving on figs and nuts (14), as the emperor was close to the actor Aliturus (μάλιστα τῷ Νέρωνι καταθύμιος, 16). The emperor in fact cannot achieve any status as the passage begins with Felix and a reference to his title, Caesar, rather than to Nero's name himself, and ends with Nero being replaced by Aliturus and Poppaea Sabina, who is presented as being responsible for releasing the imperial prisoners (16).

This imperial weakness in the face of Josephus' strength and successful appearance is continued in the later scenes featuring imperial characters. Vespasian for example is introduced to the narrative in a cloud of accusations (407–9): the Tyrians abuse Agrippa, who was in the company of Vespasian and described by Josephus as both 'a king and a friend' (καὶ βασιλέα καὶ

---

    narrative within itself and the message Josephus wishes to deliver through *Life* – and not through the actual events themselves.

8 Mason, 'Essay', 61–2, echoed by den Hollander, *Josephus*, 54.

9 The procurator M. Antonius Felix is portrayed in a negative light by Josephus, and thus stands in contrast to the positive image of the priests associated with Josephus. He is introduced in *Ant.* 20.137 as the brother of the infamous Marcus Antonius Pallas, induces the Judean princess Drusilla to violate her ancestral laws by marrying him (*Ant.* 20.143–44) and is held responsible by Josephus for the deteriorating situation in Judaea (*Ant.* 20.160–78). See also Mason, *Life*, 21n.95.

... φίλον), which implies that by extension the Tyrians were insulting the Romans themselves.[10] Philip, upon Vespasian's suggestion, is sent to Rome by Agrippa to give an account of the events to Nero but, so the narrative goes, because of the civil war Philip was not able to fulfil the mission and returns home (408-9). While Price, followed by Mason, argues convincingly that the timeline of the narrative does not add up (Nero could not have been in Rome, nor had civil war begun at this point in 67 CE), and that Josephus simply made a mistake based on ignorance and carelessness, the rhetoric impact of the story must not be overlooked, especially in light of a similar story immediately following.[11] Upon Vespasian's arrival in Ptolemais (410), another associate of Agrippa is accused by the populace, this time Justus of Tiberias. Again, Vespasian suggests how Agrippa should act – Justus was to be disciplined – but his suggestion comes to nothing as Agrippa secretly disregards Vespasian's orders. Vespasian, thus, in *Life* is introduced under a hail of accusations and ineffectiveness.

The next few passages further enhance the impression of the Flavian emperors being bested as now Josephus broaches the issue of the relationships between them; as we have seen, earlier, in our interpretation of autobiography we consider how relationships depicted in the narrative reflect on the author and main character. Even though Josephus had been captured after the siege of Jotapata, he emphasizes how he was treated by the Romans and Vespasian, especially with all honours (τὰ πολλὰ διὰ τιμῆς ἄγοντος με Οὐεσπασιανοῦ, 414). Initially, however, Josephus leaves the honours list rather vague, referring only to the marriage he was ordered by Vespasian to enter into, with a captured Judean woman.[12] Commentators concerned more with the historicity of the situation have noted the emphasis Josephus places on the woman's virginity (414);[13] when we read the statements in light of our understanding of a comparison between Josephus, the Flavians and Rome, we see that Josephus as soon as he was able,

---

10 See the relevant notes in Mason, *Life, ad locum,* on the absurdity and lack of historicity regarding the accusations levelled by the Tyrians against Agrippa and Philip. This only adds to the rhetorical impact of the first scene featuring Vespasian in action.
11 Jonathan J. Price, 'The Enigma of Philip ben Jakimos', *Historia* 11 (1991): 77-94; Mason, *Life,* 163n.1681.
12 Josephus does not return to the list of benefits received until much later in the narrative (*Life* 423); he glosses over a rather long period of time, having travelled for example to and from Alexandria in 69 CE during this period.
13 See here Mason, *Life,* 164n.1700 for κελεύω and den Hollander, *Josephus,* 80-3, for the possible historical situations and relationships between Josephus and the woman. This study does not, and cannot, offer further insight into the historical events *Life* narrates nor does it pass judgement on its historical reliability, as the primary focus rests on enhancing our understanding of the text's genre.

Josephus overturned Vespasian's orders, released his wife, and remarried a woman of his own choosing (415).

Josephus' superiority over the Flavians is raised again when Josephus narrates how Titus often (πολλάκις) tried to persuade Josephus to take for himself anything he wanted from Jerusalem (417b). At first glance this presentation seems to demonstrate Titus' generosity, and the scene has been understood as Josephus defending himself against accusations of benefitting from Jerusalem's fall.[14] In a comparative light between Josephus and Titus, however, by looking at how the scene reflects on Josephus and his relationships to the other characters in the narrative, we can see how Titus is put into a position of weakness next to Josephus by trying valiantly to convince Josephus who refuses to ask for material gain, instead choosing to free prisoners. The comparative tension is heightened in light of the Roman soldiers looting the city. Similarly, Josephus demonstrates his superiority over Titus because all it took was for Josephus to approach him once with tears in his eyes before Titus ordered three crucified prisoners to be rescued (420-1); Josephus had no need to revert to Titus' frequent attempts at persuasion. Josephus directly counters Roman actions by freeing those they had imprisoned and by rescuing what they had tried to destroy (the scrolls) – he overturns Roman actions with the blessing of a weak Titus.

The weakness of the imperial family is further revealed in the continuous accusations raised against Josephus himself (416-17; 424-5; 428b). Although Vespasian orders the first of these accusers to be put to death, the imperial warning does not appear to have been strong enough to deter others. Josephus leaves the various accusers unnamed, and Mason has aptly remarked on the rhetorical effectiveness of creating accusations to enhance one's own reputation.[15] Thus we do not need to take the statements of accusations historically. Instead, we see the weakness in the imperial position and protection compared to Josephus' enhanced reputation and status.[16]

Josephus clearly revelled in his abilities of being ironic at the Flavian imperial family's expense. We can still today see their extensive, perhaps even desperate, efforts of using their victory over Jerusalem as a founding pillar of their reign.[17]

---

14 Mason, *Life*, 165n.1717.
15 Mason, *Life*, 170n.1769.
16 *Contra* den Hollander, *Josephus*, 212, who suggests that Josephus used the motif of accusation/defence to signal the continued favour he held under the different emperors: Josephus' accusers tried to get rid of Josephus with the advent of each new emperor ('testing the waters') but he continued to be protected by imperial favour.
17 See exemplary Steven L. Tuck, 'Imperial Image-Making', in *A Companion to the Flavian Age of Rome*, ed. by Andrew Zissos (Chicester, Malden: John Wiley & Sons, 2016), 111-15, 118, with further references.

The irony behind the narrative is found in the realization that Judeans continued to exist – successfully – without their temple, superior even to the most superior Roman family, no matter how emphatically the Flavians had tried to visualize Jerusalem's defeat.

Josephus presents himself as better at being Roman and as better than the imperial family in several ways, even at autobiography itself – we have already seen how (generically perfectly) Josephus composed *Life* following his literary precedents. The imbalance of the text has been discussed frequently, as the balance between the framework and the main narrative. In this framework, the prologue and epilogue are filled with generic catchphrases and genre language, focusing the audience's attention onto the genre. Notably, it is this framework that deals with and reacts strongly to Roman themes and characters. We note a clever use of genre and literature. The celebratory layer in which, through his choice of genre, Josephus asks his audience to identify with himself on his journey can be interpreted as being directed at the Judean elements especially in Rome who were attempting to reorganize themselves. His autobiography was a reminder, a show of strength. Josephus through his autobiography has become a little bit of everything for his readers. Accomplished author, general, strategist, prophet, priest and upholder of Judean heritage. Reading *Life* in this way correlates well with the current understanding of the Judean situation in Rome. As William den Hollander recently argued, while there was no direct persecution, there nevertheless existed a state of anxiety among the Judeans in Rome.[18] By writing Judean history and asking the audience to identify with himself, arguably one of the more successful Judeans in recent history and able to beat the Romans at their own game, Josephus likely attempted to bolster their and maybe his own morale.[19] Simultaneously, the inherent ironic layer was aimed at further subversive Roman elements already criticizing the Flavian rule (see earlier). The weakness of the imperial position and its characters shines through Josephus' autobiography, and their weakness is reflected by Josephus' superiority.

---

18 Den Hollander, *Josephus*, 231–44.
19 See here, for example, den Hollander, *Josephus*, 293–304, for Josephus' relationship with the local Judean community and his situation in Rome and the atmosphere in Rome against Judeans. See also Mclaren, 'Jews in Rome', 164, for the atmosphere in Rome and in general for Josephus' attempt to boost Judean morale through his writings. For Josephus' preservation of Judean dignity as a conquered people in *War*, see Steve Mason, *Josephus and the New Testament*, 2nd edn (Peabody: Hendrickson Publishers, Inc., 2003).

Evaluation

This study has applied genre theory to *Life* and a collection of ancient texts and has shown Josephus' *Life* in a new light, as part of the development of ancient autobiography. The contribution of this study lies firstly in a more in-depth understanding of the genre of autobiography in antiquity and *Life's* relationship to the genre, of Josephus' place within the generic discourse and tradition. A genre-based approach facilitates the grouping together of a range of texts and discussing their relationship to each other and other texts, as well as allowing their interpretation and evaluation based on firm methodological foundations. Genre offers a tool for interpretation and uncovering nuances of the ancient mindset and literary sophistication. Thus, the conclusions of this study were applied to a brief re-reading of *Life* to demonstrate the value of knowing a text's genre. The boundaries of this study were delineated by the limited ancient evidence. This study does not endeavour to re-invent the wheel nor to add new, previously unknown evidence; instead, the study re-evaluated the existing evidence by asking different questions about the texts and of the knowledge we already possess. Much admirable scholarship has already been applied to *Life* and Josephus' situation in Rome and his Flavian context. This study now adds another dimension on how we can read Josephus in particular, or any literature, through a generic lens. By respecting the importance of knowing a text's genre, we gain new insights into Josephus' aims, audience, literary ability, and wider state of mind given his life-changing experiences and his ability to balance between the various aspects of Rome and Jerusalem. The study has also enhanced our understanding of how much thought and effort Josephus placed into the composition of *Life*.

Responding to disputed issues

In terms of other scholarly attempts to find a genre for *Life*, we see that a comprehensive approach based on critical literary theory was successful and can, to an extent, incorporate these previous attempts into the generic discourse. In Chapter 1 the early critical understandings of *Life* as an apologia were noted. This was based on the perceived dominance of an apologetic, self-defensive theme running through *Life* which culminates in the digression against Justus of Tiberias (*Life* 336–67). Given the results of this analysis, it is possible to read *Life*, or passages such as the aforementioned digression or a passage in which Josephus actively defends his integrity (77–83), as written in the apologetic mode rather than understanding the entire *Life* as an apologia. Scholars have of course used the term 'apologetic' in reference to *Life*; however, a clarification and distinction of the use and understanding of the term from a critical literary point of view were necessary. We must distinguish between *Life* being an autobiography in terms of genre and being read apologetically, or in the case of Neyrey's approach, encomiastically.

Although Neyrey cannot comprehensively demonstrate that *Life* fulfils all the requirements of what he calls a 'formal encomium' as he does not expand his definition sufficiently, it is now possible to accept parts of his conclusion regarding the genre of *Life*. We have seen that the concept of genre functions on different levels: genre, sub-genre and mode. Neyrey's findings, interesting in themselves, that Josephus adheres to the conventional elements (e.g. origin/birth; accomplishments; σύγκρισις), can apply to *Life* only on a modal rather than on the generic level. Josephus employs the features used to present and describe himself in a way that is characteristic for an encomium, thus they become encomiastic features which help him structure and characterize his autobiography. However, as a single feature, they cannot define the overall genre. It is also noteworthy that, of the literary comparanda discussed in this analysis, none are referred to as encomia, and in fact for the author to place himself at the centre of an encomium goes against all the methods compiled at great length by Quintilian and Plutarch when discussing how best to speak or write about oneself.

In terms of Josephus' audience, we have seen arguments raised for various audience constellations. Appreciating Josephus' compositional skills, we must consider that Josephus combined all these features, parallels and possible associations in the one text for the benefit of different audiences and their different expectations and literary awareness. The audience's reaction and process of understanding *Life* (or any text in fact) depend on their literary knowledge base, or library, as a primary frame of reference. The fact that Josephus took such great care to align *Life* with the generic parameters of ancient autobiography, and did not deviate at all from them, suggests that he intended for or expected audiences with different backgrounds and levels of education. It also suggests that Josephus wanted to ensure comprehension and interpretation for audiences equipped with differing levels of mental libraries who would respond to the different literary layers in *Life*. We must ask what Josephus wanted his audience to experience and remember from his *Life*. We must not forget that by the time Josephus was writing *Life*, more than twenty years had passed since the destruction of the temple, enough time for a whole new generation of Judeans (both local and in the Diaspora) to grow up with an adjusted understanding of and connections to Jerusalem. Encouraging the audience to identify with himself, Josephus may well have wished to strengthen the ties of his compatriots, their ties to their religion and motherland, a reaffirmation of their identity.[20]

The dichotomy between the parallel accounts in *Life* and *War* has not been discussed in this study.[21] However, it is hoped that the findings of this study in relation to the genre ancient of autobiography will be able to contribute to a discussion focusing on the autobiographical passages in historiographical works or those of other ancient genres such as inscriptions or poetry.[22] I noted the multitude of speeches and letters written by many of the authors discussed earlier in their attempts to put across their messages and achievements: Cicero, Caesar, Sulla, Augustus and Catulus are all credited with numerous additional publications and speeches to spread the same message we find in the specific texts discussed here from an autobiographical perspective. We can consider the relevant passages in Josephus' *War* (2.568–3.408) in this vein and consider the relationship and effect of the other publications in relation to the texts discussed in this analysis.

Life's literary setting

The conclusion that this study suggests is that Josephus intended to conform his work to, and align it closely with, the respective sub-genres of ancient autobiography, shaping his account to suit them both. We ask how far he was aware of his literary predecessors, and which texts he had come across that

---

20 See Adams, *Greek Genres*, who intelligently argues that Diaspora Judeans and their literature demonstrated their ties to their heritage but at the same time also their comfort and lack of shame for living in the Diaspora. This may also partly explain why Josephus offered geographical or situational explanations; while audience members raised in Judea would have been familiar with many of these details, a new generation of Judeans raised in the Diaspora would be unaware of distances between villages or other details Josephus had included. Some of the additional detail, usually attributed to have been included for the benefit of a non-Judean audience, may have proven equally helpful to a Diaspora audience.
21 For studies of the dichotomy, see best Cohen, *Josephus*; Rappaport, 'Where Was Josephus Lying?'; Rajak, *Josephus*, 154–66. See also in brief Attridge, 'Josephus and His Works', 187–92. For the autobiographical sections of *War*, see Glas, 'Self–Characterization'.
22 An intriguing parallel to a scene in the autobiographical passages of *War* can be found in the ὑπομνήματα of Aratus of Sicyon, widely held to constitute an early text in the development of autobiography. For Aratus, see most recently Marasco, 'Hellenistic Age', 104–17, with further references. Plutarch recounts a scene in which Aratus sets out to give himself up to the enemy and is held back by crying women and children (*Arat.* 42.1); Josephus recounts a similar scene, in Jotapata, of women, children and old men throwing themselves at his feet weeping and beseeching him not to leave them to face the Roman army (*War* 3.193–204, esp. 202, cf. *Life* 205–07,210). Other authors who included autobiographical units into their histories include Thucydides, Ctesias, Polybius and Ammianus Marcellinus. See further Marincola, *Authority*, 182–92, 200–4.

guided his composition of *Life* as a simultaneously conservative and innovative ancient autobiography. Several scholars, dating back to Theodor Mommsen, have suggested a variety of possible Roman sources underlying the Roman narrative in *Ant.* 19.1–273, in which Josephus narrates the events surrounding Caligula's murder and Claudius' accession. Theodor Mommsen was the first to put forward the suggestion that Josephus had used Cluvius Rufus' history, based on the intimate conversation between Cluvius and Bathybius in *Ant.* 19.91–92 that according to Mommsen could only have been known to the author himself.[23]

However, because of our general lack of information about Cluvius and his writings as well as a problematic manuscript tradition, several scholars have suggested several other possible Roman sources for *Ant.* 19, all Roman and all written in Latin – operating under the assumption that Josephus would have been able to work with Latin sources.[24] Geoffrey Lewis, approaching Emperor Claudius' autobiography from a different, unrelated angle, suggests which passages in Josephus we can trace back to Claudius' autobiography.[25] He points out that given our lack of more detailed information about the work itself, 'we are reduced simply to noting the emperor's known activities'.[26] As mirrored in Josephus' writings, these activities are limited to Claudius' accession, at which point Josephus breaks off the narrative; Lewis thus suggests the following passages: *Ant.* 19.13, 32f, 66f, 132, 154–6, 158–9, 169–84, 214, 227, 234–5, 236, 248, 251f, 258, 263.[27] While I largely agree with the passages suggested by Lewis,

---

23 Theodor Mommsen, 'Cornelius Tacitus und Cluvius Rufus', *Hermes* 4 (1870): 295–325, esp. 320–2. For Cluvius as historian, see *HRR* vol. 2, 114–15; Pliny, *Ep.* 9.19.5; Tacitus, *Ann.* 13.20.
24 Dieter Timpe, 'Römische Geschichte Bei Flavius Josephus', *Historia: Zeitschrift für Alte Geschichte* 9 (1960): 474–502; Louis Feldman, 'The Sources of Josephus' "Antiquities" Book 19', *Latomus* 21 (1962): 320–33. See ibid., 322, and his Loeb translation *ad locum* for the variant textual traditions. See also T. P. Wiseman, *Death of an Emperor – Flavius Josephus, Translated with an Introduction and Commentary* (Exeter: Exeter University Press, 1991), 111–18, for an evaluation of the evidence for and against Cluvius Rufus.
25 Lewis, 'Imperial Autobiography'. Timpe, 'Römische Geschichte', focused his search on comparisons of the unknown author with Tacitus, looking for a literary tradition and concluding the source to be 'ein annalistisches Geschichtswerk eines senatorischen Verfassers' composed under Vespasian. Feldman, 'Sources', 331–2, considers all the Roman authors known to have written about Caligula's reign, and indeed suggests Claudius' autobiography as a possible source for Josephus. Unfortunately, Feldman's discussion of the autobiography remains vague and he does not offer a detailed selection of passages in *Ant.* 19 which might be based on the autobiography. Thomas Goud, 'The Sources of Josephus "Antiquities" 19', *Historia: Zeitschrift für Alte Geschichte* 45 (1996): 472–82, picks up the idea of Claudius' autobiography in this context, but does not offer any detailed information either. He only vaguely sees the text's presence in the literary background. See Chapter 3 for this study's acceptance of Josephus' language skills.
26 Ibid., 696.
27 Ibid. His list does not align with the breakdown of Josephus' sources as proposed by Wiseman, *Death of an Emperor*, xiii. Wiseman suggests two distinct Roman sources (but not Claudius' autobiography). According to Wiseman's divisions, Josephus' main source is visible in *Ant.* 11.24–61, 62–7, 70–93, 96–105, 109–57, 161–9, 198–211, 269–73, while a secondary source is the basis for *Ant.* 11.2–14, 17–23, 94–5, 158–60, 212–36, 237–45, 246–68. See also Daniel R. Schwartz,

a case can be made for a further passage in the Josephan narrative, based on his treatment of source material generally and the context of this study.[28]

Ant. 19.263 begins with a concluding statement, summing up the previous passage, the deliberations in the Senate following the tumults after Caligula's murder: καὶ οἱ μὲν ἐν τοῖσδε ἦσαν. The focus switches to a laudatory report about a suddenly very assertive Claudius and the soldiers who run to him to pay their respect (*Ant.* 19.263-268).[29] The passage demonstrates the military support offered to Claudius, essential for any Roman emperor, and shows Claudius being strong and simultaneously diplomatic towards the Senate; solely his intervention with the army saves the consul Quintus Pomponius; Claudius can show his authority at the very outset of his reign. The scene also features one of Claudius' protégées and early favourites, Rufrius Pollio, in a positive light opposing Caligula's murderers in his new position as praetorian prefect (*Ant.* 19.267).[30]

The passage also shows Claudius defending the imperial institution and the questionable honour of his predecessor by having Caligula's murderers caught and executed. In this presentation, the passage carries with it an apologetic tone and could well represent Claudius' own version of events; although the murder of Caligula held positive consequences for Rome, freeing the city of his tyranny, Claudius could not afford to set a precedent. He executes the celebrated murderers for his own safety, and that of the institution, and apologizes for his actions. The fact that the scene has Claudius discuss the decision with anonymous friends absolves him of the sole responsibility and indicates an inner turmoil or at least the pretence of such feelings.[31] The next break (19.269) introduces new source material (λέγεται δὲ), a digression describing the deaths of Caligula's murderers (19.269-274) in more detail. The apologetic tone of the previous passage (19.263-268) correlates well with the laconic and concluding

---

Agrippa I: The Last Kind of Judaea (Tübingen: J.C.B. Mohr, 1990), 2-38, for a discussion of Josephus' source material in *Ant.* 19.

28 For a discussion of Josephus' integration of source material into his narrative, see Schwartz, 'Many Sources'.
29 Earlier pictures of Claudius are less flattering – he hides, is scared, and pleads with the soldiers (*Ant.* 19.212, 216, 218).
30 Cf. Dio, lx 23.2 for preferential treatment enjoyed by Pollio.
31 The scene has no parallel in Suetonius' biography. Dio, lx 3.4. offers a version of events similar to Josephus' narrative: Τὸν μὲν οὖν Χαιρέαν καί τινας ἄλλους, καίπερ πάνυ ἐπὶ τῷ τοῦ Γαΐου θανάτῳ ἡσθείς, ὅμως ἀπέκτεινεν· οὐ γὰρ ὅτι τὴν ἀρχὴν διὰ τὴν ἐκείνου πρᾶξιν εἰλήφει χάριν αὐτῷ ᾔδει, ἀλλ'ὅτι ἐτόλμησεν αὐτοκράτορα ἀποσφάξαι ἐδυσχέραινεν, πόρρωθεν τὸ καθ'ἑαυτὸν ἐς ἀσφάλειαν προορώμενος – 'He put Chaerea and some others to death, in spite of his pleasure at the death of Gaius. For he was looking far ahead to ensure his own safety, and so, instead of feeling grateful toward the man through whose deed he had gained the throne, he was displeased with him for having dared to slay an emperor.'

statement that informs us that Chaerea, Lupus and several others were executed (ἀπήγετο οὖν τὴν ἐπὶ θανάτῳ καὶ σὺν αὐτῷ Λοῦππός τε καῖ Ῥωμαίων πλείους), and thus stands in contrast to the at times celebratory report of Chaerea's death that follows. This break offers a suitable place for Josephus to include other traditions about Caligula's murderers and their deaths.[32]

Overall, given that the small introductory and concluding remarks (19.263,269) inserted by Josephus indicate where he changes his source material, and given the previous discussions, I would argue that this passage should be included in the debate concerning Claudius' lost autobiography. This not only expands our knowledge of literature available to Josephus and opens further avenues of research but also helps our understanding of Josephus as our conclusions feed into current, parallel scholarship connecting Josephus even more deeply with the contemporaneous classical literary and educational milieu.

Life's generic setting

We have seen that the application of genre theory to ancient literature is able to yield insightful results and allows for new interpretative possibilities. Literary theory, it has been shown, plays a vital role in the interpretation of ancient texts whose social and cultural context has long since been lost. We can see more clearly the changes, traditions and innovations in the genre and its reception, which in turn can reflect on social and cultural changes. Knowing the genre of a text will enhance our experience of the text, will develop and deepen our understanding of its contents, and will shape the expectations with which we approach the text in the first place. A contribution of this study to scholarship, re-evaluating *Life* in its generic setting, consequently lies in marking the outlines of ancient autobiography and its sub-genres, the demonstration of ancient genre awareness of a genre in development, a genre perhaps not as tangible as historiography or epic, but nevertheless sufficiently developed to allow both authors and audiences to compose, communicate and interpret. By setting *Life* in its generic context, this study contributes to a further re-reading *Life*, allowing us to see its contents in a different light as we realize that Josephus offered his audience the possibility of identifying with him and made them his co-conspirators in subtly criticizing the ruling regime and simultaneously

---

32 Schwartz, *Agrippa I*, 24–8, ascribes this passage to a Roman source he calls 'Claud', which Josephus also relied upon for *Ant.* 19.212–47, 249, 259, 274–5, and *War* 2.204–17. However, aside from defining this source as Roman, or specialized in Roman history (pp. 30, 91), Schwartz does not attempt any further investigation into the author of this source.

encouraging his previously defeated compatriots by suggesting that this Judean, at the very least, managed to conquer Rome.

This study has shown an innate understanding of the genre autobiography in antiquity, and Josephus was reacting to this awareness by choosing to compose *Life* in the way he did. We can see how deeply immersed Josephus must have been in the contemporary literary and social culture to be able to pick up on the generic relationships and implications and to reproduce a genre that was itself still evolving. By ensuring that he included numerous features highly reminiscent of other autobiographies, Josephus demonstrates his erudition. The implications of *Life*'s generic setting are valuable, both in terms of content and context. In terms of Josephus' own self-perception, Josephus places himself into the same literary tradition as his predecessors, prominent political and military figures who stood out in their time. Josephus thought of himself as being qualified to stand in this tradition and expected to be appreciated as such by his audience. The act of writing *Life* shows us the literature, or the lens, through which Josephus wanted his audience to read and understand him.

We are now coming to the end of our study, which has taken as its limits the works of non-Christian authors up to the third century CE. This does not mean to imply that we cannot trace further the development of ancient autobiography, but merely that every study must have its limits. One of the results of this study has shown that the development of ancient autobiography continued constantly and that Josephus' *Life* itself was an important part of that development. Looking at religio-cultural encounters, the development of Christian autobiography directly parallels the development of autobiography in classical culture and society. It is generally recognized in scholarship that writing about oneself became prominent in ancient Greece with a growing understanding and appreciation of the individual, driven forward particularly by the prominence of Athenian democracy. Once it became evident that an individual was individual enough to warrant specific attention, we see a rise in authors writing about themselves as well as a proliferation of biographies, with most texts datable to the first centuries BCE and CE, a time of political and cultural reorientation. Looking at the development of Christianity, we see a remarkable parallel between literary and social development. While early Christianity was considered a minority religion in the Roman Empire, along with the political and social restrictions placed upon them, no individual except for Jesus could warrant extensive literary treatment. However, with the political rise of Christianity in the fourth century, individual Christians came to recognize their power and it is exactly at this time, diachronically parallel with the development in the Greco-Roman world, that Christian autobiography and hagiography emerges.

It is my hope that the conclusions of this study and the implications, including especially the re-reading of *Life*, sketched out briefly in the final chapter, will launch new investigations into the text and our perception of Josephus; more astute readers have certainly noted other possible conclusions and implications of this study than the present author, and it is hoped that this study will prove a helpful basis for their subsequent research.

Σοὶ δ'ἀποδεδωκώς, κράτιστε ἀνδρῶν Ἐπαφρόδιτε, τὴν πᾶσαν τῆς ἀρχαιολογίας ἀναγραφὴν ἐπὶ τοῦ παρόντος ἐνταῦθα καταπαύω τὸν λόγον. (*Life* 430)

Bibliography

Adams, James Noel. *Bilingualism and the Latin Language*. Cambridge: Cambridge University Press, 2003.

Adams, Sean A. *The Genre of Acts and Collected Biography*. Cambridge: Cambridge University Press, 2013.

Adams, Sean A. *Greek Genres and Jewish Authors: Negotiating Literary Culture in the Greco-Roman Era*. Waco: Baylor University Press, 2020.

von Albrecht, Michael. *A History of Roman Literature: From Livius Andronicus to Boethius with Special Regard to Its Influence on World Literature*, translated by Frances Newman and Kevin Newman. 2 vols. Leiden, New York, Köln: E.J. Brill, 1997.

Alexander, Loveday. 'The Acts of the Apostles as an Apologetic Text'. In *Apologetics in the Roman Empire*, edited by Mark Edwards, Martin Goodman, Simon Price and Christopher Rowland, 15–44. Oxford, New York: Oxford University Press, 1999.

Alexander, Loveday. 'What Is a Gospel'. In *The Cambridge Companion to the Gospels*, edited by Stephen C. Barton, 13–33. Cambridge: Cambridge University Press, 2006.

Attridge, Harold W. 'Josephus and His Works'. In *Jewish Writings of the Second Temple Period. Apocrypha, Pseudepigrapha, Qumran Sectarian Writings, Philo, Josephus*, edited by Michael Stone, 185–232. Philadelphia: Fortress Press, 1984.

Aune, David E. *The New Testament in Its Literary Environment*. Cambridge: James Clark & Co, 1988.

Badian, Ernst. *Lucius Sulla: The Deadly Reformer. The Seventh Todd Memorial Lecture Delivered in the University of Sydney, 11 September 1969*. Sydney: Sydney University Press, 1969.

Baier, Thomas. 'Autobiographie in der späten Römischen Republik'. In *Antike Autobiographien: Werke-Epochen-Gattungen*, edited by Michael Reichel, 123–42. Köln, Weimar, Wien: Böhlau Verlag, 2005.

Balogh, Josef. 'Voces Paginarum'. *Philologus* 82 (1927): 84–109.

Barclay, John M. G. 'The Empire Writes Back: Josephan Rhetoric in Flavian Rome'. In *Flavius Josephus and Flavian Rome*, edited by Jonathan Edmondson, Steve Mason and James Rives, 315–32. Oxford: Oxford University Press, 2005.

Barclay, John M. G. *Against Apion: Translation and Commentary*. Leiden: Brill, 2007.

Barish, David A. 'The Autobiography of Josephus and the Hypothesis of a Second Edition of His Antiquities'. *Harvard Theological Review* 71 (1978): 61–75.

Barlow, Jonathan. 'Noble Gauls and Their Other in Caesar's Propaganda'. In *Julius Caesar as Artful Reporter: The War Commentaries as Political Instruments*, edited by

Kathryn Welch and Anton Powell, 139–70. London: Duckworth with the Classical Press of Wales, 1998.

Barnes, Timothy David. 'The Sack of the Temple in Josephus and Tacitus'. In *Flavius Josephus and Flavian Rome*, edited by Jonathan Edmondson, Steve Mason and James Rives, 129–44. Oxford: Oxford University Press, 2005.

Barthes, Roland. 'Death of an Author'. *Aspen* 5–6 (1967).

Bearzot, Cinzia. 'Royal Autobiography in the Hellenistic Age'. In *Political Autobiographies and Memoirs in Antiquity: A Brill Companion*, edited by Gabriele Marasco, 37–87. Leiden, Boston: Brill, 2011.

Beck, Hans and Uwe Walter. *Die frühen Römischen Historiker. Band I von Fabius Pictor bis Cn. Gellius*. Darmstadt: Wissenschaftliche Buchgesellschaft, 2004.

Beck, Hans and Uwe Walter. *Die frühen Römischen Historiker. Band II von Coelius Antipater bis Pomponius Atticus*. Darmstadt: Wissenschaftliche Buchgesellschaft, 2004.

Behr, Holger. *Die Selbstdarstellung Sullas: Ein Aristokratischer Politiker zwischen persönlichem Führungsanspruch und Standessolidarität*. Frankfurt am Main: Peter Lang, 1993.

Bilde, Per. *Flavius Josephus between Jerusalem and Rome: His Life, His Works and Their Importance*. Sheffield: JSOT, 1988.

Boemer, Franz. 'Der Commentarius: Zur Vorgeschichte und Literarischen Form der Schriften Caesars'. *Hermes* 81 (1953): 210–50.

Bolin, Thomas M. *Freedom Beyond Forgiveness: The Book of Jonah Re-Examined*. Sheffield: Sheffield Academic Press, 1997.

Bradley, Patrick J. 'Irony and the Narrator in Xenophon's *Anabasis*'. In *Xenophon*, edited by Vivienne J. Gray, 520–52. Oxford: Oxford University Press, 2010.

Braun, Thomas. 'Xenophon's Dangerous Liasons'. In *The Long March: Xenophon and the Ten Thousand*, edited by Robin Lane Fox, 97–130. New Haven and London: Yale University Press, 2004.

Breitenbach, Hans Rudolf. *Historiographische Anschauungsformen Xenophons*. Freiburg i.d. Schweiz: Paulusdruckerei, 1950.

Breitenbach, Hans Rudolf. 'Xenophon S.V.'. In *Paulys Real-Encyclopaedie der Classischen Altertumswissenschaft*, edited by August Friedrich von Pauly and Georg Wissowa. Stuttgart: A. Druckenmüller, 1967.

Brighton, Mark Andrew. *The Sicarii in Josephus' Judean War: Rhetorical Analysis and Historical Observations*. Atlanta: Society of Biblical Literature, 2009.

Brunt, Peter A. 'On Historical Fragments and Epitomes 1'. *The Classical Quarterly* 30, no. 2 (1980): 477–94.

Bultmann, Rudolf. *Die Geschichte der synoptischen Tradition. Zweite neubearbeitete Auflage*. Göttingen: Vandenhoeck und Ruprecht, 1931.

Burridge, Richard. *What Are the Gospels? A Comparison with Graeco-Roman Biography*. 2nd edn. Michigan: William B. Eerdmans Pub. Co., 2004.

Burridge, Richard. 'The Genre of Acts: Revisited'. In *Reading Acts Today: Essays in Honour of Loveday C. A. Alexander*, edited by Steve Walton, Thomas L. Phillips, et al., 3–28. London, New York: T & T Clark, 2011.

Candau, José M. 'Republican Rome: Autobiography and Political Struggles'. In *Political Autobiographies and Memoirs in Antiquity: A Brill Companion*, edited by Gabriele Marasco, 121–59. Leiden, Boston: Brill, 2011.

Cawkwell, George. 'When, How and Why Did Xenophon Write the *Anabasis*?'. In *The Long March: Xenophon and the Ten Thousand*, edited by Robin Lane Fox, 47–67. New Haven, London: Yale University Press, 2004.

Cleary, Vincent J. 'Caesar's "Commentarii": Writings in Search of a Genre'. *The Classical Journal* 80 (1985): 345–50.

Cohen, Shaye. *Josephus in Galilee and Rome – His Vita and Development as a Historian*. 2nd edn. Boston, Leiden: Brill Academic Publishers, 2002.

Cohn Eskenazi, Tamara. *In an Age of Prose: A Literary Approach to Ezra-Nehemiah*. Atlanta: Scholars Press, 1988.

Collins, John J. *Apocalypse: The Morphology of a Genre*. Semeia 14. Missoula: Scholars Press, 1979.

Collins, John J., ed. *The Apocalyptic Imagination: An Introduction to Jewish Apocalyptic Literature*. 3rd edn. Grand Rapids: Wm. B. Eerdmans Publishing Co., 2016.

Conte, Gian Biagio. *The Rhetoric of Imitation: Genre and Poetic Memory in Virgil and Other Latin Poets. Translated from the Italian with a Foreword by Charles Segal*. Ithaca and London: Cornell University Press, 1986.

Conte, Gian Biagio. *Genres and Readers. Lucretius, Love Elegy, Pliny's Encyclopedia. Transl. By Glenn W. Most. With a Foreword by Charles Segal*. Baltimore and London: John Hopkins University Press, 1994.

Conte, Gian Biagio. *Latin Literature: A History*, Rev. edn. Baltimore: John Hopkins University Press, 1994.

Conte, Gian Biagio and Glenn W. Most. '*Imitatio* (Μίμησις)'. In *The Oxford Classical Dictionary*, edited by Simon Hornblower and Anthony Spawforth, 749. 3rd rev. edn. Oxford: Oxford University Press, 2003.

Cotton, Hannah M. and Werner Eck. 'Josephus' Roman Audience: Josephus and the Roman Elites'. In *Flavius Josephus and Flavian Rome*, edited by Jonathan Edmondson, James Rives and Steve Mason, 37–52. Oxford: Oxford University Press, 2005.

Cox, James M. 'Recovering Literature's Lost Ground through Autobiography'. In *Autobiography: Essays Theoretical and Critical*, edited by James Olney, 123–45. Princeton: Princeton University Press, 1980.

Cribiore, Raffaella. *The School of Libanius in Late Antique Antioch*. Princeton: Princeton University Press, 2007.

Cribiore, Raffaella. *Libanius the Sophist: Rhetoric, Reality, and Religion in the Fourth Century*. Ithaca, London: Cornell University Press, 2013.

Damgaard, Finn. *Recasting Moses: The Memory of Moses in Biographical and Autobiographical Narratives in Ancient Judaism and 4th-Century Christianity*. Frankfurt: Peter Lang Verlag, 2013.

Daube, David. 'Typology in Josephus'. *JJS* 31 (1980): 18–36.

Dewald, Carolyn and John Marincola. *The Cambridge Companion to Herodotus*. Cambridge: Cambridge University Press, 2006.

Dilke, O. A. W. 'The Literary Output of the Roman Emperors'. *Greece & Rome* 4 (1957): 78–97.

Dobesch, Gerhard. 'Nikolaus von Damaskus und die Selbstbiographie des Augustus'. *Grazer Beiträge* 7 (1987): 90–174.

Dormeyer, Detlef. 'Die Vita des Josephus als Biograpie eines gescheiterten Herrschers'. In *Internationales Josephus-Kolloquium 2002*, edited by Folker Siegert and Jürgen U. Kalms, 15–33. Münster: LIT Verlag, 2003.

Dubrow, Heather. *Genre*. London: Methuen, 1982.

Eagleton, Terry. *Literary Theory: An Introduction*. 2nd edn. London: Blackwell Publishers, 1996.

Earl, Donald. 'Prologue-Form in Ancient Historiography'. In *Aufstieg und Niedergang der Römischen Welt*, edited by Wolfgang Haase, 842–56. Berlin: Walter de Gruyter, 1972.

Edwards, H. J. *Caesar, the Gallic War, with an English Translation by H.J. Edwards*. Cambridge, MA: Harvard University Press, 2004.

Edwards, Mark et al., eds. *Apologetics in the Roman Empire: Pagans, Jews, and Christians*. Oxford, New York: Oxford University Press, 1999.

Engels, Johannes. 'Die Hypomnemata-Schriften und die Anfänge der politischen Biographie und Autobiographie in der Griechischen Literatur'. *Zeitschrift für Papyrologie und Epigraphik* 96 (1993): 19–36.

Engels, Johannes. *Augusteische Oikumenegeographie und Universalhistorie im Werk Strabons von Amaseia*. Stuttgart: Franz Steiner Verlag GmbH, 1999.

Erbse, Hartmut. 'Xenophon's *Anabasis* (an Inaugural Address, Largely Unrevised, Delivered in Tübingen 14 Dezember 1965)'. In *Xenophon*, edited by Vivienne J. Gray, 476–501. Oxford: Oxford University Press, 2010.

Fantham, Elaine. *Roman Literary Culture from Cicero to Apuleius*. Baltimore, London: Johns Hopkins University Press, 1999.

Farrell, Joseph. 'Classical Genre in Theory and Practice'. *NLH* 34 (2003): 383–408.

Farrell, Joseph. 'Literary Criticism'. In *The Oxford Handbook of Roman Studies*, edited by Alessandro Barchiese and Walter Scheidel, 176–87. Oxford: Oxford University Press, 2010.

Feldman, Louis. 'The Sources of Josephus' "Antiquities" Book 19'. *Latomus* 21 (1962): 320–33.

Feldman, Louis. *Studies in Josephus' Rewritten Bible*. Leiden, New York: Brill, 1998.

Feldman, Louis and Gohei Hata. *Josephus, the Bible and History*. Detroit: Wayne State University Press, 1989.

Flower, Michael A. *Xenophon's Anabasis, or the Expedition of Cyrus*. New York: Oxford University Press Inc., 2012.

Fowler, Alastair. 'The Life and Death of Literary Forms'. *New Literary History* 2 (1971): 199–216.
Fowler, Alastair. *Kinds of Literature: An Introduction to the Theory of Genres and Modes.* Oxford: Clarendon Press, 1982.
Fredriksen, Paula. 'The *Confessions* as Autobiography'. In *A Companion to Augustine*, edited by Mark Vessey with the assistance of Shelley Reid, 87–98. Chichester, West Suxxex; Malden, MA: Wiley–Blackwell, 2012.
Friis, Martin. *Image and Imitation: Josephus' Antiquities 1–11 and Greco-Roman historiography.* Tübingen: Mohr Siebeck, 2018.
Frow, John. *Genre.* London and New York: Routledge, 2006.
Galimberti, Alessandro. 'The Emperor Domitian'. In *A Companion to the Flavian Age of Rome*, edited by Andrew Zisso, 92–108. Chicester; Malden: John Wiley & Sons, 2016.
Gates, Henry Louis Jr. 'Lifting the Veil'. In *Inventing the Truth: The Art and Craft of Memoir.* edited by William Zinsser. Revised and Expanded 2nd edn. Boston, New York: Mifflin Company, 1995.
Gavrilov, A. K. 'Techniques of Reading in Classical Antiquity'. CQ 47, no. 1 (1997): 56–73.
Geiger, Joseph. *Cornelius Nepos and Ancient Political Biography.* Stuttgart: Franz SteinerVerlag Wiesbaden GmbH, 1985.
Geiger, Joseph. 'The Augustan Age'. In *Political Autobiographies and Memoirs in Antiquity*, edited by Gabriele Marasco, 233–66. Leiden, Boston: Brill, 2011.
Geiger, Joseph. 'Jewish Biography'. In *Oxford Handbook for Ancient Biography*, edited by Koen De Temmerman, 59–71. Oxford: Oxford University Press, 2020.
Gelzer, Matthias. *Caesar, Der Politiker Und Staatsmann.* Wiesbaden: F. Steiner Verlag, 1960.
Gelzer, Matthias. *Kleine Schriften 3 vols.* Wiesbaden: Franz Steiner Verlag, 1962–4.
Gfrereis, Heike. *Grundbegriffe der Literaturwissenschaft.* Stuttgart, Weimar: Verlag J.B. Metzler, 1999.
Gill, Christopher. *Greek Thought.* Oxford: Oxford University Press, 1995.
Glas, Eelco. 'Flavius Josephus' Self-Characterization in First-Century Rome'. PhD diss., University of Groningen, Groningen, 2020.
Goldsworthy, Adrian. '"Instinctive Genius": The Depiction of Caesar the General'. In *Julius Caesar as Artful Reporter: The War Commentaries as Political Instruments*, edited by Kathryn Welch and Anton Powell, 193–219. London: Duckworth with The Classical Press of Wales, 1998.
Goodman, Martin. *The Ruling Class of Judaea: The Origins of the Jewish Revolt against Rome A.D. 66–70.* Cambridge: Cambridge University Press, 1987.
Goodman, Martin. 'Kosher Olive Oil in Antiquity'. In *A Tribute to Geza Vermes: Essays on Jewish and Christian Literature and History*, edited by Philip R. Davies and Richard T. White, 227–45. Sheffield: Sheffield Academic Press, 1990.
Goodman, Martin. 'Josephus as Roman Citizen'. In *Josephus and the History of the Greco Roman Period: Essays in Memory of Morton Smith*, edited by Fausto Parente and Joseph Sievers, 329–38. Leiden, New York: E.J. Brill, 1994.

Goud, Thomas. 'The Sources of Josephus "Antiquities" 19', *Historia: Zeitschrift fur Alte Geschichte* 45 (1996): 472–82.
Gray, Vivien J. *Xenophon*. Oxford, New York: Oxford University Press, 2010.
Gray, Vivien J. 'Classical Greece'. In *Political Autobiographies and Memoirs in Antiquity: A Brill Companion*, edited by Gabriele Marasco, 1–36. Leiden, Boston: Brill, 2011.
Grojnowski, Davina. 'Nehemiah, Josephus, and Self-Presentation: An Analysis of Parallels'. *Journal for the Study of Judaism* 46, no. 3 (2015): 345–65.
Gusdorf, Georges. 'Conditions and Limits of Autobiography'. In *Autobiography: Essays Theoretical and Critical*, edited by James Olney, 28–48. Princeton: Princeton University Press, 1980.
Hack, Roy Kenneth. 'The Doctrine of Literary Forms'. *Harvard Studies in Classical Philology* 27 (1916): 1–65.
Hadas-Lebel, Mirelle. 'Le récit autobiographique chez Flavius Josèphe'. In *L'invention de l'autobiograhphie d'Hésiode á Saint Augustine*, edited by Marie-François Baslez, Philippe Hoffmann and Laurent Pernot, 125–32. Paris: Presses de l'École normale supérieure, 1993.
Hägg, Thomas. *The Art of Biography in Antiquity*. Cambridge: Cambridge University Press, 2012.
Hall, Lindsay '*Ratio* and *Romanitas* in the *Bellum Gallicum*'. In *Julius Caesar as Artful Reporter: The War Commentaries as Political Instruments*, edited by Kathryn Welch and Anton Powell, 11–43. London: Duckworth with The Classical Press of Wales, 1998.
Hansen, Günther Christian. 'Einige Anmerkungen Zum Sprachgebrauch Des Josephus'. In *Internationals Josephus-Kolloquium, Brüssel 1998*, edited by Jürgen U. Kalms and Folker Siegert, 39–52. Münster: LIT Verlag, 1999.
Harrison, Stephen J. *Generic Enrichment in Vergil and Horace*. Oxford: Oxford University Press, 2007.
Hau, Lisa Irene. 'Narrator and Narratorial Persona in Diodoros'. In *Diodoros of Sicily: Historiographical Theory and Practice in the Bibliotheke* (and their Implications for the Tradition of Greek Historiography), edited by L. I. Hau, A. Meeus and B. Sheridan, 277–302. Peeters: Leuven, 2018.
Hendrickson, G. L. 'The *Memoirs* of Rutilius Rufus'. *Classical Philology* 28 (1933): 153–75.
Hinterberger, Martin. *Autobiographische Traditionen in Byzanz*. Wien: Verlag der Österreichischen Akademie der Wissenschaften, 1999.
Hirsch, Eric Donald Jr. *Validity in Interpretation*. New Haven, London: Yale University Press, 1967.
Hirschberger, Martina. 'Historiograph im Zwiespalt – Iosephus' Darstellung seiner Selbst im Ἰουδαϊκος Πόλεμος'. In *Antike Autobiographien: Werke-Epochen-Gattungen*, edited by Michael Reichel, 143–83. Köln: Böhlau Verlag GmbH & Cie, 2005.
den Hollander, William. *Josephus, the Emperors, and the City of Rome: From Hostage to Historian*. Leiden, Boston: Brill, 2014.

Horsfall, Nicholas. 'Some Problems of Titulature in Roman Literary History'. *BICS* 28 (1981): 103–14.

Howell Chapman, Honora. 'Spectacle in Josephus' *Jewish War*'. In *Flavius Josephus and Flavian Rome*, edited by Jonathan Edmondson, Steve Mason and James Rives, 289–313. Oxford: Oxford University Press, 2005.

Hurlet, Frédéric. 'Sources and Evidence'. In *A Companion to the Flavian Age of Rome*, edited by Andrew Zissos, 17–39. Chicester, Malden: John Wiley & Sons, 2016.

Hurtado, Larry W. 'Oral Fixation and New Testament Studies? "Orality", "Performance" and Reading Texts in Early Christianity'. *New Testament Studies* 60, no. 3 (2014): 321–40.

Hurtado, Larry W. 'Correcting Iverson's "Correction"'. *NTS* 62 (2016): 201–6.

Hurtado, Larry W. and Chris Keith. 'Writing and Book Production in the Hellenistic and Roman Periods'. In *New Cambridge History of the Bible Vol. 1: From the Beginnings to 600*, edited by James Carleton and Joachim Schaper, 63–80. Cambridge: Cambridge University Press, 2013.

Iverson, Kelly R. 'Oral Fixation or Oral Corrective? A Response to Larry Hurtado'. *New Testament Studies* 62, no. 2 (2016): 183–200.

Johnson, William A. 'Toward a Sociology of Reading in Classical Antiquity'. *American Journal of Philology* 121, no. 4 (2000): 593–627.

Johnson, William A. *Readers and Reading Culture in the High Roman Empire: A Study of Elite Communities*. Oxford: Oxford University Press, 2010.

Johnson, William A. and Holt N. Parker. *Ancient Literacies*. Oxford: Oxford University Press, 2009.

Jones, Christopher P. 'Towards a Chronology of Josephus'. *Scripta classica Israelica* 21 (2002): 113–22.

Keaveney, Arthur. 'Sulla, the Marsi, and the Hirpini'. *CP* 76 (1981): 292–6.

Keaveney, Arthur. *Sulla: The Last Republican*. 2nd edn. London and New York: Routledge, 2005.

Kelsey, Francis W. 'The Title of Caesar's Work on the Gallic and Civil Wars'. *Transactions and Proceedings of the American Philological Association* 36 (1905): 211–38.

Kennedy, Jay B. 'Plato's Forms, Pythagorean Mathematics, and Stichometry'. *APEIRON* 43, no. 1 (2010): 1–32.

Köpke, Ernst. *Über die Gattung der Apomnemoneumata in der Griechischen Literattur*. Brandenburg, 1857.

Koskenniemi, Eric. *Greek Writers and Philosophers in Philo and Josephus*. Leiden, Boston: Brill, 2019.

Kurczyk, Stephanie. *Cicero und die Inszenierung der eigenen Vergangenheit*. Köln, Weimar, Wien: Böhlau Verlag, 2006.

Landau, Tamar. *Out-Heroding Herod: Josephus, Rhetoric, and the Herod-Narratives*. Leiden, Boston: Brill, 2006.

Lane Fox, Robin. *The Long March: Xenophon and the Ten Thousand*. New Haven, London: Yale University Press, 2004.

Laqueur, Richard. *Der Jüdische Historiker Flavius Josephus: Ein biographischer Versuch auf neuer quellenkritischer Grundlage*. Giessen: Münchow'sche Verlagsbuchhandlung, 1920.

Lewis, Geoffrey. 'Sulla's Autobiography: Scope and Economy'. *Athenaeum* 79 (1991): 509–19.

Lewis, Geoffrey. 'Imperial Autobiography: Augustus to Hadrian'. *ANRW* II.34, no. 1 (1993): 626–706.

Lippold, Adolf. *Die Historia Augusta*. Stuttgart: Steiner Verlag, 1998.

Mächler, Stefan. *Der Fall Wilkomirski. Über Die Wahrheit Einer Biografie*. Zürich: Pendo Verlag, 2000.

Malitz, Jürgen. 'Autobiographien und Biographien römischer Kaiser im ersten Jahrhundertnach Christus'. In *Propaganda – Selbstdarstellung – Repräsentation im römischen Kaiserreich des 1. Jhr. n. Chr.*, edited by Gregor Weber, 227–42. Stuttgart: Steiner Verlag, 2003.

Männlein-Robert, Irmgard. 'The Meditations as an (Philosophical) Autobiography'. In *A Companion to Marcus Aurelius*, edited by Marcel van Ackeren, 362–81. Chichester, Malden: Wiley-Blackwell, 2012.

Marasco, Gabriele. 'The Hellenistic Age: Autobiography and Political Struggles'. In *Political Autobiographies and Memoirs in Antiquity: A Brill Companion*, edited by Gabriele Marasco, 87–120. Leiden, Boston: Brill, 2011.

Marasco, Gabriele. *Political Autobiographies and Memoirs in Antiquity: A Brill Companion*. Leiden: Brill, 2011.

Marincola, John. *Authority and Tradition in Ancient Historiography*. Cambridge: Cambridge University Press, 1997.

Marincola, John. 'Genre, Convention, and Innovation in Greco-Roman Historiography'. In *The Limits of Historiography: Genre and Narrative in Ancient Historical Texts*, edited by Christina Shuttleworth Kraus, 281–324. Leiden, Boston, Cologne: Brill, 1999.

Mason, Steve. *Flavius Josephus on the Pharisees: A Composition-Critical Study*. Leiden; New York: E.J. Brill, 1990.

Mason, Steve. '*Contra Apionem* in Social and Literary Context'. In *Josephus' Contra Apionem: Studies in Its Character and Context*, edited by L. H. Feldman and J. R. Levison, 187–228. Leiden: Brill, 1996.

Mason, Steve. 'An Essay in Character: The Aim and Audience of Josephus' *Vita*'. In *Internationales Josephus-Kolloquium 1997*, edited by Folker Siegert and Jürgen U. Kalms, 31–77. Münster: LIT Verlag, 1998.

Mason, Steve. 'Should Any Wish to Enquire Further (*Ant*. 1.25): The Aim and Audience of Josephus' *Judean Antiquities/Life*'. In *Understanding Josephus: Seven Perspectives*, edited by Steve Mason, 64–103. Sheffield: Sheffield Academic Press, 1998.

Mason, Steve. 'Introduction to the *Judean Antiquities*'. In *Flavius Josephus, translation and Commentary Books 1-4 / Translation and Commentary by Louis H. Feldman*, edited by Steve Mason. Leiden, Boston: Brill, 2000.

Mason, Steve. *Life of Josephus; Translation and Commentary*. Leiden, Boston: Brill, 2001.

Mason, Steve. 'Flavius Josephus in Flavian Rome: Reading on and between the Lines'. In *Flavian Rome: Culture, Image, Text*, edited by Anthony James Boyle and William Dominik, 559-90. Leiden, Boston: Brill, 2003.

Mason, Steve. *Josephus and the New Testament*. 2nd edn. Peabody: Hendrickson Publishers, Inc., 2003.

Mason, Steve. 'Figured Speech and Irony in T. Flavius Josephus'. In *Flavius Josephus and Flavian Rome*, edited by Jonathan Edmondson, Steve Mason and James Rives, 243-88. Oxford: Oxford University Press, 2005.

Mason, Steve. 'Of Audience and Meaning: Reading Josephus' *Bellum Judaicum* in the Contextof a Flavian Audience'. In *Josephus and Jewish History in Flavian Rome and Beyond*, edited by Josephus Sievers and Gaia Lembi, 71-100. Leiden: Brill, 2005.

Mason, Steve. 'The Importance of the Latter Half of Josephus's Judaean Antiquities for His Roman Audience.' In *Pentateuchal Traditions in the Late Second Temple Period*, edited by Akio Moriya and Gohei Hata, 129-53. Leiden: Brill, 2012.

Mason, Steve. *A History of the Jewish War A.D. 66-74*. Cambridge: Cambridge University Press, 2016.

Mason, Steve. 'Josephus's *Autobiography* (Life of Josephus)'. In *A Companion to Josephus*, edited by Honora Howell Chapman and Zuleika Rodgers, 59-74. Chichester: John Wiley & Sons. 2016.

Mason, Steve. 'Josephus's Judean War'. In *A Companion to Josephus*, edited by Honora Howell Chapman and Zuleika Rodgers, 13-35. Chichester: John Wiley & Sons, 2016.

Mason, Steve. *Orientation to the History of Roman Judaea*. Eugene: Cascade Books, 2016.

Matthews, John F. 'Historia Augusta'. In *Oxford Classical Dictionary*. 3rd edn, edited by Simon Hornblower and Antony Spawforth, 713-14. Oxford: Oxford University Press, 2003.

Mayer, Marc. 'Caesar and the *Corpus Caesarianum*'. In *Political Autobiographies and Memoirs in Antiquity*, edited by Gabriele Marasco, 189-232. Leiden, Boston: Brill, 2011.

McCutcheon, Robert W. 'Silent Reading in Antiquity and the Future History of the Book'. *Book History* 18, no. 1 (2015): 1-32.

McDonald, A. H. 'Theme and Style in Roman Historiography'. *JRS* 65 (1975): 1-10.

McLaren, James S. *Turbulent Times?: Josephus and Scholarship on Judaea in the First Century CE*. Sheffield: Sheffield Academic Press, 1998.

McLaren, James S. 'The Jews in Rome during the Flavian Period'. *Antichthon* 47 (2013): 156-72.

Mellor, Ronald. *The Roman Historians*. London: Routledge, 1999.

Misch, Georg. *Geschichte Der Autobiographie; Das Altertum*. 2nd revised edn. Leipzig, Berlin: B.G. Teubner, 1931.

Momigliano, Arnaldo. *The Development of Greek Biography*. Cambridge, MA: Harvard University Press, 1971.

Momigliano, Arnaldo. *The Classical Foundations of Modern Historiography*. Berkeley: University of California Press, 1990.

Mommsen, Theodor. 'Cornelius Tacitus und Cluvius Rufus'. *Hermes* 4 (1870): 295–325.

Münzer, F. 'Lutatius (4)'. In *Pauly's Realenzyklopädie der classischen Altertumswissenschaft. Neue Bearbeitung*, edited by Wilhelm Kroll, 2068–71. Stuttgart: J.B. Metzlersche Verlagsbuchhandlung, 1927.

Neyrey, Jerome. 'Josephus *Vita* and the Encomium: A Native Model of Personality'. *Journal for the Study of Judaism* 25 (1994): 177–206.

Niditch, Susan. *Oral World and Written Word: Ancient Israelite Literature*. Louisville: Westminster John Knox Press, 1996.

Norman, A. F. *Libanius' Autobiography (Oration 1): The Greek Text/Edited, with Introduction, Translation and Notes*. London, New York: Published for the University of Hull by the Oxford University Press, University of Hull, 1965.

Noy, David. *Foreigners at Rome: Citizens and Strangers*. London: Duckworth with the Classical Press of Wales, 2000.

Noy, David. 'Apologetics'. *The Classical Review (New Series)* 52 (2002): 138–40.

Ogilvie, Robert. *Roman Literature and Society*. Brighton: Harvester Press, 1980.

Oliver, Revilo P. 'The First Medicean Ms of Tacitus and the Titulature of Ancient Books'. *Transactions and Proceedings of the American Philological Association* 82 (1951): 232–61.

Ong, Walter J. *Orality and Literacy, the Technologizing of the Word*. London, New York: Methuen, 1982.

Pascal, Roy. *Die Autobiographie; Gehalt und Gestalt*. Stuttgart, Berlin: W. Kohlhammer Verlag, 1965.

Paul, G. M. 'The Presentation of Titus in the Jewish War of Josephus: Two Aspects'. *Phoenix* 47 (1993): 56–66.

Pausch, Dennis. 'Formen Literarischer Selbstdarstellung in Der Kaiserzeit: Die Von Römischen Herrschern Verfassten Autobiographischen Schriften Und Ihr Literarisches Umfeld'. *Rheinisches Museum für Philologie* 147 (2004): 303–36.

Pausch, Dennis. 'Libellus Non Tam Diserte Quam Fideliter Scriptus? Unreliable Narrative in the Historia Augusta'. *Ancient Narrative* 8 (2009): 115–35.

Pelling, Christopher. 'Epilogue'. In *The Limits of Historiography: Genre and Narrative in Ancient Historical Texts*, edited by Christina Shuttleworth Kraus, 325–60. Leiden: Brill, 1999.

Pelling, Christopher B. R. 'Was There an Ancient Genre of "Autobiography"? Or, Did Augustus Know What He Was Doing?'. In *The Lost Memoirs of Augustus and the Development of Roman Autobiography*, edited by Christopher Smith and Anton Powell, 41–64. Swansea: The Classical Press of Wales, 2009.

Petit, Paul. 'Untersuchungen über die Veröffentlichung und Verbreitung der Reden des Libanios (1956)'. In *Libanios*, edited by Georgios Fatouros and Tilman Krischer, 84–128. Darmstadt: Wissenschaftliche Buchgesellschaft, 1983.

Pitcher, L. V. 'Characterization in Ancient Historiography'. In *A Companion to Greek and Roman Historiography Vol. 1*, edited by John Marincola, 102–17. Malden: Wiley Blackwell, 2011.

Powell, Anton 'Augustus' Age of Apology: An Analysis of the Memoirs – and an Argument for Two Further Fragments'. In *The Lost Memoirs of Augustus and the Development of Roman Autobiography*, edited by Christopher Smith and Anton Powell, 173–94. Swansea: The Classical Press of Wales, 2009.

Price, Jonathan. 'The Engima of Philip ben Jakimos'. *Historia* 11 (1991): 77–94.

Price, Jonathan. 'Josephus'. In *The Oxford History of Historical Writing: Beginnings to AD 600*, edited by Andrew Feldherr and Grant Hardy, 219–43. Oxford: Oxford University Press, 2011.

Rajak, Tessa. 'Josephus and Justus of Tiberias'. In *Josephus, Judaism and Christianity*, edited by Louis Feldman and Gohei Hata, 81–94. Leiden: Brill, 1987.

Rajak, Tessa. 'Talking at Trypho: Christian Apologetic as Anti-Judaism in Justin's Dialogue with Trypho'. In *Apologetics in the Roman Empire: Pagans, Jews, and Christians*, edited by Mark Edwards, et al., 59–80. Oxford, New York: Oxford University Press, 1999.

Rajak, Tessa. *Josephus – the Historian and His Society*. London: Duckworth, 2002.

Rajak, Tessa. *Translation and Survival: The Greek Bible of the ancient Jewish Diaspora*. Oxford: Oxford University Press, 2011.

Rappaport, Uriel. 'Where Was Josephus Lying – in His Life or in the War?' In *Josephus and the History of the Greco-Roman Period: Essays in Memory of Morton Smith*, edited by Fausto Parente and Joseph Sievers, 279–89. Leiden, New York: E.J. Brill, 1994.

Rappaport, Uriel. *John of Gischala: From the Mountains of Galilee to the Walls of Jerusalem. The Author's Electronically Circulated Translation by R. Toueg, of His Yohanan mi-Gush Halav: Me-Hare ha-Galil el Homot Yerushalayim*. Haifa: University of Haifa Press, 2006 [Hebrew].

Reichel, Michael. *Antike Autobiographien. Werke–Epochen–Gattungen*. Köln, Weimar, Wien: Böhlau Verlag, 2005.

Reichel, Michael. 'Ist Xenophons *Anabasis* eine Autobiographie?'. In *Antike Autobiographien. Werke–Epochen–Gattungen*, edited by Michael Reichel, 45–73. Köln, Weimar, Wien: Böhlau Verlag, 2005.

Reiser, Marius. *Sprache und literarische Formen des Neuen Testaments: Eine Einführung*. Paderborn, München, Wien, Zürich: Ferdinand Schöningh, 2001.

Rich, John. 'Cantabrian Closure: Augustus' Spanish War and the Ending of His Memoirs'. In *The Lost Memoirs of Augustus and the Development of Roman Autobiography*, edited by Anton Powell and Christopher Smith, 145–72. Swansea: The Classical Press of Wales, 2009.

Richards, E. Randolph. *Paul and First-Century Letter Writing: Secretaries, Composition and Collection*. Downers Grove: InterVarsity Press, 2004.

Richards, G. C. 'The Composition of Josephus' Antiquities'. *The Classical Quarterly* 33 (1939): 36–40.

Riggsby, Andrew M. *Caesar in Gaul and Rome: War in Words*. Austin: University of Texas Press, 2006.

Riggsby, Andrew M. 'Memoir and Autobiography in Republican Rome'. In *Companion to Greek and Roman Historiography Vol. 1*, edited by John Marincola, 266–74. Malden, Oxford: Blackwell, 2007.

Roche, Paul. 'Latin Prose Literature: Author and Authority in the Prefaces of Pliny and Quintilian'. In *A Companion to the Flavian Age of Imperial Rome*, edited by Andrew Zissos, 434–49. Chichester: John Wiley & Sons, 2016.

Rood, Tim. 'Panhellenism and Self-Presentation: Xenophon's Speeches'. In *The Long March: Xenophon and the Ten Thousand*, edited by Robin Lane Fox, 305–29. New Haven, London: Yale University Press, 2004.

Roy, Jim. 'Xenophon's Evidence for the *Anabasis*'. *Athenaeum* 46 (1968): 37–46.

Roy, Jim. 'Xenophon's *Anabasis* as a Traveller's Memoir'. In *Travel, Geography, and Culture in Ancient Greece, Egypt, and the Near East*, edited by Colin Adams and Jim Roy, 66–77. Oxford: Oxbow Books, 2007.

Russell, Donald Andrew. 'De Imitatione'. In *Creative Imitation and Latin Literature*, edited by David West and Tony Woodman, 1–16. Cambridge: Cambridge University Press, 1979.

Russell, Donald Andrew and Michael Winterbottom. *Ancient Literary Criticism: The Principal Texts in New Translations*. Oxford: Clarendon Press, 1972.

Saenger, Paul. *Space between Words: The Origins of Silent Reading*. Stanford: Stanford University Press, 1997.

Sanders, Ed. *Envy and Jealousy in Classical Athens: A Socio-Psychological Approach*. New York: Oxford University Press, 2014.

Schalit, Abraham. 'Josephus and Justus'. *Klio* 26 (1933): 67–95.

Scholz, Peter. 'Sulla's *Commentarii* – eine literarische Rechtfertigung. Zu Wesen und Funktion der autobiographischen Schriften in der späten Römischen Republik'. In *Formen Römischer Geschichtsschreibung von den Anfängen bis Livius*, edited by Ulrich Eigler et al., 172–95. Darmstadt: Wissenschaftliche Buchgesellschaft, 2003.

Scholz, Peter. 'Autobiographien Hellenistischer Herrscher und Republikanischer Nobiles'. In *Die Griechische Biographie in Hellenistischer Zeit*, edited by Michael Erler and Stefan Schorn, 385–406. Berlin, New York: Walter de Gruyter, 2007.

Schreckenberg, Heinz. *Die Flavius-Josephus-Tradition in Antike und Mittelalter, Arbeiten zur Literatur und Geschichte des Hellenistischen Judentums*. Leiden: Brill, 1972.

Schürer, Emil. *The History of the Jewish People in the Age of Jesus Christ (175 B.C.–A.D. 135), Revised and Edited by Geza Vermes & Fergus Millar*. Edinburgh: Clark, 1973.

Schwartz, Daniel R. *Agrippa I: The Last Kind of Judaea*. Tübingen: J.C.B. Mohr, 1990.

Schwartz, Daniel R. 'Josephus, Catullus, Divine Providence, and the Date of the *Judean War*'. In *Flavius Josephus; Interpretation and History*, edited by Jack Pastor, Pnina Stern and Menahem Mor, 331–52. Leiden, Boston: Brill, 2011.

Schwartz, Daniel R. 'Many Sources but a Single Author: Josephus's *Jewish Antiquities*'. In *A Companion to Josephus*, edited by Honora Howell Chapman and Zuleika Rodgers, 36–58. Chichester: John Wiley & Sons, 2016.

Schwartz, Seth. 'The Composition and Publication of Josephus' Bellum Iudaicum Book 7'. *HTR* 79 (1986): 373–86.

Schwartz, Seth. *Josephus and Judaean Politics, Columbia Studies in the Classical Tradition*. Leiden, New York, København, Köln: E.J.Brill, 1990.

Schwartz, Seth. 'Memory in Josephus and the Culture of the Jews in the First Century'. In *Common Judaism: Explorations in Second-Temple Judaism*, edited by Wayne O. McCready and Adele Reinhartz, 185–94. Minnesota: Fortress Press, 2011.

Shepard Kraemer, Ross. *Unreliable Witnesses [Electronic Book]: Religion, Gender and History in the Greco-Roman Mediterranean*. New York: Oxford University Press, 2011.

Shutt, Rowland J. H. *Studies in Josephus*. London: SPCK, 1961.

Shuttleworth Kraus, Christina. 'Bellum Gallicum'. In *A Companion to Julius Caesar*, edited by Miriam Griffin, 159–74. Oxford: Wiley–Blackwell, 2009.

Siegert, Folker, Heinz Schreckenberg and Manuel Vogel. *Flavius Josephus, Aus Meinem Leben (Vita). Kritische Ausgabe, Übersetzung und Kommentar von Folker Siegert, Heinz Schreckenberg, Manuel Vogel und dem Josephus–Arbeitskreis des Institutum Judaicum Delitzschianum*. Tübingen: Mohr Siebeck, 2001.

Sizoo, A. 'Autobiographie'. In *Reallexikon für Antike und Christentum*, edited by Theodor Klauser, 1050–5. Stuttgart: Hiersemann Verlags–GmbH, 1950.

Smith, Christopher. 'The Memoirs of Augustus: *Testimonia* and Fragments'. In *The Lost Memoirs of Augustus and the Development of Roman Autobiography*, edited by Christopher Smith and Anton Powerll, 1–13. Swansea: The Classical Press of Wales, 2009.

Smith, Christopher. 'Sulla's *Memoirs*'. In *The Lost Memoirs of Augustus and the Development of Roman Autobiography*, edited by Christopher Smith and Anton Powell, 65–85. Swansea: The Classical Press of Wales, 2009.

Smith, Christopher and Anton Powell, eds. *The Lost Memoirs of Augustus and the Development of Roman Autobiography*. Swansea: The Classical Press of Wales, 2009.

Smith, Justin M. 'Genre, Sub-Genre and Questions of Audience: A Proposed Typology for Greco-Roman Biography'. *Journal of Greco-Roman Christianity and Judaism* 4 (2007): 184–216.

Smith, Sidonie and Julia Watson. *Reading Autobiography: A Guide for Interpreting Life Narratives*. 2nd edn. Minneapolis: University of Minnesota Press, 2010.

Spilsbury, Paul. 'Josephus and the Bible'. In *A Companion to Josephus*, edited by Honora Howell Chapman and Zuleika Rodgers, 123–34. Chichester: John Wiley & Sons, 2016.

Stern, Pnina. 'Life of Josephus: The Autobiography of Flavius Josephus'. *Journal for the Study of Judaism* 41 (2010): 63–93.

Stern, Pnina. 'Josephus and Justus: The Place of Chapter 65 (336–367) in *Life*, the Autobiography of Flavius Josephus'. In *Flavius Josephus: Interpretation and History*, edited by Jack Pastor, Pnina Stern and Menahem Mor, 381–96. Leiden, Boston: Brill, 2011.

Sternberg, Meir. *The Poetics of Biblical Narrative*. Bloomington: Indiana University Press, 1985.

Struthers Malbon, Elizabeth and Adele Berlin. *Characterization in Biblical Literature*. Atlanta: Scholars Press, 1993.

Sturrock, John. *The Language of Autobiography: Studies in the First Person Singular*. Cambridge: Cambridge University Press, 1993.

Sturrock, John. *Structuralism: With a New Introduction by Jean-Michel Rabaté*. 2nd edn. Oxford: Blackwell, 2003.

Stylianou, P. J. 'One *Anabasis* or Two?'. In *The Long March: Xenophon and the Ten Thousand*, edited by Robin Lane Fox, 68–96. New Haven, London: Yale University Press. 2004.

Suerbaum, Werner. *Die Archaische Literatur von den Anfängen bis Sullas Tod: Die vorliterarische Periode und die Zeit von 240 bis 78 V.Chr.* München: C.H. Beck, 2002.

Talbert, Charles H. *What Is a Gospel? The Genre of the Canonical Gospels*. London: SPCK, 1978.

Tatum, Jeffrey. 'The Late Republic: Autobiographies and Memoirs in the Age of the Civil Wars'. In *Political Autobiographies and Memoirs in Antiquity: A Brill Companion*, edited by Gabriele Marasco, 161–87. Leiden, Boston: Brill, 2011.

Thackeray, H. St. John. *Josephus: The Man and the Historian. With a Preface by George Foot Moore, The Hilda Stich Strook Lectures (Established 1926) at the Jewish Institute of Religion*. New York: Jewish Institute of Religion Press, 1929.

Thein, Alexander. '*Felicitas* and the Memoirs of Sulla and Augustus'. In *The Lost Memoirs of Augustus and the Development of Roman Autobiography*, edited by Christopher Smith and Anton Powell, 87–109. Swansea: The Classical Press of Wales, 2009.

Thomas, Rosalind. *Literacy and Orality in Ancient Greece*. Cambridge; New York: Cambridge University Press, 1992.

Timpe, Dieter. 'Römische Geschichte Bei Flavius Josephus'. *Historia: Zeitschrift fur Alte Geschichte* 9 (1960): 474–502.

Todorov, Tzvetan. *Genres in Discourse*, trans. by Catherine Porter. Cambridge: Cambridge University Press, 1990.

Toher, Mark. 'On the Use of Nicolaus' Historical Fragments'. CA 8 (1989): 159–72.

Toher, Mark. 'Herod, Augustus, and Nicolaus of Damascus'. In *Herod and Augustus: IJS Conference, 21st–23rd June 2005*, edited by David Jacobson and Nikos Kokkinos, 65–82. Leiden: Brill, 2009.

Tuck, Steven L. 'Imperial Image-Making'. In *A Companion to the Flavian Age of Rome*, edited by Andrew Zissos, 109–28. Chicester, Malden: John Wiley & Sons, 2016.

Tuckett, Christopher. 'Book Review: *What Are the Gospels? A Comparison with Graeco-Roman Biography*'. *Theology* 96 (1993): 74–5.
van Dijk, Gert-Jan. *Ainoi, Logoi, Mythoi: Fables in Archaic, Classical, and Hellenistic Greek Literature; with a Study of the Theory and Terminology of the Genre*. Leiden: Brill, 1997.
Vasaly, Ann. 'Characterization and Complexity: Caesar, Sallust, and Livy'. In *The Cambridge Companion to the Roman Historians*, edited by Andrew Feldherr, 245–60. Cambridge: Cambridge University Press, 2009.
Vatri, Alessandro. 'Ancient Greek Writing for Memory: Textual Features as Mnemonic Facilitators'. *Mnemosyne* 68, no. 5 (2015): 750–73.
Verbrugghe, Gerald P. 'On the Meaning of Annals'. *Philologus* 133 (1989): 192–230.
Villalba Varneda, Pere. 'The Early Empire'. In *Political Autobiographies and Memoirs in Antiquity: A Brill Companion*, edited by Gabriele Marasco, 315–62. Leiden, Boston: Brill, 2011.
Wacholder, Ben Zion. *Nicolaus of Damascus, University of California Publications in History*. Berkeley, Los Angeles: University of California Press, 1962.
Walcot, Peter. *Envy and the Greeks: A Study of Human Behaviour*. Warminster: Aris & Phillips, 1978.
Walter, Uwe. 'Annales and Analysis'. In *The Oxford History of Historical Writing. Volume 1: Beginnings to 600 AD*, 265–90. Oxford: Oxford University Press, 2011.
Ward, J. S. 'Roman Greek: Latinisms in the Greek of Flavius Josephus'. *CQ* 57, no. 2 (2007): 632–49.
Weber, Wilhelm. *Josephus Und Vespasian: Untersuchungen Zu Dem Jüdischen Krieg Des Flavius Josephus*. Berlin, Stuttgart: Verlag von W. Kohlhammer, 1921.
Weintraub, Karl Joachim. *The Value of the Individual – Self and Circumstance in Autobiography*. Chicago: University of Chicago Press, 1976.
Welch, Kathryn. 'Caesar and His Officers in the Gallic War Commentaries'. In *Julius Caesar as Artful Reporter: The War Commentaries as Political Instruments*, edited by Kathryn Welch and Anton Powell, 85–110. London: Duckworth with The Classical Press of Wales, 1998.
Wellek, Rene and Austin Warren, eds. *Theory of Literature*. 3rd edn. Harmondsworth: Penguin, Pelican, 1982 reprint of 1963 edn.
Wencis, Leonard. '*Hypopsia* and the Structure of Xenophon's *Anabasis*'. *The Classical Journal* 73, no. 1 (1977): 44–9.
West, David and Tony Woodman. *Creative Imitation and Latin Literature*. Cambridge: Cambridge University Press, 1979.
Whitby, Michael. 'Xenophon's Ten Thousand as a Fighting Force'. In *The Long March: Xenophon and the Ten Thousand*, edited by Robin Lane Fox, 215–42. New Haven, London: Yale University Press, 2004.
Whitmarsh, Tim. *The Second Sophistic*. Oxford: Oxford University Press, 2005.
Whitmarsh, Tim. *The Cambridge Companion to the Greek and Roman Novel*. Cambridge: Cambridge University Press, 2008.

Wilkomirski, Binjamin. *Bruchstücke. Aus Einer Kindheit 1939–1948*. Frankfurt: Jüdischer Verlag, 1995.

Williams, Michael Stuart. 'Augustine's *Confessions* as Autobiography'. In *The OxfordHandbook of Ancient Biography*, edited by Koen de Temmerman, 281–94. New York: Oxford University Press, 2020.

Wills, Lawrence M. *The Jewish Novel in the Ancient World*. Ithaca and London: Cornell University Press, 1995.

Wilson, Marcus. 'After the Silence: Tacitus, Suetonius, Juvenal'. In *Flavian Rome: Culture, Image, Text*, edited by Anthony James Boyle and William Dominik, 523–42. Leiden, Boston: Brill, 2003.

Wintjes, Jorit. *Das Leben Des Libanius*. Radhen/Westf.: Verlag Marie Leidorf GmbH, 2005.

Wiseman, T. P. *Death of an Emperor – Flavius Josephus, Translated with an Introduction and Commentary*. Exeter: Exeter University Press, 1991.

Wiseman, T. P. 'The Publication of *De Bello Gallico*'. In *Julius Caesar as Artful Reporter*, edited by Kathryn Welch and Anton Powell, 1–9. London: Duckworth with The Classical Press of Wales, 1998.

Wiseman, T. P. 'Augustus, Sulla and the Supernatural'. In *The Lost Memoirs of Augustus and the Development of Roman Autobiography*, edited by Anton Powell and Christopher Smith, 111–23. Swansea: The Classical Press of Wales, 2009.

Wittgenstein, Ludwig. *Philosophical Investigations*. Oxford: Basil Blackwell, 1968.

Yagoda, Ben. *Memoir, a History*. New York: Riverhead Books, 2009.

Yarrow, Liv Mariah. *Historiography at the End of the Republic*. Oxford: Oxford University Press, 2006.

Yavetz, Zvi. 'The *Res Gestae* and Augustus' Public Image'. In *Caesar Augustus: Seven Aspects*, edited by Fergus Millar and Erich Segal, 1–36. Oxford: Clarendon Press, 1984.

Young, Frances. 'Greek Apologists of the Second Century'. In *Apologetics in the Roman Empire:Pagans, Jews, and Christians*, edited by Mark Edwards, et al., 81–104. Oxford, New York: Oxford University Press, 1999.

Zeitlin, Solomon. 'A Survey of Jewish Historiography: From the Biblical Books to the "Sefer ha Kabbalah" with Special Emphasis on Josephus (Continued)'. *The Jewish Quarterly Review* 60, no. 1 (1969): 37–68.

Zimmermann, Bernhard. 'Exil und Autobiographie'. *Antike und Abendland* 48 (2002): 187–95.

Zinsser, William. *Inventing the Truth: The Art and Craft of Memoir*. Revised and Expanded 2nd edn. Boston, New York: Mifflin Company, 1995.

Index

Adams, Sean 15
Aeschylus 39
Against Apion (Josephus) 1
Agricola (Tacitus) 50
Agrippa, Marcus 61, 69, 112, 119, 122, 127, 131, 137, 144, 149, 172–3
Agrippa II 132, 144
Agrippina 19
Alexander 140–1
Anabasis (Xenophon) 21–2, 26, 28, 31 n.17, 59, 70–1, 73–4, 73 nn.64, 66, 74 nn.69, 72, 82–7, 89–92, 99–100, 103–6, 109–10, 114, 114 n.65, 118–20, 122, 130–4, 137–42, 145–6, 148, 152–5, 159, 162–6
   allocation of space 89–90
   audience experiences 133–4
   as autobiography 74, 74 n.69
   dramatic settings of 118
   genre perspective 73–4, 73 n.66
   geographical settings of 118
   length 99
   mode of representation 96
   opening formula/preface 84–5
   scale 105–8
   structure 100–1
   style 128–30
   verb subjects, analysis of 86–7
ancient genre theory 37–47
   development 43–4
   distinctions 37–8
   features 38–41
   imitatio in 44–7
   vs. practice 41–3
   on writing about oneself 47–54
Antidosis (Isocrates) 47
Antioch 104
Antiquities of the Jews (Josephus) 2, 5, 10, 39–42, 68–9, 80–3, 92, 96–9, 112, 124–8, 134–5, 135 n.56, 137, 141, 144, 149, 179–80
   autobiography as genre in 79, 157–8

biblical narrative 135
composition/publication, time of 144–5
epilogue of 83
length 97
Life, relationship with 2, 5, 7–11, 39–42, 68–9, 80–3, 84 n.14, 92, 96–9, 112, 124–8, 134–5, 137, 141, 144, 149, 179–80
structure 99
style 126–7
title 80
apologia 13, 22–3, 70
Aratus of Sicyon (271–213 BCE) 75 n.75
Aristides, Aelius 38
Aristotle 12, 39–41, 43–4, 54, 71, 129
audiences 139–40
Augustus 81, 99, 104, 120, 122, 131, 154
   autobiography 61
   enunciation 97
   Res Gestae 13, 58–9, 72, 75, 82, 104, 159
   style of speaking 130
Ausweichbewegung 20
autobiography 2–3, 7–16; *see also Life* (Josephus)
   in antiquity, genre of 5–6, 16–24, 60
   genre of 8, 32
   and historiography 71–6
   Misch's prescriptive approach to 6
   mode 32
   modern expectations of 7
   as platform for individual author 6
   Roman Republican 19–20
   ruler-biography for 13
   Tacitus' view of 51–2
   Wilkormiski, Binjamin 34

Barish, David 3, 7
Bilde, Per 8–9
biography 5–6, 36, 63–4, 63 n.28
Boemer, Franz 68
Book of Nehemiah 140–1

Brill, E. J. 10
Burridge, Richard 35–6, 36 n.44, 40, 98–9, 169

Caesar, Julius 61, 64–6, 84–9, 96, 99, 103, 106, 109–10, 113, 118, 120, 128–9, 134, 138, 142–7, 151
Candau, José 59
Cato 39, 46, 53, 70, 141–2
Catulus, Quintus Lutatius 49–50, 58–9, 81, 104, 106, 122, 148 n.102, 154
Cawkwell, George 145, 153
Cethegus, M. Cornelius 44
Cicero 12, 24, 38–40, 42, 44–6, 48–50, 54, 59, 65–8, 71–2, 81–2, 88, 91, 95–8, 102–6, 113, 115, 120, 122, 129–31, 142–3, 147, 151–5, 159–64, 178
Clearchus 114
Cohen, Shaye 5, 8, 8 nn.25, 29, 125, 150
commentarii/commentarius 19, 36, 36 n.41, 64–8, 98
Commentariolum petitionis (Cicero) 65
Confessions (Augustine) 21, 63, 102, 121 n.10, 143
Conte, Gian Biagio 64
Cornelius, Publius 120
Cotton, Hannah 140
Cribiore, Raffaella 62, 138–9
Ctesias 114, 114 n.66
Cyropedia (Reichel) 84

Daube, David 134–5
De corona (Demosthenes) 48, 85
decorum 7, 32, 38, 41–2
Delphi 104
Demetrius of Phaleron (350–280 BCE) 17 n.72, 42
Demosthenes 48, 52, 85
De vita sua 62–3, 81 n.7
Dio, Cassius 52
Dionysius of Halicarnassus 38, 41–2, 44, 73
Domitia 140
Dormeyer, Detlev 12–13
Dubrow, Heather 27–8

Eck, Werner 140
Engels, Johannes 68
Epaphroditus 139–41
Euripides 39

Evagoras (Isocrates) 42, 44, 47 n.72, 163 n.17
excursus 15–16
ἀπομνημονεύματα 69–71

family resemblance 29
Farrell, Joseph 39
Felix, Cornelius Sulla 58–9
Flaccus, Valerius 113
Flavians 171–5
Fortune (τύχη) 62
Fowler, Alastair 31–3, 40, 97, 163, 165–7
  developmental stages 165–7
  genre, stages of 31
  on sub-genres 33
  on transformation of generic labels 31
Fox, Robin Lane 114

Galilean city 117
Gallic Wars (Caesar) 64, 66–7, 71–2, 84–6, 99–101, 106–7, 128–9, 133, 141–2, 146, 151–2
Gates, Henry Louis, Jr. 16
Geiger, Joseph 98
Gellius, Aulus 82, 102, 120
Gelzer, Mathias 3, 7, 66
generic ambiguity 39
generic contract, between author and reader 27–8
genres 1, 3–26
  assumptions 4
  of autobiography in antiquity 5–6, 16–24
  definition 27–9
  developments of 31
  distinctions 37–8
  features 27–9
  Gallic Wars 66–7
  implications 3–4
  importance of 3, 33–4
  for *Life* (Josephus) 6–15, 33–5
  modes 32
  prose 38
  recognition 29–30, 30 n.14
  relationships of 31
  of *SHA* 4
  sub-genres 33
  theory 27–57
    ancient 37–47

methodological case studies   34–7
modern   27–34
writing about oneself, ancient comments on   47–54
geographische Fachliteratur   20
Goodman, Martin   140–1, 140 n.79
Gospels (Burridge)   35–6, 40
Greek encomium   11–13
Gregory of Nazianzus   62–3
Gusdorf, Georges   15–16

Hack, Roy Kenneth   42
Hadas-Lebel, Mirelle   11
Hägg, Thomas   63, 70
Harrison, Stephen J.   39, 42 n.59, 43 n.63
Herodotus   1 n.2, 60–2, 69, 72, 84, 91, 99, 104, 107, 123, 140–1, 143, 146
Herrscherautobiographie   20
Hirsch, Eric Donald Jr.   29, 33
Hirschberger, Martina   14
Hirtius, Aulus   66, 99, 129, 146
Historia universalis (Herod)   107
historiography   1–2, 1 n.2, 4, 15
  and autobiography   71–6
  generic conventions   11, 107
  Judean War (*War*; Josephus)   1, 8, 21, 32, 80
  Sulla's work and   60, 82, 106–7
Horace   38, 40, 42
Huzar, Eleanor   131

imitatio   44–7
irony   129, 170–1, 175
Isocrates   17 n.72, 37–8, 42, 44, 47

John of Gischala   2, 85, 135–6
Josephus (Thackeray)   124–6, 124 n.18, 128 n.33
Josephus, Flavius   1
  Against Apion   1
  Antiquities of the Jews   2, 5, 10, 39–42, 68–9, 80–3, 92, 96–9, 112, 124–8, 134–5, 137, 141, 144, 149, 179–80
  career   7
  characterization of himself   135
  first-person narrative   96–7
  Judean Antiquities   1, 7–11
  as Judean aristocrat   139–40
  Judean War (*War*)   1, 8, 21, 80

Life   1–26, 33–5, 79–93, 95–115, 117–56 (*see also Life* (Josephus))
literary milieu   57–77
Judean Antiquities (Josephus)   1, 97–9
  Life, relationship with   5, 7–11
Judean War (*War*; Josephus)   1, 8, 21, 32, 80
Julian (331–363 CE)   61–2
Justus of Tiberias   2, 7, 9, 85, 89, 135–6

Kim Yong-Un   3

Laqueur, Richard   80, 111
Lewis, Geoffrey   18–19, 82
Libanius of Antioch (b. 314 CE)   46, 59, 61–3, 82–7, 104, 110, 120, 123, 154
  allocation of space   90–2
  geographical settings   118–19
  Oration 1   26, 46, 57, 61–2, 82, 84, 90–2, 97, 101, 104, 110, 118–23, 130, 134, 143, 147, 152, 154
  oratorical success   122
  style   130
Life (Josephus)   1–26, 33–5, 79–93, 95–115, 117–56, 163–5
  allocation of space   87–92
  Antiquities, relationship with   2, 5, 7–11, 39–42, 68–9, 80–3, 84 n.14, 92, 96–9, 112, 124–8, 134–5, 137, 141, 144, 149, 179–80
  as apologia   13, 22–3
  atmosphere   132–4
  authorial intention/purpose   148–55
    apologetic   151, 153–5
    didactic   150, 153
    encomiastic   148–9, 151
    exemplary   149, 152
    informative   149–50, 152
    memory/raise awareness, preserve   150, 152–3
    polemic   151, 153–5
  as autobiography   2–3, 7–16
  vs. *Bios Kaisarios* (*BK*)   112–13
  as celebration of character   8
  characterization, method of   108–10, 108 n.42
  composition/publication, time of   144–8
  as 'erste erhaltene Autobiographie der Antike'   12

evaluation 176–83
  disputed issues, response
    to 176–8
  generic setting 181–3
  literary setting 178–81
external features 95–115
genres for 6–15, 33–5
in Greco-Roman context 5
internal features 117–56
Judean War (*War*), relationship
  with 1, 8, 21, 80
length 97–9
literary context 8
literary units 103–4
mode of representation 95–7
opening formula/preface 83–5
quality of characterization 134–9
re-reading of 169–75
  characters 170–1
  Flavians through author 171–5
scale of 104–8
scholarly opinion on 6–16
setting, geographical/dramatic 117–19
social setting (audience,
  occasion) 139–44
sources in 111–14
structural imbalance 7
structure of 99–102
style 124–32
title 80–3
tone of 132
topoi 119–24
  ancestry 119–20
  birth/childhood/education 120–1
  career/retirement, end of 123–4
  deeds 121–2
  divine intervention 122–3
  virtues 122
translation 10
verb subjects, analysis of 85–7
Lucceius 48–9, 122, 143
Lucian of Samosata 40–1

Maecenas 61, 131, 144
Maechler, Stefan 34
Marcellinus, Ammianus 72
Marius, Gaius 58–9
Martyr, Justin 23, 70
Mason, Steve 3, 5, 8, 10–11, 83–4,
  100, 109, 112, 119–20, 124–6,
  125 n.22, 132, 135, 139–40, 147,
  149–50, 165, 170–5
Mayer, Marc 67, 151–2
McLaren, James S. 149
Mellor, Roland 66
memoir(s) 15–16, 19
Memorabilia 70
Misch, Georg 6, 73–4, 101
modern genre theory 27–34
  definition 27–9
  developments of 31
  importance of 33–4
  modes 32
  recognition 29–30, 30 n.14
  relationships of 31
  sub-genres 33
Momigliano, Arnaldo 17

Natural History (Pliny) 44–5, 52, 95
Neyrey, Jerome 11–12
Nicolaus of Damascus 15, 20, 53, 60–1,
  102, 104, 107, 110, 118, 120–1
  autobiography 87, 107, 122
  title 81
  travels 118
  Universal History 61
  βίος 59–64, 76, 101, 107, 129
Norman, A. F. 62, 97, 143
novel 31, 47–8, 84–5, 161–2

optimism 133
Oration 1 (Libanius) 26, 46, 57, 61–2, 82,
  84, 90–2, 97, 101, 104, 110, 118–23,
  130, 134, 143, 147, 152, 154

pattern 158–62
Pausch, Dennis 4, 19–21
Pelling, Christopher 3, 23–4, 43, 55, 102
Peloponnesian war (431–404 BCE) 73
pessimism 133
Petit, Paul 97, 129–30, 143
Phaedo (Plato) 70
Philip 105
Plain of Elatea 104
Plato 42, 48, 70, 80, 85, 102, 153
Pliny 44–5, 52, 95
Plutarch 11, 22–4, 26, 35, 37, 50–3, 58–9,
  63, 68, 70–1, 74–7, 81–4, 96, 100,
  104, 122, 130–1, 138, 141, 144,
  146, 149, 153–4, 163, 177

poetry   37–9
Polybius   44, 53, 72
Powell, Anton   154
Precepts of Statecraft (Plutarch)   11
progymnasmata   12
propriety   42
prose genres   38
Pythagorean biographies   63

Quintilian   12, 39–40, 42–6, 50, 53–4, 129, 131

Rajak, Tessa   3, 11
Rechenschaftsbericht   68–9, 111, 113
Rechtfertigungszwang   154
recitatio   95, 95 n.2–3
Reichel, Michael   84
Res Gestae (Augustus)   13, 58–9, 72, 75, 82, 104, 159
Riggsby, Andrew   37, 129
Roman aristocracy   10–11
Romanitas   133, 141
Roman Republican autobiographies   19–20
Rood, Tim   137–8, 151, 153
Rother, Carolus   129–30
Rufus, Rutilius   51–2, 59, 82

Samaria   117
Scaurus, Aemilius   20, 51–2, 59
Scholz, Peter   17–18
Schwartz, Daniel R.   150
Schwartz, Seth   150
scriptores historiae augustae (*SHA*)   4, 4 n.9
self-consciousness   6
self-examination   6
self-praise   22, 52–3
Seventh Epistle (Plato)   48, 102
SHA; see *scriptores historiae augustae* (*SHA*)
Shutt, R. J. H.   7
Siegert, Folker   95–6
Smith, Christopher   120, 131
Smith, Justin   36
Socrates   104
St. Augustine   62–3
sub-genres   33
Suetonius   35, 61, 65, 77 n.80, 81, 81 n.7, 96–7, 99, 101, 113, 113 n.63, 120, 130–1, 140, 144, 147, 154

Sulla, Lucius Cornelius (138–78 BCE)   60, 68, 75–6, 81–2, 84, 90–1, 96–9, 102, 104–7, 113, 115, 120–3, 130–1, 142, 146, 153, 166, 178
as *felix*   75
genealogy   75

Tacitus   19, 19 n.79, 24, 50–2, 129, 138
Tatian   23
Tertullian   23
texts outside pattern   163
Thackeray, H. St. John.   124–6, 124 n.18, 128 n.33
Thucydides   72–3
Todorov, Tzvetan   27, 30
Toher, Mark   107, 153

Universal History (Nicolaus)   15, 61

Varneda, Pere Villalba   14–15
Vespasian   105
vitae   59
vita/βίος   59–64
Vorlage (Cicero)   65, 98–9

Wacholder, Ben Zion   81 n.5, 129
Weber, William   3
Wencis, Leonard   100
Whitmarsh, Tim   13, 22, 22 n.97, 162
Wilkormiski, Binjamin   34
Wills, Lawrence   40
Wittgenstein, Ludwig   29

Xenophon   21–2, 26, 28, 31 n.17, 59, 70–1, 73–4, 73 nn.64, 66, 82–7, 89–92, 99–100, 103–6, 109–10, 114, 114 n.65, 118–20, 122, 130–4, 137–42, 145–6, 148, 152–5, 159, 162–6

Yavetz, Zvi   154

Zenon   70–1

ἀπομνημονεύματα   69–71
βίος   6, 6 n.17
ὑπομνήματα   65, 67–71
   excursus, ἀπομνημονεύματα   69–71
   Josephus' usage   68–9